The Stigma of Genius

Studies in the Postmodern Theory of Education

Joe L. Kincheloe and Shirley R. Steinberg
General Editors

Vol. 111

PETER LANG
New York • Washington, D.C./Baltimore • Boston • Bern
Frankfurt am Main • Berlin • Brussels • Vienna • Canterbury

Joe L. Kincheloe, Shirley R. Steinberg,
and Deborah J. Tippins

The Stigma of Genius

Einstein, Consciousness,
and Education

PETER LANG
New York • Washington, D.C./Baltimore • Boston • Bern
Frankfurt am Main • Berlin • Brussels • Vienna • Canterbury

Library of Congress Cataloging-in-Publication Data

Names: Kincheloe, Joe L., author. | Steinberg, Shirley R., author.
Tippins Deborah J., author.
Title: The stigma of genius: Einstein, consciousness, and education /
Joe L. Kincheloe, Shirley R. Steinberg, and Deborah J. Tippins
Description: New York: Peter Lang, 1999.
Series: Counterpoints; v. 111 | ISSN 1058-1634
Includes bibliographical references and index.
Identifiers: LCCN 99022327 | ISBN 978-0-8204-4431-4 (paperback: alk. paper)
Subjects: LCSH: Einstein, Albert, 1879–1955—Views on education.
Education—Philosophy. | Teaching. | Critical pedagogy. | Genius.
Gifted children—Education.
Classification: LCC LB875.E562 K56 1999 | DDC 370/.1—dc21
LC record available at https://lccn.loc.gov/99022327

Bibliographic information published by **Die Deutsche Nationalbibliothek**.
Die Deutsche Nationalbibliothek lists this publication in the "Deutsche
Nationalbibliografie"; detailed bibliographic data are available
on the Internet at http://dnb.d-nb.de/.

Cover art by Roymieco A. Carter

The paper in this book meets the guidelines for permanence and durability
of the Committee on Production Guidelines for Book Longevity
of the Council of Library Resources.

© 1999, 2018 Peter Lang Publishing, Inc., New York
29 Broadway, 18th floor, New York, NY 10006
www.peterlang.com

All rights reserved.
Reprint or reproduction, even partially, in all forms such as microfilm,
xerography, microfiche, microcard, and offset strictly prohibited.

Printed in the United States of America

From Joe and Shirley:

To our brilliant nieces, Sharisse, Michelle and Aimee—geniuses all

With love and thanks to our own postformal teachers:
Clint Allison, University of Tennessee—those damned Vols!
Joe

Kathy Berry, University of New Brunswick
Shirley

Collectively to our students/friends who have made the difference and will continue to do so in their careers.

Carol, Celeste, Rochelle, Tonjua, Leila: GWOC

....

From Deborah:

In celebration of the creativity and vision of elementary science teachers in Georgia's Clarke County and Barrow County school districts

To "Nicky" and "Tip," my first teachers

To Charlotte and Bill Taylor, whose lives have touched so many—and their constant reminder that learning is more than books

To Elizabeth, a Texan at heart and friend for a lifetime

To Kathy, whose metaphor for learning is almost as inspiring as her tennis game

To my colleagues and friends at West Visayas State University, Iloilo City, the Philippines

To Samantha Leigh—no words necessary!

Table of Contents

Introduction: ix
Rubber Sheets, Bowling Ball, and BBs —
Interconnectedness and a New Consciousness

Chapter One   1
Einstein's Lessons for Learners

Chapter Two   27
Einstein the Student, Einstein the Teacher

Chapter Three   49
Einstein and the Purposes of Schooling

Chapter Four   77
Rolling the Epistemological Dice

Chapter Five   95
The Nature of Genius

Chapter Six   117
Einstein's Unique Thinking Style

Table of Contents   viii

Chapter Seven   141
Einstein's Search for Unity

Chapter Eight   155
What About Teaching?

Chapter Nine   175
And Beyond Modern Education...

References   199

Index   211

Introduction:
Rubber Sheets, Bowling Ball, and BBs— Interconnectedness and a New Consciousness

Einstein often used the notion of a rubber sheet stretched over a baking dish to explain the complex notion of space. When a bowling ball or a bb is placed on it, the sheet is bent or warped around the objects. This distortion exemplifies what massive objects such as the sun or the moon do to the fabric of space. This is one of the basic concepts of Einstein's General Theory of Relativity. The rubber sheet is flat when no objects are placed upon it; Einstein referred to this as the absence of gravity. When the bowling ball depresses the sheet, the curvature around the depression represents a gravitational field. A bb rolled along the sheet will fall into the trough just as an asteroid will fall to Earth if it gets too close to its gravitational field. We saw the movie, *Armageddon*; we know what we're talking about. The more massive the object the greater the bending of space. The bowling ball will distort the sheet more than the bb.

So, according to Einstein, mass causes a depression in space. If a comet, for example, moves too close to a star it is drawn into its gravitational well and seized. Thus, entities in space follow the shape of the universe when they fall to Earth. They are not pulled by some gravitational force! While the rubber sheet is merely a metaphor and reduces the complexity of Einstein's relativity, it does help us appreciate the structural unity of space, matter, and motion. (A tricky part is that we have to add time to that unity as well.) Gravity, therefore, is simply a part of the structure of the universe—and, amazingly, Einstein figured that out. Objects fall into the valley in space-time produced by the bowling ball/sun. In this context the orbits of the sun's planets can be better conceptualized:

Mercury and Venus as well as Neptune and Pluto "roll" around the indention in space caused by the sun's gravity trough.

The General Theory of Relativity even asserted that if a massive object in space is disturbed, it will cause ripples in space like ripples from a rock splashing in a pond. In space these "gravity waves" are illustrated again by the rubber sheet, as we imagine dropping a ball bearing on it. BBs and bowling balls placed on other portions of the sheet will be affected by the dropping of the ball bearing. Einstein asked us to use our rubber sheet to imagine a massive object that revolves. In this situation the "gravity well" it produces in space is not just a depression in the rubber sheet but a spinning indentation that twists space. Such twisting induces other objects around it to move in particular ways. While The General Theory of Relativity is, undoubtedly, very complex and mysterious, the point we are making about it to introduce our book is quite simple. The simplicity of our point, however, should not undermine its revolutionary significance. Follow the logic of our point and its importance for cognition, consciousness, and education—relationship and interconnectedness are more important concepts than Western science traditionally realized.

As Einstein sought to understand the force of gravity, he discovered that there is no such thing as "nothingness" in the structure of the universe. Space like everything else *is something*—it is an intrinsic part of the fabric of the cosmos. Space is neither empty nor separable from matter. The *relationship* between space and matter is central to making the universe what it is. In light of Einstein's assertion the old Newtonian notion of gravity was destroyed; but most importantly to our point, the Newtonian universe and the Newtonian *way of looking at the universe* was overturned. When Newton developed his Universal Theory of Gravitation in the 1600s, he focused on gravity as a thing-in-itself. If gravity, as he believed, was simply a force, why would one look at it in any other way? Thus, he and especially those who come after him followed the emerging scientific method and removed gravity from its context so it could be efficiently analyzed. And this was exactly their mistake ("Astronomical Instruments," 1999; "Gravitational Radiation," 1998; "Still right....,"1998; Evans, 1997; Woods and Grant, 1998; Peoria Astronomical Society, 1998).

Einstein operating in the first decades of the twentieth century was able to escape the Newtonian mistake that had misled physicists for a quarter of a millennium by one conceptual move. Instead of searching for gravity as a *thing*, he saw it as a *relationship*. Einstein saw gravity *in relation* to other aspects of the universe. Indeed, he understood that the relationship between matter and space—illustrated by the rubber sheet, bowling balls, and bbs—is exactly what makes the world what it is. What we experience as gravity is not a force made up of tiny gravitons but a reflection of the structure of the universe

Introduction xi

moving us along a path existing in curved, multidimensional space. Space, he figured, is not the package in which the universe is stored—it is a central part of creation. For those who understood the basic idea of Einstein's theory, the world could never be viewed the same way again (Levenson, 1997; Woods and Grant, 1998).

OUR POINT: EINSTEIN'S RELATIVITY INDUCES US TO SEE THE IMPORTANCE OF RELATIONSHIP IN A VARIETY OF DOMAINS

Despite sci-fi's fascination with anti-gravity machines, Einstein's General Theory of Relativity tells us that you can't simply turn gravity on and off. To do so one would have to change the nature of the universe. Gravitational change, Einstein asserted, would involve a geometrical change. Thus, the General Theory of Relativity with its reductionistic but insightful notion of space and rubber sheet forces us to change not only our view of the universe but also, we argue, our conception of the microcosms of the social, the psychological, and the educational—to name only a few. Drawing on Einstein's emphasis on relationship in the physical universe and moving it to an appreciation of interconnectedness in infinite domains, we begin the process of rethinking our educational consciousness at the beginning of the new millennium.

Writing in the nineteenth century, the philosopher George W. F. Hegel was conceptually uncomfortable with Newton's absolutist explanation of gravity and the way things work. Most importantly for our educational and psychological concerns, Hegel was unimpressed with the manner in which Newton reached his conclusions. From Hegel's perspective every entity's existence could only be understood in relation to other things.In his philosophical view the concept of relationship took on an importance not valued by Newton and his scientific descendants. Relationship was so significant to Hegel that he described the interaction between entities as a living process. In such a process all things in the world were affected and shaped by all other things—just as in Einstein's theory mass worked on space and space worked in mass ("Einstein on spacetime," 1998).

If Hegel was correct then all things are "in process," parts of a larger activity. When the world is viewed in this manner, Newtonian science's concept of cause and effect crumbles. Does gravity *cause* the apple to fall and hit the scientist in the head? Not exactly, if we answer the question with the General Theory of Relativity in mind. Such a recognition of universal interconnectedness is a central concept in our analysis of higher order cognition, and in our critique of modern education. Much of what passes for teaching in elementary, secondary, college, and graduate education at the beginning of the twenty-first century does not take into account this basic Einsteinian notion. Too many educators and psychologists have not learned what Einstein taught us about thinking and the importance of relationships. Operating without the benefit of this lesson we fall into the *irrationality of conventional reason*. We see the importance of the world in things in-themselves, in isolation from their contexts, removed from the larger processes that provide their meaning. Informed by Einstein's lesson education and the thinking it teaches become more than the accumulation of fragments of data. In the call for educational standards over the last two decades, we have seen the effects of this failure to learn Einstein (and Hegel's) lesson: we judge educational quality by the quantity of data accumulated (Woods and Grant, 1998; Madison, 1988).

LIFE AS A PROCESS:
INTERCONNECTEDNESS AND THE ORIGINS OF POSTFORMALISM

The focus on relationships connecting space, time, and matter that eventuated in Einstein's revolutionary theories can also change our consciousness, cognition, and education. As we pursue modes of thinking that account for changes and interactions in the physical, social, and psychological domains, we begin to gain dramatically different and more complex perspectives on that which surrounds us. In this concept of interactive processes the etymology of our concept of postformalism or postformal thinking is revealed. (We will describe postformalism in detail later in the book.) At this point, however, it is important to explain Einstein's role in leading us to new ways of making meaning, to new appreciations of both being and becoming (Kovel, 1998).

Using Einstein's example of thinking in physics and Hegel's dialectical insights, we are led to critical and post-Newtonian forms of analysis. In this context we begin to appreciate the hidden processes that place the physical, social, psychological, and educational worlds in a sea of constant change. Newtonian and Cartesian (the scientific principles of René Descartes) ways of seeing often provide a metaphorical photograph of an entity. This photograph is an isolated moment in time, a still life that may miss the significance of the larger dynamic of which it is but a part. When we see—as postformalism labels it—facts as a part of a larger process, we begin to understand how things move beyond what they are but still retain their identity. For example, while gravity no doubt exists, it moves far beyond its existence as an entity involved merely with the attraction of one object to another when conceived as a part of an inclusive whole—the structure of the universe. Imagine the difference between a science lesson taught to middle school students about gravity that takes this processual feature into account and one that doesn't.

The process-based thinking delineated here is a form of holistic analysis that insists on the inseparability of mind and body, politics and economics, consciousness and cultural context, facts and values, the biological and the social, and gravity and matter. What education in its disciplinary organization or in its fragmentation of information treats as

Introduction

separate, the postformalism we advocate considers parts of larger wholes. There is nothing wrong, process analysts maintain, with separating entities for the purpose of labeling and analysis as long as this step is followed by the act of putting them back together. Step one: gravity is defined as the attraction of one object for another; step two: this attraction is viewed as a result of the interrelationship among space, mass, time, and motion. Thus, this mode of analysis can be described as examining an entity from differing vantage points: 1) gravity as experienced by an earthling throwing a baseball into the air and watching it return to Earth; and 2) gravity from the perspective of one who views (or like Einstein is capable of imagining) the universe as a whole and frames it in such a perspective. Understanding both modes and their relationship is important in the postformal effort to make sense of gravity (Bookchin, 1995; Kovel, 1998; Levins, 1998).

Thus, informed by these ways of seeing, the postformal thinking advocated in this book assumes that little in the universe is as it appears to be. Postformalists argue that considering an entity only as a thing-in-itself can be viciously misleading. The reason we chose to examine Einstein's educational life and thought involves his phenomenal ability to avoid this Newtonian Cartesian quicksand and to model a rigorous form of higher order cognition that can lead us out of the cognitive and educational briar patch in which we are presently ensnared. The implications of such a critique of Newtonian-Cartesian logic (conventional reason) are sobering and are not offered frivolously. Based on Einstein's mode of thinking and numerous analyses of the limitations of mainstream Western science, we are contending that there are important flaws in accepted forms of logic, research, and knowledge production.

Do not misread our assertion. We are not arguing that we throw out the Newtonian baby with the bathwater—that is, we are not arguing that mainstream science is of no benefit. Of course, it is; its contributions are significant and well documented. Our argument involves the notion that we can do better, go further, and address the limitations inherent in the Newtonian-Cartesian system—in particular, the limitations Einstein had to overcome to develop his frame-shattering theories. In many ways *The Stigma of Genius: Einstein, Consciousness, and Education* is a call for an authentic new rigor in cognition and education. It is an effort to illustrate ways of transcending conceptually impoverished definitions of high educational standards grounded on recall of fragmented bits of knowledge—long on memorization and recitation, short on understanding, interpretation, applicability/transferability, and connectedness. When students and teachers move into the processual postformal realm they gain the ability not only to explain the dynamics that move events but, like Einstein, develop the capacity to transform them in progressive ways (Kovel, 1998; Woods and Grant, 1998; Lawler, 1995).

STIRRING THE IMAGINATION: EINSTEIN AS THE EXEMPLAR OF GENIUS

In his delineation of the relationships that shape the structure of the universe, Einstein may have made the greatest leap ever in the effort to grasp the order of the cosmos. For this contribution Einstein is held in unequaled esteem by millions of people around the world. At the beginning of the twenty-first century those riddles he couldn't explain remain at the top of physicists' research agenda. Profound debates continue over the implications of and possibilities raised by Einstein's descriptions of the universe. In retrospect it is hard to believe that he single-handedly initiated a *coup d'état* in physics in only seventeen years. By 1919, four years after he issued the General Theory of Relativity, the British eclipse expedition had validated his notion of curved space by observing how the gravitational well of the sun modified the course of starlight reaching the Earth. That such an outlandish theory could be confirmed elicited a worshipful response to Einstein from the popular press—a reaction that for the most part continues into the twenty-first century ("Astronomical instruments," 1999; "Teacher's guide," 1997; "Albert Einstein," 1997; Levinson, 1997).

New discoveries over the last few decades continue to fuel the Einstein mystique. Disagreement continues as to whether he was always correct, but he was right so often that respect for his genius rarely wanes. In the 1990s NASA has launched satellites to explore the space enigmas that Einstein theorized. In 1995 the space agency launched the Rossi X-ray Timing Explorer (RXTE) for such a purpose. By 1997 it had empirically confirmed that black holes and neutron stars with their phenomenal mass were (as Einstein predicted) dragging space and time with them as they spin. The validity of such predictions is amazing to us. In light of such brilliance Einstein may be more than a scientist—maybe he was an artist of science, as his friend Banesh Hoffman once described him. Such a concept prompts us to probe its meaning. To be an artist of science may involve employing a method of cognition that moves beyond the conventional reason of Newtonian-Cartesian thinking. One of the purposes of this book involves exploring that cognitive style. As previously mentioned, postformalism emerged from such explorations. If there is an artistic aspect to science, we figured, then there is a need to reconsider the formal thinking of the traditional scientific method (Koerner, November 17, 1997; Peyton, 1996).

Of course, we are not alone in our amazement concerning the mind of Einstein. People around the world are still smitten with the possibilities offered by The General Theory of Relativity: time travel, extended life in speed of light space flights, worm holes in spacetime, alternative universes, etc.... Such awe inspires screenwriters to include him in movies such as *Insignificance* where Marilyn Monroe discusses relativity with him, or *IQ* where recognizing in his special way the importance of both intellect and

Introduction

passion he plays matchmaker for his niece and an auto mechanic, or in Steve Martin's *Picasso at the Lapin Agile* where he meets Picasso and a time-travelling Elvis Presley at a Paris bar.

One doesn't have to look far to see Einstein's image almost anywhere on the planet at the turn of the millennium: in Japan his face is used to sell a video game called 3DO; in "head shops" in the US, Canada, and Australia his face adorns tee-shirts and posters; in Hungary he appears in advertisements for the phone company; in South Africa he is used to hawk insurance. A quick browse of the web will expose numerous companies using Einstein's name and image to sell "pathways to success" and cognitive growth (Woods and Grants, 1998; Fox, December 16, 1994; Taylor, September 17, 1998; Paterniti, 1997; Wenger and Poe, 1995). For example, in "Quantum Learning and Peak Performance Through the Use of Remembrance and Einstein's Dream:"

> Albert Einstein wrote that music, especially Mozart's, made him acutely aware of the mathematical structures music. This awareness, in turn, focused his concentration. He would listen to Mozart, therefore, while conducting research; the Sonata for Two Pianos in D Major, his favorite piece. The validity of Einstein's personal observation was proven in a recent experiment at the University of California at Irvine. There students listened to Mozart for 10 minutes and were then tested for recall. Their IQ scores climbed an average of nine points! Now you can experience this "Mozart Effect" by using "Remembrance and Einstein's Dream" to stimulate your own brain, to reach quantum-learning and increase your level of mental peak performance.

For better or for worse, Einstein's name stirs our imagination. Millions of us who watched *The Twilight Zone* as kids remember the mystique of the introduction to the show with Rod Serling's voice over swirling black and white images, one of which was $e=mc^2$. Matter is energy, Einstein told us via the famous equation. Granite is energy, Georgia red clay is energy—nothing is solid, nothing is as it appears to be if we believe Einstein. We remember our first encounter with the concepts of black holes and worm holes. With the rubber sheet in mind, scientists familiar with Einstein's theories imagined a black hole amassing more and more matter into a smaller and smaller locale. At some point, they theorized, the distortion of space (the rubber sheet) would become so great that a hole could be ripped in it.

Imagine poking a pencil into the rubber sheet and making a hole. If we gather the rubber sheet and fold it (distorted space) and keep pushing the pencil through the first hole, we can eventually poke another hole at another point on the sheet. In this manner we have created a worm hole in space. The shortest distance between the two holes is not a straight line through traditional notions of space and distance; the quickest and shortest path between the two points is the worm hole. The idea is so compelling that NASA has provided limited funding to explore the idea for future space flights. Imagine using a worm hole to beat a light ray taking the traditional, straight line "scenic route" to a far distant planet in another galaxy. These are the types of fanciful concepts Einstein's work continues to unleash. So powerful are the feelings he evokes that many have moved both him and his ideas into spiritual realms (Freedman, 1998). We would not deny the spiritual implications of many of his understandings of the interconnectedness of the universe.

EXPOSING UNACKNOWLEDGED RELATIONSHIPS:
THE DIFFICULTY WITH IDENTIFYING GENIUS

At the same time Einstein inspires, he baffles and frightens. New ideas, especially those that conflict with common sense and traditional understandings of reality, always produce some anxiety. Such was Einstein's effect as a young man, especially as a student. The title, *The Stigma of Genius*, emerges in this context as Einstein and his ideas angered his teachers and professors. This unfortunate tendency, the rejection and sometimes the persecution of genius, even the defining of genius as madness, continues to manifest itself into the social and educational world of the new millennium. Teachers and professors often loathed Einstein, viewing his interpretations of subject matter as inappropriate and disrespectful. After he fled Germany and moved to Princeton, many Americans came to hate him and the FBI saw him as a dangerous Communist sympathizer. His son, Hans Albert, was physically attacked in response to his father's viewpoints and scores of Americans called for the physicist's deportment (Paterniti, 1997).

With the way genius is stigmatized, the manner in which the gatekeepers of the academic disciplines reacted to Einstein's perspectives, it is amazing that any of his work made it into publication. Indeed, a central argument of this book is that within the traditional scientific, psychological, and educational paradigms, genius is often unrecognized and dismissed. Thousands of Einsteins, we maintain, are discouraged by negative reactions to their brilliant counter-readings of the word and the world. Throughout the book we will point out how this process takes place every day in schools around the world. A change of consciousness must occur to put an end to this pattern of human destructiveness. One of the most important ways to initiate such a transformation involves exposing the limitations of Newtonian-Cartesian ways of perceiving in the social, political, psychological, and educational spheres in a manner similar to Einstein's exposé in physics.

Just as Newton envisaged a physical world where time, space, matter, and motion are separate entities, psychologists and educators have accepted a view of humans where the social, the political, the mind, intelligence, and performance in school are things-in-themselves. Once we begin to challenge the assumptions of old paradigm psychology and education, the manner in which intelligence is defined and measured becomes more and more clear. Understanding that social and epistemological dynamics shape both the mind itself and the way the mind is perceived, we learn that we cannot separate psychology's measurement of individuals' so-called intelligence from the historical circumstances of the social groups to which they belong.

Thus, old paradigm psychology measures the socio-political circumstances of various groups: the status of the group, its self-esteem, its power relative to other groups, its economic success, its acceptance in the larger community, etc....In this context Brigett Berger (1995) argues that intelligence tests used in schools around the world measure what she calls a "modern consciousness"—a coterie of abilities that enable one to negotiate the complex cultural terrain of contemporary life with its technological innovations and rule-driven, rationalistic bureaucracies. This is the way of seeing the world put forward by Newton, Descartes, and Sir Francis Bacon in their contributions to the scientific method. It was this modernist scientific method that Einstein challenged—a method saturated with impulses to centralize, concentrate, and accumulate. This modernist scientific method laid a foundation that allowed science, technology, and bureaucracy to transform both the physical world and the Western psyche.

The better standardized test takers can operate in modern Western society, the higher their intelligence will be deemed to be. Take the variable of time, for example. Since the advent of the Newtonian-Cartesian-Baconian scientific revolution, Western societies have been trapped in a social time warp of speed that dramatically affects perceptions of intelligence. While premodern (prescientific revolution) cultures may have associated haste with waste, modern cultures believe that speed reflects alertness, power, and success. Pondering, reflecting, or musing might be valued in some cultures, but not in the modernist West. In a study involving male undergraduates in college, Robert Knapp and John Garbut (1965) found that individuals who scored the highest on standardized tests were those who placed the most value on speed. Students from traditional, indigenous, and agrarian cultures tend not to place as high a value on speed as urban, white, and mainstream ones. Thus, for *cultural* reasons, not issues of *cognitive ability*, traditional, indigenous, and agrarian students do not tend to score highly on standardized measurements of intelligence.

Add to this list middle-class students such as Einstein who for psychological more than cultural reasons do poorly on such measurements. Because Einstein perceived relationships that others did not, because he was able to see the invisible, the tacit, because he operated with a cognitive style that differed from the procedures of validated Newtonian-Cartesian thinking, he was not deemed intelligent. Thus, from a new paradigmatic, prevailing postformal perspective definitions and measurements of intelligence have to be viewed in *relation* to the social, political, epistemological, and psychological assumptions that construct them. Just like gravity intelligence cannot be understood as a thing-in-itself. When viewed in conceptual isolation, a misleading picture is produced that harms those individuals who come from backgrounds or possess dispositions that fall outside psycho-social privileged groups. Indeed, the identification of genius is complex and problematic.

Serious implications emerge from these issues. Non-postformal thinkers are often rewarded by old paradigm psychology and education for *not* recognizing relationships that change how a phenomenon is understood. I (Joe) can remember many times in school receiving "Ds" or "Fs" for asserting new interpretations of social or physical phenomena. Many times the students I had helped tutor the night before on the conventional explanation of the phenomenon and the professor's personal perspective on it would make an "A" or a "B" on the same exam. Traditionally "good students" (*unlike me*) learned the Newtonian-Cartesian lesson early: schooling tends to emphasize isolated things-in-themselves. And the best way to succeed is to employ the lowest form of cognition, rote memorization, and give back factual data in the same form it was delivered.

DISSECTING EINSTEIN'S BRAIN:
EVEN IN DEATH HE COULDN'T ESCAPE THE OLD PARADIGM

As his teachers identified intelligence with quick recall of unproblematized "facts," Einstein like millions of other talented students grew increasingly alienated from school. His disposition to play with ideas, to consider them in a variety of unusual contexts was out of step with the pedagogy of late nineteenth century German schools (Peyton, 1996). Such nineteenth-century-education thinking is perpetuated at the turn of the third millennium by seemingly never-ending calls for more standardized testing. Such testing induces teachers to defensively "teach to the test" and such a procedure exacerbates the fragmentation that already exists by forcing students to memorize unconnected and often meaningless data. Our objection to such testing/accountability is often portrayed by conservative spokespeople as opposition to "raising standards." Nothing could be further from the truth. Our objection emerges from our desire for an *authentic rigor* that emphasizes higher order cognitive abilities and challenges both students and teachers to become serious scholars. Such a vision is not quixotic—it is practical and with hard work it can be accomplished.

Without this postformal challenge schools perpetuate this pseudo-rigor that teaches students to compartmentalize knowledge and to ignore the developmental, "in-process" nature of the interconnected world. As our friend Donaldo Macedo (1994) argues— schooling of this type stupidifies. Such perspectives seemed to haunt Einstein throughout his life and even after his death. Called to perform an autopsy on the scientist after his

Introduction

death in 1955, Dr. Thomas Harvey stole Einstein's brain for his personal research into the nature of genius. As the years passed, no reports emerged from Dr. Harvey and the circumstances surrounding and whereabouts of Einstein's brain were largely forgotten. In the late 1990s an elderly Dr. Harvey admitted that he had chopped the brain into nearly 200 pieces and over the years had given about one-third of it away to various scientists.

Harvey's and his fellow researchers' purpose was to study the physical fragments of Einstein's imagination to find out how the brain of a genius differed from regular mortals. From their Newtonian-Cartesian perspective Einstein's unique ability was a physiological dynamic—he must have possessed a more efficiently functioning brain. The old paradigm perspective emerges yet again: intelligence or genius is a thing-in-itself. It is "caused" by a larger capacity brain that can store more data. The idea that Einstein's brilliance might have emerged from an unquantifiable set of unique experiences that induced him to use his resources in imaginative ways never seemed to occur to Dr. Harvey and his colleagues. For decades they unsuccessfully attempted to locate genius in the conceptual isolation of the brain's physical structure. The macabre symbolism of Einstein's fragmented brain resting in two glass jars in a dark room of Harvey's house is not lost upon postformalists (Paterniti, 1997).

This brain fiasco illustrates the old paradigm's inadequacy in the complex study of human intelligence. Traditional psychology perpetuates the modernist myth that the universe is totally knowable and controllable. The cognitive science operating in this context is reductionistic in its contention that complex psychological phenomena can best be appreciated by reducing them to their constituent parts and then piecing them together according to causal laws. The assumptions of the Newtonian-Cartesian paradigm is omnipresent in enterprises as diverse as Harvey's brain experiments, standardized testing, and the call for educational standards by political and educational leaders. The word, paradigm, comes from the Greek word for pattern, a scheme for understanding the nature of the cosmos. Just as Isaac Newton saw the physical world in terms of predictable mechanical forces in a clockwork universe, many political and educational leaders of the present still perceive the psychological world in terms of predictable generalizations that can be derived by isolating intelligence and studying its variables in a controlled setting. Despite Einstein's success the old paradigm continues to shape the social, political, psychological, and educational domains.

The terror of the absolutism of the old paradigm, its refusal to question its fragmentary ways of perceiving, is still a powerful force as the new millennium opens. The conventional reasoning of the traditional paradigm helped confront the tyrannical authority of the church and the so-called divine right of monarchs to exploit their subjects; and for such accomplishments we are thankful. We do not understand the limitations of the ways of seeing that achieved these great successes: simply put, the paradigm made too great a claim for the truth of its descriptions of reality. Because of its absolutism and perceived arrogance, many individuals during the last decades of the twentieth century grew uncomfortable with the tradition.

The conventional reason of the old paradigm came to be seen by such people as perpetuating an unquestionable authority, impersonal social institutions, an emotionless science, amoral managerial systems, and faceless, insensitive bureaucracies. Such perceptions were part of a postmodern sentiment that we will discuss throughout the book. An important aspect of this postmodern sensibility involves its recognition of conventional reason's inability to understand the ways it often invents reality to validate its theses about it. For example, the "intelligence" described by psychometricians is not a *discovery* but an *invention*. With this idea in mind we do not submit that postformal thinking is a discovery; it too is an invention. One important difference between postformalism and Newtonian-Cartesian cognitive theories is that we understand the inventive status of our construction.

EINSTEIN AND TWENTY-FIRST-CENTURY EDUCATIONAL CHANGE

Drawing upon Einstein's argument that problems can't be solved by the same type of thinking that generated them, we call for new forms of social, political, psychological, and educational thinking—a postformal consciousness. Sometimes such a new consciousness as many of Einstein's notions conflicts with common sense. Einstein argued that objects moving at high speeds increase their mass. We argue that breaking a subject down into discrete parts, teaching these parts, and then measuring how well students learned them is not a productive way of teaching. In this process the connections between the parts, questions concerning where the parts (the data) came from, the purposes of knowing such information, and examples of its use in the world are lost. The shortest educational distance between two points may not be a straight line. We are interested in the worm holes in the socio-educational rubber sheet. That which is observable in commonsense, everyday frames of educational reference may be relatively insignificant. Many educational leaders who spend decades in schools never see the effects of power, sociocultural relationships, and psychological dispositions on student performance.

Of course, the way we make sense of Einstein's messages for educators or the implications of the way he thought about reality for cognitive theory is a matter of interpretation. We understand that many well-intentioned people will strongly disagree with us—maybe the conversation between us will be valuable. Our point is that the relationship between Einstein and education is not some simplistic, gee-whiz set of points, but a com-

Introduction

plex, ever-changing, imaginative process that must be analyzed and reanalyzed. We claim no final authority or truth for our reading. From our conceptual frame we view Einstein's insights as subjugated psychological and pedagogical knowledge. A key element of postformal thinking involves the notion that we learn important lessons from those who are different in some way from ourselves. The power of difference expands each person's conceptual horizon and socio-psychological, and cultural understanding.

Individuals, postformalists maintain, who belong to different racial, ethnic, gender, religious, or socio-economic groups can learn from one another if provided the space to exchange ideas and analyze mutual difficulties. As such a powerful force, difference must not "just be tolerated" but cultivated as a spark to human creativity. Postformalists are especially interested in understanding the perspectives of those who have been marginalized along the axes of race, class, gender, sexuality, or religion. Taking their cue from liberation theologians in Latin America, postformalists often begin their analysis of an institution such as schooling by listening to those who have suffered as a result of its existence. These "different" ways of seeing allow postformalists to tap into the cognitive power of difference—a power that allows individuals access to the deep patterns (gravity in relation to the structure of space) of racism, class bias, and sexism and the way they shape the quality of everyday life.

With these understandings in mind, postformalists seek a dialogue between Eastern and Western cultures, as well as a conversation between the relatively wealthy northern cultures and the impoverished southern cultures of the planet. In such a postformal context of difference forms of knowing, such as the understandings of blue collar workers, which have traditionally been excluded by the Newtonian-Cartesian West, move educators to new vantage points and unexplored planetary perspectives. Understanding derived from the perspective of the excluded or the culturally different allows for an appreciation of the nature of justice, the invisibility of the process of oppression and the difference that highlights our own social construction as individuals. Such cognitive cross-fertilization often reveals the tacit assumptions that impede innovations of all varieties. For example, home builders who study Native American, Japanese, or African ways of building houses may gain creative insight into their craft. After studying the way Zuni Pueblos addressed problems of living space, they might be empowered to tackle space problems in ways conventional Western builders hadn't considered.

This book situates Einstein and his implications for education in this type of schema; Einstein's contribution to the power of difference was not a cultural feature—it was a psychological dynamic. Einstein's mode of thinking, his cognitive style was unique: he confronts us with other methods of making sense of the world. In this context we are making a key assumption about cognition: intelligence is not simply genetically determined—it can be learned. Einstein believed that he had learned his cognitive ability. If Einstein learned to be smart, then so can we. With this concept in mind, postformalists become detectives of intelligence. Einstein's mind, his theories and his thinking, become the postformal "crime scene" where we perform investigations into what he was doing that made him so intelligent.

Geniuses are not that much different from the rest of us. In our lives, we have sought the company of those we consider extremely intelligent. As we learn from them, we come to understand that they make mistakes, follow false leads, and have areas in their lives where they know very little. The same was true with Einstein. As brilliant as he could be, he was very innocent, almost childlike, in many areas of his life. Einstein, however, like many other brilliant people had a passion for knowing that helped him focus his attention, that gave him confidence to push on when he was wrong. Good teaching, in part, involves the ability to inspire such passion. In order for teachers to gain that ability, they must have the passion themselves—they must be scholars.

EINSTEIN AND A POSTFORMAL EDUCATION FOR THE "GIFTED MAJORITY"

Knowing this, postformalists believe that they can provide a just, inclusive, and rigorous education for the "gifted majority." We have carefully studied the out-of-school abilities of students who are deemed failures in school. In those domains in which such students are interested, they exhibit sophisticated cognitive abilities—far greater than my own. Such "weak students" are gifted in unusual ways that are quite difficult to detect with the tools used by mainstream educational psychology. Sorted and tracked by language-based tests, many students who come from homes where reading does not take place and self-reflection about language is not encouraged score poorly. Little follow-up research is done on such students and they are relegated to the "school hell" of the lower tracks.

In many previous employments of Einstein in education he has been used as a model of genius that works to exclude the very students who possessed cognitive abilities similar to his. Educators promoting exclusionary forms of gifted education have invoked Einstein to support an elite form of tracking that runs ideologically counter to the political values the great scientist promoted throughout his life. Jeffrey Peyton (1996) has helped develop an "Einstein Curriculum" that is based on the notion that "Einstein was not a child prodigy." Appreciating Einstein's flaws, Peyton argues that many students in schools today fit the Einstein profile. Instead of making Einstein a model for the gifted elite, Peyton sees him more as a representative for "problem students" or those who are "learning disabled." We agree. Einstein is much more powerful as a symbol for those students who don't show up as gifted but who have the ability to change the world (Peyton, 1996). Viewed from this perspective there are millions of Einsteins floundering in classrooms around the world. With the will and the insight, we can provide them with the passion and focus to accomplish greatness.

The postformal education promoted here and in the rest of the book is frightening to many educational leaders, advocates of some forms of elite gifted education in particular, because of its Einsteinian concerns with issues of power and justice. To expand upon these concerns we refer to critical theory and critical pedagogy throughout the book. Indeed, an Einstein-inspired education that takes his political views seriously will unfortunately make many uncomfortable. In the spirit of the interconnectedness that his work drew upon, Einstein understood that educators cannot separate the personal from the social, the ethical from the rational, or the cognitive from the political (Bookchin, 1995).

These understandings separated him from many mainstream thinkers of his and our times. Newtonian-Cartesian conventional reason when applied to the social, psychological, and educational realm made this "error of fragmentation" again and again in its search for value-free objectivity. This cognitive/epistemological issues is not some arcane philosophical abstraction that stands apart from the "real world." It continues to shape our lives in powerful ways in the twenty-first century. To expand our consciousness and to reform our educational system, we must clearly understand this important concept of relationship and interconnection. This is why the example of Einstein's conception of gravity and the interrelationship of the universe—space, time, matter, and motion—is so important.

RECLAIMING RIGOR AS WE RETHINK RATIONALITY:
EINSTEIN AND THE COGNITION OF COMPLEXITY

As postformalists advocating a culturally contextualized and socially just form of cognition, we are often faced with criticisms grounded on the belief that justice and quality are mutually exclusive concepts. We vehemently reject such an assumption. Using Einstein as a referent, we are interested in redefining rigor via postformal thinking. In the Newtonian-Cartesian paradigm rigor has often been defined as the careful following of prearranged procedure, as in researchers following the scientific method. For example, given the Newtonian notion of gravity one can follow the correct methodology and calculate to numerous decimal places the pull the Earth exerts on the moon. While a student should not be shielded from such rigor, we learn from Einstein that this is not the end of an analysis of what rigorous thinking might entail.

Moving into the postformal realm of rigor in this example of gravity, we begin to question the Newtonian model of the universe that produced his conception of gravity. Are there other models, we might ask. Let's compare the Newtonian and the Einsteinian view. What are the challenges to Einstein's reconceptualization of Newton's world? Are these questions and the analysis they elicit not a form of rigor? And are they conceptually of a different order than procedural rigor? Moving such an example into the educational domain, does rigorous educational thinking induce us to think about the relationship between schools and society? Do schools have special functions in democratic societies? Do we have to have a vision of educational purpose in a democratic society, the historical role of schooling, and the changing cultural context in which contemporary education finds itself before we can rigorously explore educational reform?

When such questions are addressed, postformalists maintain, then we can begin to appreciate the complexity of educational reform. Just as Einstein understood the complex relationships that had to be understood before a new concept of gravity could be developed, postformalists analyzing school policy must appreciate the ways education is shaped by the interaction of the social, political, economic, and psychological realms. This complex dynamic is what is missing in the public conversation about education—a conversation that lacks rigor. Like Einstein understood that the physical world is filled by irregularities and warps, postformalists appreciate the complexity of social, psychological, and educational networks. Contrary to the assumptions behind the rigorous analytical procedures taught in modernist research paradigms, the world is characterized by unstructured problems that don't lend themselves to linear applications of conventional reason (Suber, 1997; Woods and Grant, 1998).

The world is more complex, less symmetrical than Newton, Descartes, and Bacon assumed it to be. Understanding this, many mathematicians have moved into a new science of complexity and chaos theories. These innovations have been based conceptually on the notion of interrelationship in much the same cognitive mode that Einstein developed his theories. In this new arena of complexity we have to transcend traditional disciplinary boundaries to account for interrelated phenomena that pay no heed to the modernist fragmentation of knowledge (Levins, 1998). Thus, postformalists in education seek insights from a plethora of disciplines and pay special attention to the disciplinary critique of transgressive fields such as cultural studies.

If we are capable of understanding Einstein's General Theory of Relativity's four dimensional universe via the conceptual window of gravity and its relation to the rubber sheet of space, we can create a rigorous new education that takes into account contextual complexity. We can build a conceptual bricolage of social theory, political analysis, cognitive theory, critical pedagogy, systems theory, quantum mechanics, hermeneutics, critical epistemology, feminist studies, subjugated/indigenous knowledges, and many other ways of seeing that can be practically applied to thinking about education. Without lapsing into some paralyzing relativism, we can begin to view our world from many van-

Introduction xxv

tage points and grow to understand the many-sidedness of truth (Woods and Grant, 1998). The social, psychological, educational, and physical worlds we see are constituted by conflicting relationships that are sometimes contradictory. At the dawning of the new millennium, it is essential that we as a society get over the fear of such complexity and embrace a new rigor to introduce our young people to the challenges it offers. We will now trace Einstein's clues as to how we might accomplish this daunting task.

REFERENCES

"Albert Einstein" (1997) <http://sci.hkbu.edu.hk/math/einstein.html>

"Astronomical instruments" (1999) <http://www.scinet.org.uk/database/physics/Instruments/p008270.html>

Berger, B. (1995). "Methodological fetishism." In R. Jacoby and N. Glauberman (eds.), *The Bell Curve debate: History, documents, and opinion*. New York: Random House.

Bookchin, M. (1995). *The philosophy of social ecology: Essays on dialectical naturalism*. 2nd. Montreal: Black Rose Books.

"Einstein on Spacetime" (1998) <http://webplaza.pt.lu/public/fklaess/html/spacetime.html>

Evans, J. (1997). "Relativity and black holes." <http://www.physics.gmu.edu/classinfo/astr228/coursenotes/in_ch19.htm>

Fox, M. (December 16, 1994). "Matthau's formula: Einstein plus Yiddish equals movie magic." *Jewish Bulletin; Ethnic News Watch*, 143, 49, p. 27.

Freedman, D. (1998). "Faster than a speeding photon." *Discover Magazine,19*, 8, pp. 70–80.

"Gravitational radiation." (1998) <http://zebu.uoregon.edu/~imamura/122/jan12/gw.html>

Knapp, R. And J. Garbut (1965). "Variation in time descriptions and need achievement." *Journal of Social Psychology*, 67, pp. 265–81.

Koerner, B. (November 11, 1997). "A new wrinkle in time." *US News on-line*.

Kovel, J. (1998). "Dialect as praxis." *Science and Society*, 62, 3, pp. 474–80.

Lamb, B. (August 4, 1996). "Booknotes transcript: Interview with Denis Brian." <http://www1.c-span.ort/mmedia/booknote/lambbook/transcripts50023.htm>

Lawler, J. (1995). "The Marxian dialectic—dialectic investigations by Bertell Ollman." *Monthly Review*, 46, 9, pp. 48–51.

Levenson, T. (1997). "Q: How smart was he? A: (Really smart)."

Levins, R. (1998). "Dialectics and systems theory." *Science and Society*, 62, 3, pp. 375–89.

Macedo, D. (1994). *Literacies of power: What Americans are not allowed to know*. Boulder, CO: Westview Press.

Madison, G. (1988). *The hermeneutics of post-modernity: Figures and themes.* Bloomington, IN: Indiana University Press.

Morgan, G. (1999). "Images of organizations." <http://www.imaginiz.com/ioonotes/ ioochapnotes 7–8.html>

Paterniti, M. (1997). "Driving Mr. Albert: A trip across America with Einstein's Brain." *Harper's Magazine,* 295, 1969, pp. 35–60.

Peoria Astronomical Society (1998). "Beyond the event horizon: An introduction to black holes." <http://www.astronomical.org/astbook/blkhole.html>

Peyton, J. (1996). "The Einstein Curriculum." *Puppetools* <http://www.puppetools.com/einstein.htm>

"Quantum Learning and Peak Performance." (1998). <http://dnamusic.com/quantum.htm>

"Still right after all these years." (1998). <http://news3.news.wisc.edu/052einstein/frame_drag4.html>

Suber, P. (1997). "Legal reasoning after postmodern critiques of reason." *Legal Writing,* 3, pp. 21–50.

Taylor, P. (September 17, 1998). "Theatre: Two geniuses go 'phut' in Paris." *The Independent* (London).

"Teacher's Guide: Einstein Revealed." (1978). *Nova on-line.* <http://www.pbsorg/wgbh.nova.teachersguide/einstein/index.html>

Wenger, W. and R. Poe (1995). "The Einstein factor." *Success,* pp. 55–62.

The Stigma of Genius:
Einstein, Consciousness,
and Education

Einstein's Lessons for Learners

In November of 1950 teenager Peter Van Dore wrote Albert Einstein about his (Van Dore's) inability to get along in high school. "Even though I have one of the highest IQs in school," Van Dore wrote:

> I just cannot seem to get along with the teachers. I like to learn, but I enjoy finding things out for myself. When the teachers start drilling the facts into me, my head seems to shut up like a clam. I am however trying to get so that I can go to MIT (Van Dore, 1950).

Always ready to answer the letters of individuals seeking his advice, Einstein responded a few days later:

> Do not be afraid if you have difficulties in school; there are enough conformists in this world (Einstein, 1950).

Albert Einstein has always been a mythical figure, the eccentric genius who serves as patron saint to creative and frustrated high school students. As I daydreamed in a high school algebra class, trying to reconcile its complete disconnection to any aspect of my lived world, I was comforted by the knowledge that Einstein loathed algebra too. Despite the fact that he revolutionized our comprehension of reality, Einstein couldn't cut it in school. He has never successful, from elementary school all the way through graduate school. Neither the schools of his time and place nor our schools today have learned how to handle genius. Most of the time they are unable to identify genius, if indeed they even desire to identify it, especially when it expresses itself uniquely.

Einstein's life exemplifies the stigma of genius that still lives in our educational institutions. Like Einstein, many of our best and brightest find that schools not only undervalue but actually punish their creativity, intuition, and attempts at interpretations. Einstein's teachers failed to recognize his talents and sometimes treated him with condescension and contempt. His questions were ignored by his teachers, who often regarded them as threats to their authority. He was told that he would never amount to anything and that his presence spoiled the respect of the class for the teacher, he had a "bad attitude."

Such teacher perceptions forced him to leave school at the age of fifteen. In many ways Einstein considered this a blessing; he began to take personal responsibility for his education. As a result, he learned to be self-disciplined and self-directed, gaining insights far more advanced than his more "successful" classmates. During this time, he later reported, he not only came to understand existing scientific interpretations but also developed the ability to solve problems and see connections between what appeared to be dissimilar phenomena.

If education is to be of any value at all, Einstein argued, it must perpetually challenge accepted meanings. Rather than guarding their own territory, teachers must zealously guard the student's freedom to challenge orthodoxy in every academic and social domain. Educators must assume a questioning, challenging role. They must create situations in which students can question the officially certified "facts." Through these challenges students and teachers gain the ground from which new questions can be asked, and through new questions new "ways of seeing" can be developed. New insights lead to breakthroughs, to seeing relationships that were never seen before.

THE RELUCTANT SYMBOL

While Einstein's presence in the classroom may have "spoiled the respect of the class for the teacher," his cultural presence spoiled many people's respect for traditional values and beliefs about humanity's place in the universe. Thus, Einstein symbolized a sea change, a shift to new paradigms, a belief that at least Newtonian physics and nineteenth-century Western common sense were inadequate (Hauptman and Hauptman, 1987, 126; Leshan and Margenau, 1982, 21). With the theory of relativity Einstein upset the universe. Prone to upset those around him, he had really done it this time. He represented the idea that to "go beyond," we must go beyond common sense, go beyond what our sight and hearing say is true. But more must be said. While it is true that Einstein came to symbolize a generation's rebellion against tradition (for that matter maybe several generations), he was never comfortable with the role.

Einstein's Lessons for Learners 3

The thinker who helped destroy the rational harmony of the universe spent much of his life attempting to convince his colleagues that the universe is unified, harmonious, and comprehensible, albeit in a different unity than they might desire. Einstein's debates over the philosophical implications of quantum theory are legendary in the world of physics. Like most celebrated figures, Einstein cannot be appropriated one dimensionally for a particular cause, there is too much ambiguity for such simplicity. Indeed, maybe ambiguity is a key to understanding the mythology that has developed about him. Like Einstein, our late-twentieth-century notion of postmodernism is ambiguous, perplexing, and sometimes paradoxical. Could Einstein once again be the alarm clock that awakens us to a disconcerting postmodern cosmos?

WHAT IS POSTMODERNISM?

This question has been asked and not answered many times in the last decade. Before we go any further, a discussion of the term is required, not a definition, a discussion. We begin with modernism. Matei Calinescu equates modernism with the development of capitalism and its doctrine of progress, faith in the benefits of science and technology, time that can be bought and sold as a commodity and is absolute and measurable, a cult of reason (logocentrism), and a cult of action and success (Calinescu, 1987, 41).

Postmodernism, though it can never by its nature be precisely defined, has something to do with questioning these tenets of modernism. More specifically, the postmodern school of thought subjects to analysis those social forms previously shielded by the modernist ethos, admits previously inadmissible evidence derived from new questions asked by previously excluded voices, challenges hierarchical structures of knowledge and power that promote "experts" above the "masses," and seeks new ways of knowing that transcend empirically verified facts and "reasonable" linear arguments deployed in a quest for certainty (Hebdige, 1989, 226). When grounded in a critical system of meaning that is concerned with analyzing knowledge for the purpose of understanding oneself and one's relation to society more critically, naming and then changing social situations that impeded the development of egalitarian democratic communities marked by a commitment to economic and social justice, and contextualizing historically how worldviews and self-concepts come to be constructed; postmodernism becomes a powerful tool for progressive social change (Kincheloe, 1991, 1993, 1995; Giroux, 1988, 1991).

One more complication please. Do not confuse what we have just described, postmodern as critique, with postmodernism as social condition. Though the two are intimately connected, this is the point where many individuals become lost on the postmodern landscape. The "disconcerting postmodern cosmos" to which Einstein awakened us involves the postmodern social condition. Jean Francois Lyotard uses postmodernism to refer to the general condition of contemporary Western civilization. The "grand narratives of legitimation" (i.e., all encompassing explanations of history such as the Enlightenment story of the inevitable victory of reason and freedom) in the postmodern world are no longer believable; they fail to understand their own construction by social and historical forces. Reason is undermined because of its cooptation by those in power who speak with the authority of a science that is not subjected to self-analysis. Certainty is shattered as it is employed to control individuals who don't possess the correct tools to achieve it (Giroux, 1991, 19–20). Thus, the postmodern condition has arisen from a world created by modernism; the postmodern critique attempts to take us beyond the nihilism and ennui of the modern world.

WHY POSTMODERNISM?
Why would we even talk about postmodernism in this context, in a book about Albert Einstein and education? The reasons are related to the purposes of the book: 1) postmodernism allows us a new way to understand Einstein's importance to thinking and to education; 2) postmodernism grants us a method of analysis whereby we can see the hidden structures that shape the world of Western education; 3) postmodernism opens new dimensions of the relationship between Einstein and education; 4) postmodernism empowers us to extend Einstein's social and educational critique both conceptually and temporally into the contemporary era; 5) postmodernism enables us to appreciate Einstein's genius cognitively, in the process formulating new ways of knowing and higher orders of thinking; and 6) postmodernism provides us the analytical tools to deconstruct (to expose the tacit assumptions embedded within) the way that genius is represented. Is genius more often associated with particular cultures and social classes? Who can be geniuses, scientists? inventors? teachers? nurses? Are women's ways of knowing compatible with dominant definitions of genius? How is genius represented in the popular media? How might genius be seen as a handicap?

WHAT KIND OF STUDENTS DO WE WANT?
Einstein provides us with a role model for the postmodern student who is trapped in modernist schools that are concerned with measurable standardized outcomes and that unquestioningly accept officially approved information. Such students, like Einstein, quickly see through the facades, the grand narratives of school success, of shallow popularity. "Those who succeed," Eugene O'Neill wrote, "and do not push on to greater failure, are the spiritual middle classers. Their stopping at success is the proof of their compromising insignificance" (Ferguson, 1980, 118). Indeed, to the postmodern student, success is never a place to rest; the challenge is in the risk, in transcending.

Tragically, students in contemporary schools who are considered successful tend to be those who do not question the social order of the school, who rate low on both creativity and mental flexibility (Kincheloe and Steinberg, 1993).

Einstein became the model of the student endowed with civic courage who is unafraid to speak out or to take a moral stand. In the 1950s, he spoke and wrote of mass produced students unable to develop character and social coherence (Einstein, 1954a). During the McCarthy era he wrote letters of recommendation for victimized students and teachers whose "cowardly institutions" had left them twisting in the right-wing wind (Einstein, 1954b). He responded to those who praised moderation among students, declaring that such students don't "have enough character and interest to take any clear position" (Einstein, 1951). Thus, he challenged students to move beyond the comfort of commonsense, to seek liberation from the constraints of the conventional, to take the emancipatory leap.

EINSTEIN AND EMANCIPATION

Just what is this emancipatory leap? Einstein intuitively understood what we have come to call consciousness construction. Few realize the extent to which the Western world and the United States specifically has allowed itself to be taught to see or hear the world. The Miss America Pageant, for example, teaches us "beauty," "femininity," the nature of "poise," and the success of "safe" and trite answers to the problems of the world. Many men's and women's conceptions of feminine beauty, for example, are constructed by the pageant and by similar forces. Women with body shapes and sizes that differ from the "national" normal are often condemned to a life of unsuccessfully attempting to mold their physiques to the "proper" standards. Indeed, so much has this system become quantified that for the last few years computers have been programmed to predict which contestants will make the finals; these predictions have a high degree of accuracy. Women with Eastern European, Native American, Native Australian, or African heritages are deemed imperfect, outside the boundaries of "true" beauty; though inevitably the pageant ensures a superficial bow to egalitarianism by including one or two Latin Americans, African Americans, or possibly an Asian American from Hawaii; maybe one or two of the "ethnic" contestants are allowed to make it to the semi finals.

We even learn what things *sound* like. Yet how many students realize that the sound roosters make, for example, varies in different cultures: North America, "cock-a-doodle-do"; France, "cocorico"; Germany, "kikerikee"; Israel, "kukeriko." Thus, what is often referred to as commonsense involves a set of learned constructions of reality. Einstein defined commonsense as that collection of prejudices accumulated by age eighteen (Leshan and Margenau, 1982, 25, 27).

Contrary to "common sense," knowledge is not innocent; it is tacitly embedded and generated in particular situations by which economic, social, and historical forces mix with power and personal relations to produce worldviews, structures of belief and self-images. Such an understanding of knowledge allows teachers to begin to appreciate how oppression works, how patterns of subordination begin to develop.

For example, a teenaged Baptist girl from Alabama goes to church at the insistence of her parents on a Wednesday night. Even though logically she is unmoved by the appeal of the theology, emotionally, she dedicates her life to Jesus when the minister challenges the congregation to be "saved." Consider the many forces at work here: a child's desire to please her parents, who she knows will be happy with her salvation; an enculturated desire to be a good girl, a model of *feminine* piety; the underlying pressure of a school peer group in the popular crowd, members of which are all involved in youth programs in the Baptist Church, which socially may be the only "game" in town. To discuss the girl's decision on the basis of the appeal of the fundamentalist theology misses the point. The girl's actions are not based on a linear and rational, cause and effect process; her action is the result of a complex interplay of social forces, only a few of which we have mentioned here. As Michael Apple has maintained, beliefs "win ascendancy" not by way of logical appeal but by working on feelings, and their connections to the perceived needs, hopes, and fears of individuals (Giroux and McLaren, 1989, xxix).

With these ideas about consciousness construction in mind, we can begin to understand that schools are not simply places where instruction takes place and bits of neutral knowledge are transferred, they are contested cultural sites. Certain ways of speaking are legitimate, others are not, e.g., standard white English as opposed to black English; particular forms of knowledge are certified, others are not, e.g., science and technology and anthropological understandings of culture; specific histories are taught, others are not, e.g., that of European males, and not that of European or non-European women; certain patterns of authority are employed, others are not, e.g., patriarchal authoritarianism rather than democratic participation. Under the guise of transmitting a common culture, schools dignify and reinforce a dominant culture replete with particular ways of knowing and experiencing (Kincheloe and Steinberg, 1997; Kincheloe, Steinberg and Hinchey, 1999).

Schools don't study these issues; they don't study consciousness construction. When one examines the reform proposals submitted by various governmental agencies, one is hard pressed to see one reference to such concerns as a part of schooling. Writers such as E.D. Hirsch or Allan Bloom have no use for culture as an object of study, Bloom believes that such study leads to a "closing" of our minds (Aronowitz, 1989, 206). Indeed, most popular late-twentieth-century analysis of education accepts without question the standard cultural and school organization.

If we are to free our students' minds and emancipate ourselves we must understand these processes, these organizations, and their effects. The emancipatory risk inevitably will involve confrontation with the forces that have shaped our society's consciousness. Yet such confrontation allows us to see who we are and who we want to be. Armed with an understanding of how we have come to see the world and ourselves, we begin the long journey toward self-direction. As Einstein did early in his life, we learn to teach ourselves. Using Michel Foucault's concept of genealogy, we trace the formation of our subjectivities. We begin to see ourselves at various points in the web of reality, ever confined by our placement but liberated by our appreciation of our predicament. Thus, in the spirit of postmodern critique we begin to understand and disengage ourselves from the metanarratives that have become the dominant ways of seeing. Our ability to see from a variety of perspectives forms the basis of a long-running meta dialogue with ourselves. This inner conversation leads to a perpetual redefinition of our images of both self and world (Kincheloe, 1991, 46, 173).

WHAT ABOUT GENIUS?

After immersing ourselves in postmodern critique and thinking about the nature of emancipation, we have an admission to make: we don't know what genius is. In fact, the very word makes us a little uncomfortable because of the way it has been used. It is not our purpose to redefine genius and to delineate specific educational steps for its cultivation, a theme that has permeated much of the gifted and talented literature in teaching. We want to look at the concept "genius" as a cultural artifact, as a concept that has much to tell us about who we are and what we want to become. Admittedly, we agree with Einstein that higher-order intelligence (which has something to do with the artifact "genius") involves the ability to see connections among a variety of events. Einstein, for example, recognized common threads that wove his lifestyle, his values, and the laws of nature together into a unique fabric. This sophisticated intelligence has something to do with the ability to see what no one else has seen before and to see possibility where others see only despair. At the same time, higher-order intelligence has the ability to make the conventional members of society anxious, if not hostile. Indeed, there has always been a dual response to genius, a concurrent glorification and vilification.

As Einstein often put it, let's play with a thought experiment for a moment. It's 1905 and you're a professor of physics at the University of Berne. You pick up the phone to hear a twenty-four-year-old stranger who works at the Swiss National Patent Office ask if you would listen to some ideas about space and time that he has developed: a clock at the equator ticks at a slower rate than an identical clock placed at the North Pole; astronauts on a high-speed space journey would return to Earth younger than their contemporaries; an electron's mass enlarges with increased velocity. Remember, the stranger does not even hold an academic job, a background check would confirm that he was an eccentric who had been a poor student. You hang up. You might even bring up the call over dinner with friends to ridicule the young crackpot. How quick we are to dismiss the insightful.

But continue the thought. The young man serendipitously gains attention with his bizarre ideas. The ideas shake up our commonsense view of the world; they destroy our scientific, philosophical, and religious certainties. Imagine what one might read about him in the newspapers. Richard Lloyd Jones, an Oklahoma newspaperman, wrote the following editorial about Einstein in 1951 (at the height of America's postwar antiintellectualism):

> He had to scram out of Germany. America opened her arms to him, generous America, hospitable America opened her arms and took him in. We are appreciative. Here was a fellow who could teach us a lot about complicated equations that nobody could understand and is of little use to those who do. We give the fugitive citizenship.
>
> Einstein was soon a citizen of the United States. And then he began to find fault with us. He didn't like a lot of the things we were doing, had done or hoped to do. He might have known a lot about the fourth or the forty-fourth dimensions, but he didn't have brains to comprehend George Washington, to understand Tom Paine, to find intellectual comradeship with Thomas Jefferson or John Adams. He began to lend his name to subversive enterprises. It takes brains to have appreciation. It takes brains to comprehend intellectual courage and the moral powers that made America. Einstein hasn't got the brains. His brains are as disordered as his uncombed hair. And we have too many scrambled brains like his.
>
> What is the measure of an "intellectual"? Are we to call an ingrate an "intellectual"? Are we to call an intellectual one who, however gifted in some technical capacity, cannot comprehend the spiritual powers without which no freedoms were ever proclaimed . . . . Most of our intellectuals are not smart enough to be Americans (Jones, 1951).

Apart from the fact that editor Jones, in his attempt to read Einstein out of the American dream, embraced Tom Paine (whose anarchist views were too extreme even for the French Revolution), the newspaperman also put forth a worldview that was historically incorrect, socially racist, and culturally deadening. One is reminded of the southern legislators who voted to round off the value of pi since the fraction was too hard to memorize.

Schools often reflect such reactionary, order-producing, anti-intellectual aspects of the larger society. Traditionally, they have been quite inhospitable to the cultivation of creative intelligence and higher-order thinking. Charles Dickens well understood this tendency in the middle of nineteenth-century England. In *Hard Times* he wrote about how Mr. Gradgrind banished flowered carpets from his school because they allowed students to become accustomed to false images and thus to improper flights of fancy and imagination. Gradgrind explained his perspective toward creative genius in the first paragraph of the novel:

> Now, what I want is Facts. Teach these boys and girls nothing but Facts. Facts alone are wanted in life. Plant nothing else, and root out everything else. You can only form the minds of reasoning animals upon Facts: nothing else will ever be of any service to them (Quoted in Hardison, 1989, 20, 21).

In the same spirit, schools of the 1980s and 1990s entered into a neo-Dark Age. It is an epoch during which Reaganistic longings for a more ordered world bear as much relevance to truth as did the 1984 "Morning in America" commercials; where theological and social fundamentalists exert perpetual pressure on the curriculum; and where Reaganistic longings, fundamentalist pressure, and the testing movement combine to render consciousness expansion and higher-order thinking (Gradgrind's flowered carpets) an evil, if not at times Satanic, act. Fundamentalist preachers, supported by presidents and members of Congress, regularly refer to attempts to teach sophisticated thinking as attempts of anti-Christians to control the minds of the young. Thus, schools pursue blandness, working to turn out faceless students who go through the system quietly, unable to question the world around them. The "gifted" few who gain access to the world of imaginative leaps, curiosity, synthesis, and flashes of insight are the only exceptions, the only ones considered capable of handling such challenges.

Indeed, genius (or rather what is generally perceived as genius) evokes negative reactions regardless of time or place. Innovators are flies in the ointment of the dominant culture. They are members of a monkey wrench gang who disturb the drowsy status quo. They reject the comfort of consensus as they point and giggle at the emperor's nakedness. To fail to see the emperor's new clothes, to question the one correct way of seeing, is perceived by conventional members of society as an overt rejection of reason (Mr. Jones' ungrateful intellectual is not smart enough to be an American). Questioning accepted wisdom leads to a "catastrophic anxiety," an inability to deal with the chaotic and unpredictable world that Einstein's work seemed to create. This loss of certainty wreaks havoc when it is transferred to a school context, and evokes extreme expressions of educational catastrophic anxiety (Ferguson, 1980, 301; Leshan and Margenau, 1982, 20).

Hermann Hesse wrote of the great struggle between rule and spirit that is performed year after year, from school to school. School leaders devote great amounts of time "to nip the few profound or more valuable intellects in the bud." Those who are detested by the teachers and principals, he continued, the students who are punished and expelled "are the ones who afterwards add to society's treasure." The tragedy, Hesse concluded, are the ones who don't make it through, those who "waste away with quiet obstinacy and finally go under" (quoted in Ferguson 1980, 301).

Too often school is not a place where intellect is protected and cultivated, where interpretive ability is encouraged. In school, learner consciousness and the world are separate entities; the world is simply "out there" to be categorized, sorted into neat boxes, not displayed like a flowered carpet. Thus, schools of the late twentieth century operate in a nineteenth-century world. The world of the school is still a pre-Einsteinian universe. This nineteenth-century view of rationalism holds that consciousness arrived late on the scene of history and found the world to be a tidy and well-organized place. Consciousness did not help *construct* reality; it discovered it, and can now only help catalog it. Constructivism contends that the knower and the known cannot be separated, that consciousness of the knower is an important part in the creation of the world as we know it (Leshan and Margenau, 1982, 24). Imagine how hard it is for creative thinkers such as Einstein to fit into a day-to-day life in which their passion and their interpretive abilities are superfluous.

Is it no coincidence that both Einstein and Newton turned out their most creative work in isolation from school. In a letter to fellow scientist Max Born, Einstein recommended that a brilliant young student of Born's pursue work outside of school while independently working on theoretical physics. Einstein thought that the student could be far more productive and creative away from the prevailing assumptions of academia (which then and now hold to the dominant meta narratives of nineteenth-century science) and the unneeded pressures of testing and competition endemic to schools. The requirements of testing, Einstein argued, lead to superficiality and kill the spirit of learning (Einstein, 1952). The orgy of testing of the 1980s and 1990s continues to impede student learning. One teacher reported that now he takes his junior high pupils to a pond, gathers samples of water, and spends much time helping the students analyze all the life forms that are present. If a standardized science examination were to be required, however, this teacher could no longer take the students to the pond. It would take too much time away from teaching them how to pass the test (Reynolds, 1987, 174; Bohm and Peat, 1987, 77).

A COGNITIVE REVOLUTION

Creativity, contrary to prevailing wisdom, is not the province of artists, musicians, writers of literature alone. Its development is crucial to everyone and to all of society. The restriction of creativity and higher-order thinking to limited venues is a manifestation of limited imagination, of the decline of higher-order thinking in the contemporary world, of the postmodern condition, of a *cognitive illness*.

One of the main purposes of the postmodern educator is to cure this cognitive illness, in this book we will look to a variety of sources for the cure. The world of Einstein's mind is one important source. Piaget's work was extremely helpful to our attempt to understand what constitutes higher-order thinking, with its description of concrete and formal thinking. Drawing upon our understanding of emancipation and postmodern critique we are empowered to pursue ways of knowing and levels of cognition that go beyond Piagetian formalism. Adults do not simply reach a final cognitive equilibrium beyond which no higher level of thought can develop. There must be modes of thought that transcend the formal operational ability to construct abstract conclusions, understand cause and effect relationships, and employ the methods of nineteenth-century science to explain reality. After Einstein we know too much to define formal operations as the zenith of human cognitive activity (Kincheloe, 1991, 44; Kincheloe et al. 1999).

Formal thinking implies an acceptance of a Newtonian-Cartesian machinelike worldview, a perspective that is trapped within a cause and effect, hypothetical deductive system of reasoning. The formal thinker uses a science that breaks a social or physical system down into its basic component parts in order to understand its function. Emphasizing certainty and prediction, formal thinking organizes verified facts into a theory. The facts that don't fit into the theory are set aside or reconfigured, and the theory that is developed is the one best suited to eliminate contradictions in what we know.

Schools and test makers, assuming that this formal thought represents the highest level of human thought, focus their efforts on its cultivation and measurement (though sometimes they fail to get beyond concrete thinking). One of the major flaws with the endless parade of reforms presented by William Bennett and Lamar Alexander is the failure to recognize this assumption (Bennett was the enforcer for Ronald Reagan who viewed education as an Andy Hardy movie, and Alexander was an enforcer for Bush whose concept of education is the noblesse oblige of St. Paul's and the Yale of pre-1960). Students like Einstein who have moved beyond formality are rarely rewarded and are sometimes even punished in schools built upon such reforms.

What Kincheloe has described as postformal thinking is comfortable with the uncertain, tentative knowledge that emerges from postmodern critique (Kincheloe, 1991, 44, 45; Kincheloe and Steinberg, 1993). Einstein distinguished between ingenuity and intuition, ingenuity still operates within a formal structure, intuition operates at a postformal level. Ingenuity involves puzzle solving, a key function of a Newtonian scientist in his or her attempt to generate a clever hypothesis. Intuition guides the revolutionary scientist in his or her journey into the postmodern jungle. In no way are the two processes always separate, there is constant interaction and communication between the two modes of thinking (Voorhees and Royce, 1987, 29).

Ideas such as Kincheloe's postformality are what Einstein was talking about when he urged us to become involved with the Great Search. In his spirit we are calling for educators to become involved in a new renaissance, a creative surge grounded not simply in psychology but in a historical and social worldview of the various dimensions of power relations. This postmodern cognitive revolution recognizes the need for emancipation, the danger of the postmodern condition, the value of postmodern critique, and the many implications of postformality. Those who want step-by-step procedures for the initiation of our creative surge will be disappointed with our work. The cognitive revolution we envision does not lend itself to a recipe-like list of procedures. We can be confident that there will be profiteers who will attempt to provide a slick package of steps for the creative surge. Yet, too often such procedures become rigid conventions in the infrastructure of consciousness and eventually come to block the very creativity they were supposed to promote (Bohm and Peat, 1987, 265–266).

Creativity and sophisticated thinking have rarely played an important role in calls for social and educational change, for reform. Unfortunately, society changes only when a critical mass of individuals react to a set of problems that have been allowed to build up. The postmodern condition demands social imagination, a new way of seeing that understands that thinking and the survival of our species are inseparable. We have developed important methods for the study of the "world out there" but we have failed in the attempt to study "me in here." Ensnared by this Newtonian-Cartesian model of thought, we have arrived at a situation in which we gather more and more data about matter and energy but fail to increase our insight into the minds that put our information about matter and energy to use. An obvious example involves our significantly increased ability to wage war over the past two thousand years, while at the same time we have learned little about the causes of war (Leshan and Morgenau, 1982, xiii). Einstein commented specifically about this reality when in 1952 he argued that education must work harder to "develop the social side of humans." If we don't tame the egotistical drives of the species we will surely destroy one another, he concluded (Einstein, 1952).

Einstein also argued that when humans experience themselves, their consciousness, as separate from one another, they have fallen victim to a form of mass delusion that has destructive implications. This delusion becomes a kind of mental prison that restricts our social imagination, binds us to simple personal desires, and limits our affection to a few individuals close to us. Part of our emancipation involves freeing ourselves from this prison by expanding our realm of concern to all living creatures and the whole of nature in its interrelated complexity. In this book on the sociopolitical implications of time, *Time Wars*, Jeremy Rifkin expands this theme, arguing that emancipation involves the transfer of our private experience of empathy into public policy. In an empathetic social order, natural time takes precedence over the artificial rhythm of the industrial order with its time clock and its possessed time. Rifkin argues that the empathetic social order recognizes the interconnection of humans and as a result protects them from the modern culture's tendency to rob them of their pasts and futures. An emancipatory education is grounded upon this understanding and seeks to contextualize information and student lives accordingly (Resnick, 1980, 862; Rifkin, 1987, 226).

Thus, the recognition of the socioeducational effect of such structures as time is the epitome of postformal thinking. Individuals tend to be so obstinately attached to the tacit infrastructure of their culture that they unconsciously resist attempts at social change. Postformal thinking attempts to bring these hidden infrastructures to consciousness so that men and women can make conscious choices concerning their lives (Bohm and Peat, 1987, iii). Educators, for example, often move through sixteen to twenty years of schooling without ever being induced to think about their own thinking and that which has shaped it. This is one of Einstein's most important lessons; he models a postformal thinking that frequently confronts the assumptions that shaped his perspective, the very questions he asked. An important aspect of higher-order thinking, Einstein's in particular involved the ability to ask unique questions. Such questions emerge from the capacity to identify both new orders and new categories in old orders.

From where does this capacity to identify new orders come? The key, we believe, revolves around the notion of contextualization. Science and education in the modern era have consistently split off problems into increasingly specialized areas, in the process ignoring the larger context that provides unity to all things. This tendency is so much a part of modernism that it has affected our general approach to life as a whole. Viewing a problem from many contexts (e.g., historical, racial, socioeconomic, gender, geographic place, temporal, nontemporal, emotional, spiritual, etc.) allows us to see relationships that were invisible before. Armed with the recognition of a set of new relationships, we are able to sophisticate our inquiry, to ask unique questions that open the door to new recognitions. Indeed, the theory of relativity itself was developed by viewing electrodynamics in the context of mechanics. This contextualization allowed Einstein the ability to question the speed of light, beginning from an unusual perspective. The answers he found, of course, were phenomenal (Bohm and Peat, 1987, 11–14; Clark, 1971, 117). Let us expand our analysis of the importance of context by examining in more detail the historical Einstein.

CONTEXTUALIZING EINSTEIN

In the middle of the fourteenth century the bubonic plague swept across Europe, killing at least one-fourth of the population and changing the social order of the West forever.

Many realized that the medieval way of seeing was no longer adequate. Every technique derived from the medieval organization of knowledge was employed in the attempts to control the plagues, including prayer, mysticism, scapegoating, and magic. When pressured by a critical problem impervious to solution, a dominant culture's organization of reality will either collapse or a new one will develop. Under the pressure of such mass sickness, Western society began to develop a new way of seeing, a way that enabled it to understand and control the outside environment, the *res extensa*, the world of matter and energy. Thus, the Aquinas-Aristotle synthesis of Greek science and Christianity was overthrown and the way was paved for modern science (Bohm and Peat, 1987, 108; Leshan and Margenau, 1982, 30–31).

The foundation of modern science rested on the separation of the knower and the known which became a cardinal tenet of the Newtonian-Cartesian way of organizing the world. René Descartes' analytical method of reasoning, often termed reductionism, asserts that all aspects of complex phenomena can be best appreciated by reducing them to their constituent parts and then piecing these elements together according to causal laws (Mahoney and Lyddon, 1988, 192).

All of this took place within Descartes' separation of the mind and matter. Known as Cartesian dualism, human experience was divided into two distinct realms: 1) an internal world of sensation; and 2) an objective world composed of natural phenomena. Drawing on dualism, scientists asserted that the laws of physical and social systems could be uncovered objectively; the systems operated apart from human perception, with no connection to the act of perceiving. Descartes theorized that the internal world and the natural world were forever separate and one could never be shown to be a form of the other (Lavine, 1984, 124; Lowe, 1982, 163; Kincheloe, 1991, 27). We understand now, but could not have understood then, that this separation of mind and matter had profound and unfortunate consequences. Our ability to confront problems like the plague undoubtedly improved, as our power to control the "outside" world advanced. At the same time, however, we accomplished little in the attempt to comprehend our own consciousness, our "inner experience" (Leshan and Margenau, 1982, 31).

Thus, the Newtonian-Cartesian compass pointed the way to modernity with its centralization, concentration, accumulation, efficiency, and speed. Bigger became better as the dualistic way of seeing reinforced a patriarchal, expansionist, sociopolitical order grounded in the desire for power and conquest. Such a worldview served to dehumanize, to focus attention on concerns other than the sanctity of humanity.

Sir Francis Bacon, who along with Newton and Descartes was influential in defining modernist science, exhibited a radical discomfort with the inner world of men and women, with the essence of humanity. For example, Bacon argued that the imagination was a vain and unproductive entity that should be controlled by the strength of reason. Poetry, he said, distorts what is real, because it encourages the rational mind to surrender to the imagination. A metaphor joins things not naturally connected, creating a misleading and dangerous set of images in the mind of its reader. Despite such protestations, Bacon himself used metaphors as he explained the benefits of reason. Reflecting the patriarchal expansionism of modernity, Bacon used metaphors of warfare and enslavement: reason must "deliver and reduce" the mind; once the mind is "conquered," reason destroys its innate poetic tendencies and "buckles and bows" it to reality (Rifkin, 1987, 11; Hardison, 1989, 18–19).

Descartes, Newton, and Bacon laid a foundation that allowed science and technology to transform the world. Commerce increased, nationalism grew, and Europeans could conquer other civilizations at a rate previous unimagined. The rise of modernistic science was closely followed by a decline in the importance of religion and spirituality. An obsession with progress provided new goals and values to fill the vacuum left by the loss of religious faith. Even the family was affected as the new order shifted its allegiance to the impersonal ties of commerce, industry, and bureaucracy (Bohm and Peat, 1987, 109–110). Rationality became a new deity, and around this god the credo of modernity was developed: the world is rational (logocentric) and there is only one meaning of the term. All natural phenomena could be described within the boundaries of this monolithic rationality whether we were studying atoms or the solar system, dreams or engines, learning or gunpowder. No exceptions.

Every part of the universe was quantitative; thus, the goal of science and education was to develop more precise systems of measurement and to commit the results of such measurement to the mind of the learner. Equally important to the modern world was the concept of linearity, of cause and effect. Modernists could not imagine an uncaused event, the past leads mechanistically to the present, which leads to the future. If the past, present, and future were related in such a mechanistic manner, then the universe was clearly predictable. If we have collected our data sufficiently, we can logically forecast the future. Pierre Simon Laplace, the eighteenth-century philosopher, extended this logocentric linearity, arguing that the individual who was cognizant of the position and velocity of all the atoms in the universe could predict every possible future event (Leshan and Margenau, 1982, 4–6).

While Laplace was a caricature of developing modernity, the logocentric narrowness of the worldview did serve to reduce and fragment the world to the point that individual were blinded to particular forms of human and every physical experience. Modern science fragmented the world by attempting to analyze everything into independent elements that could be studied in isolation. Teachers, for example, study in colleges of education that view schools as institutions separate from the rest of the society. For the purpose of simplifying the process of analysis, disciplines of study are divided arbitrarily without regard for larger context. The Reagan-Bush reforms were well within the tradition of modern fragmentation because they were formulated outside of the wider cultural and political concerns of justice, equality, and social vision. As the politicians mandate test-driven curricula, they create a new form of the cognitive illness. Finding its roots in this fragmented world view, right wing reform has produced a "factoid syndrome" by which students learn isolated bits and pieces of information for tests without concern for relationships between the facts or their application to the problems of the world.

Such fragmented thinking and education has weakened our ability to see relationships between our actions and the cosmos. As we come to value autonomy over participation, isolation over communion, we begin to view natural phenomena as objects for exploitation and manipulation. This has led us to see science as a tool of prediction and control that suffers little remorse when in the name of progress and short-term profits it leads to a rape of nature (Rifkin, 1989, 259).

If we continue to isolate and analyze the various components of the physical world, many scientists argued, we will soon gain an absolute understanding of nature; it will be the end of history. Students of human and social science have taken up the same banner, arguing that we will eventually construct mechanical models of the human mind and human societies. Such perspectives are based on the assumption that we all possess a common frame of reference. The fact that they reflect a particular worldview (or dominant ideology) that emerged from a particular time and place is rarely considered in the world of schooling. Thus, this quest for absolute and certain knowledge obscures more than it uncovers because of its refusal to examine the assumptions that guide it (Gordon, Miller, and Rollock, 1990, 15).

Our unexamined educational quest for certainty results in a twelve- to sixteen-year training program for Newtonian-Cartesian modernity. Modernist schools emphasize quantities, distance, and location, not qualities, relationships, or context. It is enough to know that $2 + 2 = 4$. Why bother to understand that $2 + 2 = 20$ in another number-based system, or that putting two of something together with two or more creates a larger one that may be better (a movement toward a progressive goal or worse a monopoly of industry)? Modernist assumptions are tacitly embedded in various aspects of school life. The tests typically given in North American schools, for example, prepare students to think in terms of linear causality and quantification, the foundations of modernism. Because we are not educated to think in terms of exposing the tacit assumptions in our practices and conventions, many teachers are oblivious to the fact that they are propagating a specific ideology when they design their tests and teach their classes.

"What do you mean I'm promoting a particular ideology?" many would ask; "I'm simply trying to teach these children to think objectively." All of us have at least once questioned the way exams are designed in our school experience. Most of us have felt compromised by having to choose one correct answer. There are other factors at work here, we have thought. It seems misguided to try to isolate this phenomenon, this answer, from the world around it. But we eventually capitulate and provide the "correct" answers to questions involving names, dates, and places (and even reasons for events as specified by the teacher or the text), answers that are unambiguous and that lend themselves to precise measurement. True or false, fill in the blanks, multiple choice, and matching tests are all grounded in Newtonian-Cartesian cause and effect linearity, for all sets of given conditions there is only one correct final state, one *right* answer (Leshan and Margenau, 1982, 7; Rifkin, 1989, 262–63; Bohm and Peat, 1987, 24).

The appearance of Einstein's special theory of relativity in 1905 laid the groundwork for a new way of seeing the world. Many of the aberrations that resisted Newtonian explanation were resolved by the theory, the mechanical rules that seemed so inviolate when viewed from a commonsense perspective were not really universals. Einstein showed that such rules were irrelevant at both the macrolevel (galaxies) and the microlevel (electrons). In a flash it became possible to understand nature in ways other than as a clockwork, although uncertain, the possibilities were infinite (Ferguson, 1980, 27).

Thus, the groundwork was constructed for scientific and cultural movement into the unknown. Though challenging and exciting, many found it frightening and confusing, and reactions of various types from the religious to the occult to the political began (and continue) to emerge. External meaning grew more and more elusive, no longer grounded in commonsense certainty. Metaphysical frameworks were questionable and knowledge became ephemeral, as the world began to be seen less as an absolute reality and more as a construct of the knower. The absolute reality that was once so accessible became only a faint dream of the past and ever-receding chimera (Hardison, 1989, 7, 49; Hauptman and Hauptman, 1987, 125). Even certainties such as linear, uniformly flowing time were shattered, as Einstein demonstrated that time depended on the speed of the observer (Bohm and Peat, 1987, 108).

What we are describing is the beginning of the fitful, ambiguous, nonlinear movement from modernism to postmodernism, a movement that is still occurring at the end of the twentieth century. The fitful, ambiguous, nonlinear nature of this long-term shift is illustrated by the paradoxical development of twentieth-century educational psychology and pedagogy. Ironically, as physiologists and psychologists were purging all references to consciousness from their descriptions of neurophysiological processes, physicists such as Einstein were producing convincing evidence that the mind is essential to our understanding of the physical world, that, indeed, consciousness is inseparable from the physical. Slowly, as the evidence from the physicists began to accumulate, many began to realize that this modern denial of mind placed us in a situation much like the medieval Europeans; our dominant way of seeing could no more solve the social and educational problems of the present era than the use of prayer, magic, scapegoating, and mysticism could cure the bubonic plague (Talbot, 1986, 149).

There is great reluctance among many, including experts within the educational establishment, to accept the possibility that modern science is incapable of solving many of our pressing social and human problems. Understandably, people cling to the modernist creed that everything that is real is real in the same sense; consciousness, our inner experience, cannot be fit into the same logical system that is used to understand the physical world of concrete objects (Leshan and Margenau, 1982, 7).

Postmodern critique opens our eyes to multiple readings of the world and ourselves. This means that we can no longer accept simple, unidirectional, linear reality. The complex reality of postmodernism demands recognition of multiple causes and the possibility of multiple frames of reference, different vantage points in the web of the universe. Just as Einstein showed that reality took on a different appearance depending on the location of the observer, postmodern analysts argue that in any realm of experience the knower cannot be separated from the known. If we stand on the railroad track the departing train grows smaller; if we stand on the back of the train, the distant rails come together. Neither is actual reality (the train is the same size; the rails are still parallel), but both are an actual reality to the viewer. Thus, consciousness is not formed as the result of some simple cause and effect process; the world is not simply "out there" to be perceived by the human mind. As a result, teaching involves far more than the transmission of officially approved knowledge from teacher to student. Like Walt Whitman, we must take ourselves and our students and become one with the world.

Such contentions defy classical commonsensical notions; they imply that the shortest distance between two points is *not* always a straight line. The violence, chaos, and instability of the twentieth century long ago destroyed our certainties and pulled the metaphysical rug out from under us. In their attempts to cope with such a situation, men and women have either turned in desperation to fundamentalist religion, astrology, the occult, drugs, neopatriotism, or back to basics education, or have run away to live in isolation. Viewed in a larger historical context, the advent of the fragmented world, the postmodern condition, can be studied as the culmination of a panoply of challenges to current tradition.

The Earth was the center of the universe, until the scientific discoveries of Kepler and Copernicus convinced us that this wasn't so. Then came Darwin with his rejection of the belief that humans were made directly by God in His [sic] image. Reason was our supreme expression as humans, always there to guide us through our trials until Freud discovered the unconscious and the irrational. Our mores and folkways reflected eternal truth about human nature and provided us with unquestionable ways of living until anthropologists discovered a variety of social organizations that seemed to work as well as if not in some ways much better than, ours. With Einstein the idea that the physical world was stable and predictable fell by the wayside, and with it the assurance that truth was easily identifiable by the application of the logical scientific principles developed by Bacon, Descartes, and Newton. Should we be surprised when people retreat from the implications of Einstein's work and the arrival of the postmodern universe (Leshan and Margenau, 1982, 26)?

This retreat is made more difficult and complex because of the consistent promise of progress that has accompanied modernism. Obviously, we are better off materially than ever before, freer from the ravages of *some* diseases, capable of communicating in ways previously unimagined, but at the same time the long-term environmental and social damage concurrently produced may overwhelm these temporary advances. Thus, modernity has pulled men and women in opposite directions, rendering them unable to decide whether to flee or fight. Is this the best of times or the worst of times? How can educators deal with the destruction of the environment by industry and society, racial hatred, the limited vision of modern science, or the blindness of nationalistic fervor when schools are ideologically controlled by these very things? Cartesian dualism, the separation of mind and matter, continues to inflict its damage, rendering us incapable of exposing the tacit structures that construct our worldviews, our self-images. Franz Kafka understood this tragic dualism when he wrote in his diary:

> The clocks are not in unison, the inner one runs crazily on.... The outer one limps along at its usual speed. What else can happen but that the two worlds split apart (Quoted in Hauptman and Hauptman, 1987, 127)?

Despite the platitudes that issue from our seats of government, from the pulpits of those who preach a nationalistic religion, and from the whitewashed history and government classes in our schools, occidental culture as the dominant and cultural power is in decline. Despite its many creative accomplishments, the postmodern West has so far failed to address the conditions that have brought about the decline. The cognitive disease remains not only untreated, but undiagnosed by those who hold the seats of power. Hope persists, however, in the minds of those who speak and write of new ways of thinking and of acting. The crisis itself provides opportunity in that it has pushed wise individuals to envision the creative surge, the characteristics of the cognitive revolution. Such a revolution will serve to reconnect us with nature, renew our sense of outrage toward injustice, put us in direct contact with life as a whole, and establish multidimensional bonds with other human beings. As the cognitive revolution gains momentum, the intellectual and civic courage, the cosmic consciousness of Einstein can serve as inspiration for those carrying the banner. Contextualized in terms of modernity and postmodernity, Einstein takes on a role that may help in our attempt to save humanity.

EINSTEIN, THE POSTMODERN CRITIQUE, AND LESSONS FOR LEARNERS

Einstein once described intuition as a sacred gift and rationality as a servant. Modern science and education have worshipped the servant and profaned the sacred (Samples, 1979, 222). Those who have analyzed Einstein's scientific work maintain that any attempt to understand his discoveries on a purely rational basis will fail; nonrational aspects of human potential are sprinkled throughout Einstein's thinking (Fleming, 1987, 81). Einstein intuitively understood the limits of reason; he realized that scientific discoveries were not made by a logical series of successive steps. He destroyed the concept of an objective reality free from the mind of the explorer. Although he was reluctant to accept all of the implications of his work, those who followed him realized that the reality we observe is our own organization. Like water, reality is a compound with consciousness as one of its elements. Thus, we can't imagine what the compound would be if consciousness was not present. Nietzsche was right with his "fallacy of the immaculate perception," which maintained that it was misleading to believe that what we see is what is true (Leshan and Margenau, 1982, 25). Indeed, it is easier to trace the steps of rationality than those of intuition.

Once we realize that consciousness and outside reality are inseparable, we come to understand that the manner in which our consciousness constructs this outside reality takes on a new importance. How are such constructions made? What influences the process? Both questions become central to students of education. As we become aware of these aspects of the interplay between consciousness and reality, we begin to see the world as a complex, weblike configuration of interacting forces. Our consciousness exists inside, not outside the web. No one in this configuration of the world can achieve a Godlike perspective, no one can jump outside the web and look back at it from afar. We must recognize our confinement, our limited vantage point.

To recognize how our particular location in the web shapes our conception of reality, we need to understand our historicity (our context, or place in space and time). Modern cause-and-effect scientific research tends to ignore the way our historicity works to construct our consciousness. This results in a view of reality, ourselves, and our relationship to outside reality that has been reduced to a static framework. Such simplicity does not work, we are seeing only one portion of the picture. Post-Einsteinian, postmodern science rejects the possibility of an ultimate correct description of reality. There is no more a final description of reality than there is a true shape of a lump of clay. It is absurd to ask: "What is the ultimate shape of a lump of clay?" The same idea applies to intelligence, "what is true intelligence?" A postmodern teacher or learner who asks such a question opens up the possibility of new forms of thinking that were previously unimagined.

Whether we like it or not, Einstein forced us to ask, "What is true intelligence?" The scientific community and the interested lay public were fascinated by the question. The educational community has tried to suppress it. A brief example from Einstein's involvement with quantum theory may illustrate how scientific innovation influences in general our construction of reality and thus holds implications for a variety of fields, education included. On the surface, quantum mechanics should have little to do with neurobiology. Recent discoveries, however, have indicated that the nervous system can respond to individual quanta of energy. As a result, neuroscience's current reliance on Newtonian conceptions of space, time, and causality may be inadequate.

Learning theorists will have to go through the same process (some have already), as they reconceptualize the nature of memory from a linear Newtonian conception to a more holographic quantum perception. When physicists at the end of the nineteenth century asked the question, "What are the basic building blocks of nature?" they implicitly suggested that matter was made up of some material that was similar to our conception of bricks. Quantum physics taught us that not only were subatomic structures something totally different from our commonsense reality but that the answers to our questions involve concepts that transcend our Newtonian visual imagination (Bohm and Peat, 1987, 71–72; Talbot, 1986, 13, 38).

How do we learn to shift perspectives in a way that moves us beyond the Newtonian-Cartesian world of surface appearances, of Western common sense? This ability to shift perspectives facilitates not only problem-solving but problem identification as well. Students who develop the ability to reframe a problem usually recontextualize their thoughts about it, allowing for an approach from a different angle. Profoundly influenced by Einstein's work in physics, poet William Carlos Williams pondered the benefits of shifting perspective in literature. Combining the multiple frames of reference common to both Einsteinian physics and Cubism, especially Duchamps' *Nude Descending a Staircase*, Williams constructed *Kora in Hell: Improvisations* in 1920. Williams broke free from the linear constraints of Newtonian time as he combined the thoughts of several people within an instant. His shift of perspective allowed him to draw many broken things into a dance giving them thus a full being.... The stream of things having *composed itself* into wiry strands that move in one fixed direction, the poet in desperation turns at right angles and cuts across current with startling results to his hang dog mood (Mandell, 1987, 137).

Williams' cutting across the current is a profound metaphor for our attempt to define a cognitive revolution. When we cut across the current of our commonsense linear flow of time, we subvert our Newtonian ways of seeing, the belief in absolute space, time, and motion. As with Einstein and Williams, Schopenhauer and Heidegger, we are empowered to see new, unanticipated realities. Such a shift in perspective allows us access to new data; we are no longer chained to information that was validated by its easy fit into Western commonsense reality (Briggs and Peat, 1984, 277).

Educational science, for example, because it operates within Newtonian-Cartesian boundaries, has only examined specific portions of the world of teaching and learning. That which has been regarded as noise by traditional analysts may be heard quite differently by those who cut across the current of linearity. A school's public address system, typically ignored by the product-oriented traditional researcher, may take on new significance when there is a shift in perspective. A woman teaching the second grade may perceive a gender-related condescension toward an elementary school's predominately female staff embedded in the authoritarian edicts issued by the male principal over the PA system. What was once noise that had to be filtered out of "real" educational research becomes an important expression of the dynamics of power that operate in an elementary school. Before the shift in perspective, an observer might have seen life in the elementary school only in terms of those specific acts that involved student performance on standardized tests. Postformal thinkers see and hear beneath the surface, the prescribed; they uncover deep structures that shape our lived worlds. They go beyond the fragmentation endemic to commonsense ways of knowing and of learning (James and Ebbutt, 1981, 90; Wood, 1988, 146).

We recognize that our minds are constructed to view reality from a "correct" framework, a perspective that serves to fragment perception in a way that removes that which is being observed from its various contexts. In the spirit of Einstein, we combat this reductionism by developing the ability to see from multiple frames of reference, the more the better. Imagine what insight we could gather if it were possible to commission da Vinci, O'Keeffe, Magritte, and Van Gogh to paint the same scene. Not only would we see it from several revealing perspectives, but in our comparative viewing of the various paintings we would discern even further insight into the limitations of our original perception.

Think of intelligence in this context. When we are unable to shift our perspective about intelligence in a way that removes us from the blinders of Newtonian-Cartesian modernity, we see intelligence from only one limited frame of reference; genius becomes a static and petrified entity. Caught in the modern time warp of speed and efficiency, we are convinced that speed and intelligence are inseparable. Premodern cultures might contend that haste makes waste, but modern educators believe that speed reflects alertness, power, and success. Always in a hurry, modern women and men speak of slow and fast students. Pondering, reflecting, or musing might be valued in some cultures, but not in cultures of the modern West.

In a study involving male undergraduates, psychologists Robert Knapp and John Garbut found that the highest scorers on standardized exams were those who placed the most importance on the value of speed. Students from many traditional, indigenous, and agrarian cultures do not place a high value on the notion of speed. Thus, for cultural reasons, *not* cognitive ones, such students do not tend to score highly on the dominant modes of educational evaluation. Like Einstein, students from these cultural backgrounds are more open and vulnerable and less controlling and manipulative in their student roles. They view life more in terms of an aesthetic experience than as a contest.

In addition to this, researchers have discovered a correlation between one's socioeconoimc class and one's temporal orientation (Rifkin, 1987, 71-72). As a result, we discover one more way that culture and class influence school performance. Because educators often see from the unidimensional modern perspective, such hidden sociocultural and economic factors are unseen and individual students are deemed cognitively inferior. Hence, the status quo is perpetuated, as economically disadvantaged and culturally different students are condemned to school failure. Once we step outside the limited modern paradigm and view intelligence from a variety of frameworks, our resulting shift in perspective allows us to see students from outside the mainstream culture in a new way. We see forms of intelligence previously overlooked; indeed, teachers begin to learn from the uniqueness of such students.

Many would argue that the high performance of particular Asian students on such standardized tests destroys the connections that educational analysis have drawn between culture and school performance. For instance, the Japanese family, in its attempt to uphold family honor, makes sure that its children perform well in school. Japanese children are acculturated to perform well on tests, even at the expense of creativity. Although students from Japanese culture score high on standardized tests, their scores tend to cluster around the mean. Fewer Japanese students score at the bottom, but fewer score at the other extreme as well. The narrow, formal, and rigid training of Japanese children produces intellectual discipline but discourages intellectual creativity (Doyle, 1989, 117).

Just as the fish is unaware of the water, modern educators have been blind to the characteristics of modernism. When they are able to step outside the comfort of modernism, educational leaders and teachers are empowered to reflect on how it has shaped their perspectives toward the world, learning, and their personal role in the process. Like archaeologists and anthropologists who are granted sight by the conspicuous unfamiliarity of the customs they are exploring, educators have the potential to make the familiar strange. In the process, they uncover hidden historical forces that have helped shape the educational world.

Early in the modern era, for example, we begin to see the restructuring of the public's conception of what schools were designed to accomplish. In the 1770s social commentators began to assert that schools should be training grounds for industrial work. At the earliest age possible, many argued, children should be habituated to labor and fatigue (Thompson, 1967, 84). By the time of the earliest public school movements in the United States in the 1840s, educators had adopted the scheduling concepts of industry and had adapted the classroom to the rhythms of the factory. The time structures used to govern schools have remained virtually the same ever since.

Efficiency, introduced by industrial management theorist and modern prophet Frederick W. Taylor, became the gospel of both the workplace and the school. With the hyperrationalized time and motion studies, which in the contemporary era are calibrated to one-hundred-thousandths of a second, Taylor's efficiency promoted a separation of knowledge of work (conceptualization) from the menial task itself (execution). This separation produced generations of deskilled workers; workers who pushed bread into a plastic bag on an assembly line for eight hours at a time; men and women who lost all spiritual connection, all personal identification with the products of their labor.

All of this was accomplished in the name of time efficiency and economic profit. None of this has seemed outrageous or even significant in the development of school goals to educators who are blinded by their familiarity with the tacit assumptions that underlie modernism. Like workers in Taylor's efficient factory, teachers who are supervised and evaluated by the efficiency models still used in contemporary schools are deskilled, they are stripped of their role in the conceptualization of the teaching act. Such teachers become mere executors of managerial plans, blue-collar workers who are training deskilled blue-collar students (Garman and Hazi, 1988, 670–72; Wirth, 1983, 12; Callahan, 1962).

When students like Einstein and other postformal thinkers shatter the accepted narrative sequences, they are able to see historical developments that were previously deemed irrelevant. The influence of time that is organized for efficiency, for instance, has not been traditionally viewed as a dominant theme in the shaping of school goals (Hauptman and Hauptman, 1987, 126). But when we think of time in alternate contexts, when we shift our perspective, such a motif emerges as a major factor in the shaping not only of schools but in the construction of our consciousness, our way of making sense of our lives. Thus, we have engaged in one of the most important acts common to postmodern critique, deconstruction.

Deconstruction can be defined in many ways: as a method of reading, as an interpretive strategy, and as a philosophical strategy. For our purposes it involves all three of these definitions, because it views the world as texts to be decoded, to be explored for unintended meanings. Jacques Derrida has used deconstruction to question the integrity of texts, meaning that he refuses to accept the authority of traditional, established interpretations of the world. He has characteristically focused on elements that others find insignificant. His purpose is not to reveal what the text really means or what the author intended, but to expose an unintended current, an unnoticed contradiction within it. Deconstruction, like the work of Einstein, reverses the hierarchy of cause and effect, the temporality of traditional cause-and-effect rationality. Cause has always been considered the origin that is logically and temporally prior to effect in Western logic. Deconstruction upsets the certainty of this easy hierarchy by asserting that the effect is what causes the cause to become a cause. Such a displacement requires a significant reevaluation of common sense in the mundane, in everyday language. In many ways it is the extension of Einsteinian relativity into new dimensions of reality (Culler, 1981, 14–15; Culler, 1982, 85–88).

When the world is viewed as a text, deconstruction holds important implications for education. No longer can the reader be passive, a pawn of producers of texts. Whether the text is produced by an author or by tradition, "areas of blindness" are embedded in it, areas that, when exposed, reveal insight into the nature of how our consciousness is constructed. All texts are silent on certain points, and the task of deconstruction reveals the meanings of such silences (Scholes, 1982, 13). By employing deconstructive strategies, teachers and students gain a creative role that transcends the attempt to correctly answer questions about what the author meant. After deconstruction, we can never be so certain and comfortable with the stability of the world's meanings.

Deconstruction represents the contemporary postmodern extension of a century of attempts in art, literature, psychology, and physics to penetrate surface appearances, to transcend the tyranny of common sense, to expose the unconsciousness of a culture. Within a deconstructive framework, consider what has happened to the Western concept of reality in the twentieth century. The work of Albert Einstein, Werner Heisenberg, Sigmund Freud, and Karl Jung has served to destroy the fixed meaning of reality. We have come to learn that, like fiction, science is a text. It produces "truth" no more absolute than the truth of Mozart or Dickens, it is an inventive act. As Arthur Koestler wrote: "Einstein's space is no closer to reality than Van Gogh's sky" (Koestler, 1970, 253).

Scientists impose their own order on chaos, just as sculptors, writers, and composers impose theirs. The order imposed always refers to particular aspects of reality and is always grounded in the observer's frame of reference. Frames of reference are historical entities that differ from period to period in the same way that a Gilbert Stuart portrait differs from one by Pablo Picasso. Undeconstructed reality once had a specific (and ultimate) meaning. New problems, whether in science or education, could not be considered outside the boundaries of this reality. Thus, the manner in which we would confront the unencountered was prescribed in advance, those expressions which did not fit the prevailing view were ignored. We could only see or hear what we were told existed. The curriculum of our lives (not to mention our schools) was standardized and set in concrete.

Our encounters with Einstein and the deconstructive elements of the postmodern push us beyond petrified reality. Our concept of postformal cognition allows us to see beyond the given and to deal with the possibility of the ensuing uncertainty. There is more to learning than the accumulation of fragmented knowledge. Questions of why are at least as important as questions of how. Process often takes precedence over measurement (Briggs and Peat, 1984, 277–78; Rifkin, 1989, 264).

We have learned much from Einstein, but even these lessons are but simple beginnings. The cognitive revolution will change the face of schooling. No longer can education be conceived of as the collection of sets of isolated causal relationships. The world is a web of multidimensional and interrelated phenomena that move in diverse and unpredictable ways. Postmodern schooling will teach us ever-changing ways of living within Einstein's "reality," new ways of living with each other. In light of these ideas let us examine Einstein's life as a student and a teacher in more detail, constantly searching for more insight into the role of schooling in a postmodern world.

Einstein the Student, Einstein the Teacher

Modern educational wisdom speaks of fitting the school to the student in a way that accommodates the education of students in all sectors of the educational system. A paradox exists, however, when hidden structures of the school are exposed, structures that emphasize epistemologies that define learning as "mastery" of isolated bits of knowledge, marginalize conceptual knowledge, define divisions among students according to ability levels, and fail to understand women's ways of knowing, indigenous people's ways of knowing, and other subjugated knowledges. In the context of decreasing budgets for education, the nation is calling for reform that emphasizes increased accountability and demands improved learning and higher achievement in science and across the curriculum. The way in which educators might accomplish this task is made more elusive with the realization that different sectors of society have different meanings for increased learning. "For many, the vision for increased achievement involves traditional classes taught in the manner of exemplary teachers. Such a vision minimizes the personal experiences which children bring with them to school, the diversity in experiences, voices, traditions, and histories. For others, increased achievement involves curriculum reform and is associated with images of radically transformed classrooms and new roles for teachers and learners" (Robin, 1991). Amidst this background of reform, predominant models of schooling need to be examined in the light of alternative viewpoints and explanatory frameworks. For too long teachers have been expected to change, while their voices have been silenced about what can be done. Even critically aware teachers have been silenced by the myth of political neutrality in education that serves to label them as subversives. Cochran-Smith (1991) has described these teachers who are struggling for voice as "teachers who work against the grain." Teachers and students are essential to the culture of reform and the rethinking of alternative visions of schooling. In effect, the concept of democracy has been bastardized into a democracy in which everyone is allowed input about methods and styles of teaching; everyone, that is, except the teacher. As teachers begin to think of reform as an integral activity of teaching, it becomes increasingly important to explore what it means to be a teacher and what it means to be a student in a postmodern society.

WHAT DOES IT MEAN TO BE A TEACHER?

"Metaphors provide bold, rich, and distinctive windows" into the world of the classroom teacher (Fox 1989, 233). They are one way we can explore more fully what it means to be a teacher. Metaphors guide the way we approach the classroom. They are associated with salient roles and beliefs. They are at the center of the meanings associated with teaching and learning and help teachers to make sense of the events they have experienced.

Teaching roles have frequently been conceptualized using metaphors such as bricklayer, drill sergeant, clerk, babysitter, technician, and captain of the ship. Sets of beliefs are associated with these metaphors and frequently are translated into practice. But it is not enough to identify metaphors and associated teaching roles and practices. Our perception of why teachers do what they do must be rooted in an understanding of the actions that are both historically and contextually situated. Alternative metaphors and images for teaching are needed. Giroux suggests the need for a new metaphor, teacher as transformative intellectual.

> ... we should see them (teachers) as engaged and transformative intellectuals, professionals who reflect on the pedagogical principles that inform their practice, connect pedagogical theory and practice to wider social issues, and work together to share ideas, exercise power over the conditions of their labor, and embody in their teaching a vision of a better and more humane life (Giroux 1989, 729).

When we are guided by an image of teachers as transformative intellectuals, new and different ideas of what it means to be a teacher emerge. We can begin to think of teachers as knowledge makers, knowledge users, theory generators, theory translators, researchers, and reformers. We begin to think of learning as occurring through complex interactions that are embedded in contexts that take place through immanent activity by the teacher. As a transformative intellectual, the teacher constructs personal meaning from extant knowledge in a way that inextricably connects emotion, intellect, and will.

TEACHERS AS KNOWLEDGE MAKERS AND KNOWLEDGE USERS. If we view teachers as learners, it becomes clear that teachers engage in active construction of knowledge to change classroom practices. Teachers have valuable expertise that enables them to create, interpret, and construct a curriculum that builds upon students' prior knowledge and conceptual understanding. They do not need to rely on knowledge that is "transferred" from outside researchers, master teachers, teacher educators, administrators, or specialists, as is the case in traditional approaches to education based on objectivism. An objectivist view of knowledge leaves no room for teachers to make sense of their own experiences or to confront the social forces that serve to suppress their attempts to do so. Nor should our view of teaching be limited to a rationalist perspective, by which teaching is conceptualized as an applied science that utilizes the best principles and practices derived from research. A reconceptualization of what it means to be a teacher must include a critical dimension as teachers raise questions and challenge long held assumptions about their practice at a level that connects social vision to educational purpose. A critical approach to teaching must include reflection about teaching in the social context in which learning occurs. Within this tradition, both teachers and students are empowered to construct knowledge that is elicited from their personal experiences, histories, and cultural resources.

TEACHERS AS THEORY GENERATORS AND THEORY TRANSLATORS. Teaching is transformed when teachers become theorists, articulate their intentions, test their assumptions, find connections with practice, and explore the ways in which educational goals are socially constructed. As teachers question and reflect on their own practices, they will begin to generate their own emerging theories of teaching and learning.

TEACHERS AS RESEARCHERS. Teachers approach their classrooms with unique agendas of inquiry that reflect the culture in which they live and work. These research agendas continually evolve as teachers collaboratively reflect on their experiences and read, write, and reflect critically in relation to content and pedagogy. In the process, teachers become theoretically vested as they seek to understand the ways in which ideology shapes their self-images and ultimately their conception of teacher professionalism.

Many decision-making situations in the classroom lack clear paths to solution and may even lack clear definitions of the problems at hand. A primary result of this uncertainty is teachers' self-doubt, which is nourished by a second inherent characteristic of teaching: isolation within the classroom (Kagan and Tippins, 1991; Lieberman, 1982; Rosenholz, 1989). In many schools at which cultural isolation is the norm, teachers' cultural isolation from each other can create serious obstacles to change. Teachers, as researchers, can develop a collaborative culture in which those learning to teach, those already teaching, and those working within teacher education reflect upon the complex dilemmas embedded within classroom practice. They can facilitate change in an environment of isolation. "The intent of such collaborative work is to break down the isolation so endemic to the structure of experience in education and to transform the ways we understand how knowledge is produced" (Britzman 1991, 240). Teachers engaged in action research have an opportunity to create dialogue that is necessary to unlock and change beliefs and epistemologies and provide a framework by which to critically analyze practices in relation to ideological and historical orientations.

TEACHERS AS REFORMERS. William Bigelow, a secondary teacher, shared a vision of education in which teachers participate as agents of transformation in the process of teaching and learning.

> As a teacher I want to be an agent of transformation, with my classroom as a center of equality and democracy, an ongoing, if small, critique of the repressive social relations of the larger society.... I hope my classroom can become part of a protracted argument for the viability of a critical and participatory democracy.... At the outset I said that all teaching should be partisan. In fact, I think that all teaching is partisan. Whether or not we want it to be, all teachers are political agents because we help shape students' understandings of the larger society (Bigelow, 1990, 437, 441).

Critical teachers in the classroom are concerned with the relationship of schooling to economic and political structures. They recognize that teaching is not neutral, apolitical, or nonracist, and they seek to understand and reveal hidden values and priorities that are not always at the level of conscious intention. They endeavor to confront dilemmas associated with race, class, and gender that can only be understood through the emancipation of silenced voices.

PERSONAL TEACHING METAPHORS

The metaphorical language that provides an image of "teachers as transformative intellectuals" is a powerful linguistic tool. Since metaphors can both free and restrict the actions of teachers, it is important for teachers to examine the personal metaphors they use to describe teaching and learning. In our attempt to understand what it means to be a teacher in the context of postmodern condition, we explored how Greg, a middle-school science teacher, used metaphor to more fully understand what it is to be a teacher.

As a member of a teacher researcher team, Greg participated in uncovering and exploring assumptions about teaching and learning by examining his personal teaching metaphors. In one teacher researcher discussion, Greg talked about the metaphors that guided and constrained his teaching of middle school science:

Einstein the Student, Einstein the Teacher 31

Greg: You know, we were talking about metaphors the other day, and I see the teacher as a gardener. That's what my metaphor has been. Whether I follow it or not, the teacher is a gardener in this way. I'll try to explain it to you. The students are plants and some of them are tender and some of them are well developed. But they all start out as seeds which germinate and grow. And sometimes plants need watering and taking care of. And sometimes they need to be just left alone to grow. Sometimes they need support. They need different things. But in the end, like a fruit, you pick it, and you pick what you like, and it's good. You weed it and throw out what's bad and you develop this plant. That's how I see the teacher as a gardener.

Team member: Let me ask you a little bit about that, because I'm interested in metaphors and the way they're used. How do you use the metaphor? Is it a string of words or is it an image? Do you actually see yourself there as a gardener?

Greg: I actually see myself there. And instead of tying up plants, I substitute that for the image of the student is upset or something, and needs support. Or the student is not having a good day and needs support. Or somebody to talk to, support. Or even if they are not sure what they are learning, support. And the weeds are like things that are totally off the wall. And you have to pull those out one at a time. Sometimes they grow back because you don't get at the root of the problem. But you keep working, and get rid of the weeds. Fertilizer, I see that like helping a kid find things out. And the watering, my image is like taking off the cap of the head and pouring the water in, that's my watering. Filling the empty vessel. So I do that every now and then. And when the student is finally developed, you pick the fruit.

Team member: Who picks the fruit?

Greg: Well, that's the problem. As a gardener, the gardener picks the fruit. But here I see the plants, and they pick their own fruits. And they're picking each other and kind of making a salad. And you have Joe over here who's a green bean and Mary over here is a cucumber. You throw them altogether and you have a nice garden salad. I do get that visual image of it. And then there are also those days where I see the teacher as disciplinarian, the prison warden. The teacher is up in front of the room with the keys and nightstick saying sit down, shut up. But I don't play that one out. But there are those days when I see myself as a warden. And sometimes, when the kids are all going different ways, I'll see the teacher as an air traffic controller. You five are going to the library, and you want to go to the bathroom, I see myself directing traffic. I'm in the middle of a room looking for a downed plane, and sometimes they come and sometimes they don't.

Most teachers have several metaphors that guide their practice. The metaphors they use to describe their teaching practices can vary with the classroom context and the multiple roles teachers play. They empower teachers to weave patterns and make important connections that provide insight into complex relationships. Although Greg described several metaphors that were useful to him in conceptualizing his role as a science teacher, his use of the gardener metaphor to make sense of his teaching role most strongly influenced his classroom practices. Because Greg's gardener metaphor was associated with beliefs compatible with constructivism, he began to experience dissonance relative to "watering the plants" and "picking the fruit." He was later able to associate beliefs about control with this metaphor and express the need to reconceptualize his role in terms of a new metaphor and a set of beliefs. How might Einstein's life as a teacher help us in the attempt to formulate new teaching metaphors?

EINSTEIN THE TEACHER
Like many classroom teachers, Einstein's life as a teacher also was characterized by conflicting metaphors. An examination of Einstein the teacher can help us gain further perspective about what it means to be a teacher. Modern educators have a great deal to learn from Einstein. Postformal thinking provides us with a new and different lens through which to view Einstein's perspectives on the role of education in society.

THE ROLE OF EDUCATION. It is interesting to examine Einstein's perspective on the role of education in society, if for no other reason than because it is so out of step with prevailing ideas about the subject. Many of Einstein's educational views would be considered radical and dangerous in our present social climate. As such, they grant insight not only into Einstein but into ourselves and our time as well. When Einstein is seen from a broader perspective, it becomes apparent that his view of education's social role fits quite neatly into his worldview. It is part of his larger sense of egalitarianism and distrust of authority.

Einstein's view of the role of education in a society rested squarely upon the shoulders of his politics. A fervent socialist and qualified pacifist, Einstein's educational perspective rested on the assumption that the capitalistic ruling class has the church, the press, and the schools under its thumb. From a historical perspective Einstein argued that most modern political states found the roots of their existence in conquest. The conquerors established themselves, legally and economically, as the privileged class of the conquered country. Once in power, Einstein continued, the conquerors grabbed a monopoly of land ownership and established a priesthood from their own ranks. The priests, he said, controlled education, "made the class division of society into a permanent institution and created a system of values by which people were thenceforth, to a large extent unconsciously, guided in their social behavior" (Einstein, 1954).

Einstein had faith that socialism would help liberate humanity from what Thorstein Veblen called the predatory phase of human development. Since socialism is directed toward a social ethical goal, its adoption would move humanity away from selfish capitalism and toward a more cooperative spirit. Work would be directed toward the achievement of humane goals, not toward the physical needs of a greedy entrepreneurial class. With these ideals in mind Einstein argued that modern anthropology has told us, through comparative analysis of so-called primitive cultures, that human social behavior may vary greatly." The difference depends on "prevailing cultural patterns and the types of organization which predominate in society" (Einstein, 1954). Those of us, he contended, who are striving to move humanity past its predatory stage pin great hopes on the findings of the anthropologists: humans are not condemned because of their nature to "annihilate each other or to be at the mercy of a cruel, self-inflicted fate."

Education must wrest itself from the grip of the archaic capitalist social system, he asserted. Once free from the tyranny of capitalism, education could then serve to produce independently acting and thinking individuals who hold community service, not wealth accumulation, as their ultimate goal (Loria, 1979). The real source of evil in modern society is the economic anarchy of capitalism. We see before us a huge community of producers, the members of which are unceasingly striving to deprive each other of the fruits of their collective labor, not by force, but on the whole in faithful compliance with legally established rules.

In this system private capital is concentrated into the hands of the privileged few. This concentration is the result of both competition among capitalists and technological development and its division of labor. Together competition and technology encourage the establishment of larger units of production at the expense of smaller ones, and this creates an oligarchy of private capital that cannot be controlled by a democratically organized political society (Einstein, 1954). Members of the legislatures, he continued, are selected by political parties that are financed by these private capitalists. For all practical purposes, the influence of these capitalists separates the interests of the people from the legislature.

The underprivileged section of the population, in particular, has little power to influence the legislative bodies and as a result is left to twist in the wind, unprotected from the manipulations of the entrepreneurs. Under these conditions, the large capitalists control, directly or indirectly, the main sources of information: the press, radio, and education. Thus, the education of the common citizen is controlled by the prevailing capitalist powers. It becomes extremely difficult, if not impossible, for the individual citizen to arrive at objective conclusions and to make enlightened application of his political regents.

This crippling of individuals and stifling of their intellectual freedom Einstein considered to be the worst evil of capitalism. The entire system of education suffers from this evil, he asserted. An exaggerated spirit is pounded into the student, and he or she is trained to worship success in the material sense as a preparation for his future life (Einstein, 1954).

The only way Einstein saw to eliminate this soulless competition-based educational system was through the establishment of a socialist economy. The socialist economic system would be accompanied by an educational system that would emphasize the development of humanistic goals. Einstein's definition of these humanistic goals involves the recognition and promotion of innate abilities of the individual and the replacement of education's glorification of power and material success with a glorification of community service and the responsibility of each individual to humanity (Einstein, 1954).

This competitive capitalistic spirit, Einstein argued, brings out the human lust for hatred and destruction. Educators might be able to use the expertise of psychoanalysis, he wrote to Freud, to help temper these traits. The psychosocial role of education, Einstein contended, transcends the intellectual role. In a progressive spirit, he called for education to teach people the responsibility of community service as opposed to the inculcation of the competitive desire to rule.

Education does not fulfill its mission when it only teaches an individual a vocational specialty. Schools must address the acquisition of values and ask students to explore the question of what is beautiful and morally good. Modern education, he argued, must examine the motives of human beings and place curricular emphasis on the humanities. Overemphasis on capitalistic competition and premature specialization under the justification of immediate practicality destroys the humanistic spirit on which a culture's livelihood is based (Loria, 1979).

Consistent with this anti-humanistic spirit of capitalistic competition is modern education's glorification of militarism and romanticization of war. One of the first reforms that Einstein would undertake would be the rejection of education for militarism and the inculcation of narrowly defined patriotism. Our schoolbooks, for example, hide the horrors of war, while inculcating "hatred in the veins of children. I would teach peace rather than war. I would inculcate love rather than hate" (Berger, 1979).

While there are finite limits to what humans can learn in the humanistic search for truth, the process itself is liberating, as it frees us from the bonds of self-centeredness. As students search for truth in the warmth of a humanistic atmosphere, the process makes them "comrades of those who are the best and the greatest" (Dukas and Hoffman, 1979). If society is to allow its students to stand beside and learn from the "best and the greatest" thinkers, then educators must zealously protect the freedom of the curious spirit. It is this sacred curious spirit that is so vulnerable to the restrictions of authoritarian and social prejudices in modern education as well as from nonphilosophical routinizing and habit in general" (Einstein, 1954). It is a miracle that authoritarian methods of instruction, he reflected, have not already completely strangled the desire to learn (Sagan, 1978).

Indeed, freedom of inquiry is a fundamental educational principle, a freedom that Einstein was denied in most of his formal schooling. The rigid method of the Munich Gymnasium and the Zurich Federal Institute of Technology produced a dislike of school on a personal level. When combined with this broader intellectual disdain of the goals of schooling within a competitive capitalist society, his negative perspective toward schooling became entrenched. Emerging from this negativism was the implied belief that the education that is the freest and most valuable takes place outside the walls of the school. One example of this attitude appears in a sensitive response to a letter from an Italian immigrant who came to America in poverty and had educated himself: "Your letter shows me that wisdom is not a product of schooling but of the lifelong attempt to acquire it" (Dukes and Hoffman, 1979).

THE EMERGING TEACHER. Einstein did not become a teacher overnight. He took a long time to recover from the indignity of not receiving an academic appointment upon his graduation from the Zurich Institute. From his August 1900 graduation until May of 1901, except for a brief stint as an assistant to a Professor Alfred Wolfer in Zurich, Einstein was unemployed. In December of 1900 his hopes for employment were raised by his first publication in the *Annalen der Physik*. Einstein expected that he would soon land a teaching position with the publication of an article in a prestigious journal. He sent copies of the article to several well-known physicists along with his application for employment. But to no avail; the prestigious scientists had little interest in the iconoclastic young physicist with a few positive recommendations from the Zurich professors.

In the spring of 1901, he was offered a temporary position teaching mathematics at a technical school at Winterhuer, Switzerland. "I am beside myself with joy," he wrote a friend after receiving news of his appointment (Clark, 197, 67). When two months had ended no one had been sufficiently impressed with the substitute teacher to retain his services.

Soon he landed another temporary teaching position in Schaffhausen. Here he was appointed as tutor to two young students by a teacher who owned a dormitory. Happy to be teaching in any capacity, Einstein gave his full energies to his new job. Overzealous, overconfident, and impolitic, Einstein asked that the teaching of the two students become his sole responsibility when he discovered the rigid methodology of the regular teaching staff. Einstein was almost immediately dismissed (Clark, 1971, 13).

It was at this point that Einstein was offered a position at the Patent Office in Berne. In this same period he completed his thesis and sent it to the University of Zurich. In the early twentieth-century, however, it was impossible for a man to be appointed professor without having served as *privatdozent*. No comparable academic position existed in Britain or the United States. The *privatdozent* was an intern of sorts, lecturing as little or as much as he liked and receiving only nominal fees from the students he served. In 1907, Professor Kleiner, who had been involved in the initial rejection and subsequent acceptance of Einstein's thesis, proposed that Einstein should apply for a post of *privatdozent* at the University of Berne. With the loose structure of the position Einstein could retain his job as examiner at the Patent Office. Once again, Einstein gathered his application materials together and sent copies of his publications to the physics faculty. Confident that with Kleiner's help he would be appointed, Einstein was shocked when he was rejected. The Berne physicists saw him as a nonconformist, an arrogant young man who displayed insufficient respect for superiors, a blunt conversationalist, an awkward Jewish scholar, and a man approaching the age of thirty who still preferred the company of students. Though he was viewed with disdain and initially rejected, the decision was reversed at Kleiner's continued insistence.

Thus, Einstein began his teaching career in the winter of 1908 and 1909 with four students. The following term the number shrank to one. Though his time as a *privatdozent* was unimpressive, his articles were beginning to gain recognition and he was traveling to scientific conferences around Europe to present papers on his startling theories. It was ironic that the new man causing all the furor at the scholarly conferences was a mere "doctor" without a professorship to his name. The University of Zurich had established a chair in theoretical physics in 1908 and Professor Kleiner wanted Einstein. Kleiner, who had aided Einstein for so long, was quite excited about bringing the young professor to Zurich. His enthusiasm was squelched, however, when he visited Berne to see Einstein lecture to some beginning physics students. Kleiner felt that the lecture was very weak and totally inappropriate for the students in question. Kleiner asserted that it was no wonder few people attended Einstein's lecture; it elicited reverence and loyalty from some, rejection and condescension from others.

Whatever the reaction, we cannot understand Einstein as a teacher without an understanding of his egalitarianism. Einstein collaborated as an equal partner with students, listening patiently and genuinely to their ideas. He refused to make any distinction between the way he talked to the rector of the university or to a member of the custodial staff. The objects of his satire were not limited to any one group, he was ready to direct his sharp humor at anyone, regardless of his or her station. His attire became a symbol for his egalitarian spirit. In his later years as a professor he donned baggy pants and a sweater when suits were mandatory for college professors. On ceremonial occasions he refused to wear the required dress clothes, arguing that when men wear formal suits they create a climate that separates them from realities of life. "There is an atmosphere of well sounding oratory that likes to attach itself to dress clothes. Away with it," he said (Clark, 1971, 4, 9, 13).

This egalitarian spirit was manifested in his keen interest in the objections and questions of the students. He was extremely helpful to students, not as a professor, but as a friend. His time was willingly devoted to helping them and when they were mistaken he was incredibly patient in pointing out their mistakes. More than his egalitarian spirit motivated him to give so much of his time to teaching, simply put, he loved his subject. One of his graduate students said, "I have never known anybody who enjoyed science so sensuously as Einstein. Physics melted in his mouth." This love of science was his passion and thus his catalyst. Unlike many of his peers, he was not moved by ambition or vanity and had no need to impress or intimidate his students. He would illustrate his lectures with imaginative comparisons in order to make the material comprehensible to everyone involved. In addition to his creative explanations, he sized up his audience's level and tailored his lecture material accordingly. He would play the clown to evoke the interest of his students. In Zurich, students claimed that he was a born actor. Friends always admitted that there was a lot of ham in Einstein. Whether he was clowning in class or writing encouraging notes to bright students brought to his notice, Einstein was always concerned as a teacher with stimulating his students and sharing his scientific passion with them. Intellectuals, he claimed, have too often lacked the gift of stimulating their audiences. Apparently he set out to change that sad reality (Clark, 1971, 7, 13–14, 26).

THE FLIP SIDE OF THE COIN. If we accept this glowing picture of Einstein's teaching, we may certainly assume that he did serve as an intellectual who stimulated his students in unique, creative, and humanistic ways. But innovation and iconoclasm always elicit negative responses. Sometimes a great deal.

Many of his students and colleagues did not consider him to be a good teacher. His subject matter, they argued, was too original and too difficult to be explained at the students' level. Einstein found it quite distasteful to provide students with a systematic set of lectures that were designed to supply them with a mere body of facts about physics. He preferred, instead, to build a synthesis of facts and concepts, often using examples that revolved around his research interests of the moment to illustrate the connections between facts and concepts. He left the teaching of the set curriculum to other professors. As a result, his lectures were perceived by many to be scattered, uneven, and often incomprehensible (Clark, 1971, 13, 25).

Neophytes in physics often commented that he was neither inspiring nor stimulating as a teacher. They thought he looked more like a poor Italian musician than a dignified German professor. His marked Ulmer dialect was a source of ridicule and provided students and cabaret comedians with an endless supply of comic material as his fame spread. Young students often found it difficult to grasp even the meaning, not to mention the significance, of his articles and theories. They found his written works, like his lectures, to be too compressed, too exacting, and too abstract for their preference. The extrapolative distance between the specific and the general was seemingly unbridgeable to the neophyte, because he always, one student claimed, omitted simple, explicit definitions. It was not uncommon, confused students claimed, for him to stop in the middle of writing down on the blackboard a relation or a theorem and become lost in his thoughts. Minutes later he would emerge from the trance with a new hypothesis whose ingenuity, one student argued, "even the ignoramuses recognized as commensurate with the explosion of a supernova!" In these moments of creative brilliance even his student detractors forgot what was described as his "many foibles, his clumsiness, his lack of rapport with the majority of the class, his oddities, and his frequently almost inaudible delivery. Soon the moment of brilliance would pass and student acceptance would fade, and the neophytes would again resent the incomprehensibility of their instructor. He wrote and wrote, the students contended, without realizing whether his ideas made any sense to us or not." Einstein recognized how unfavorably some of his students regarded him, commenting, "how wretchedly inadequate is the theoretical physicist as he stands before nature, and before his students" (Clark, 1971, 30–31).

INCOMPREHENSIBLE LECTURER OR PROVACATEUR? If we are to analyze Einstein's role as a teacher effectively, one question that demands examination revolves around the basis of his teaching methodology. Einstein argued that physics should be taught as a drama of ideas and not as a battery of techniques. The evolution of ideas and the building of new ideas should be emphasized; teachers should concentrate on the history of the human attempt to understand the physical world. In the process, he asserted, students will discover new vantage points from which to view science and will realize that contemporary outlooks on science have no lasting significance. He was afraid that we have traditionally forsaken this view of science and have always replaced it with factual inculcation that is justified as necessary preparation for graduate work and research. He lamented the unfortunate tendency to fall back on the unexamined method that teaches students to memorize formula and does not allow them the opportunity to explore the way great minds developed their theories or the freedom to devise experiments of their own. This tendency, he argued, is analogous to the same strange need of history teachers to memorize dates (Clark, 1971, 10–12).

Einstein's view of the role of historical thinking in the study of physics and other subjects was quite sophisticated and thus often misunderstood. We must appreciate his view of history, for such an understanding is central to our grasp of his teaching methodology. Some authors have spoken directly of Einstein's disdain for history, and in so doing they have missed the point. Felix Gilbert, for example, writes of Einstein's rejection of history.

Gilbert brought six volumes of Gibbon's work *Decline and Fall of the Roman Empire* when he visited Einstein to play chess. Three days later Einstein returned the books saying "I can't read that stuff." At first, Gilbert speculated that Einstein's egalitarianism was offended by Gibbon's ironic and superior tone as he portrayed the bloody and cruel events of the late classical and early medieval times. But Gibbon's cavalier and aristocratic perspective was not the problem, Gilbert reasoned. Very simply, he maintained, Einstein's rejection of Gibbon was part and parcel of his general attitude toward history." Gilbert mistakenly assumed that "Einstein found the study of the past a very irrelevant occupation because it did not matter to him to know whether and how the present was tied to the past." He bases this interpretation on Einstein's statement: "For us, convinced physicists, the distinction between a past, a present, and a future has the character of a tenaciously held illusion." Gilbert, it seems, drew a conclusion exactly opposite of what Einstein meant by his statement. Einstein saw a past, present, and future as one continuum not given to separation and compartmentalization. Time was a whole, interconnected and inseparable, and could only be understood as such. Gilbert's initial thesis about why Einstein rejected Gibbon was much closer to the truth. It was the way history was presented that Einstein rejected, not history itself. It was the way that history was taught that offended Einstein. The past to Einstein was not a discreet entity; it was a living part of the present, a guide to theoretical understandings, and a prerequisite for future research and discovery. If Einstein's perspective on the essential role of historical research in physics was not enough to convince those who argued that Einstein eschewed historical study, all we have to do is examine his publications. He wrote many articles that dealt directly and indirectly with the history of science. Indeed, the history of scientific epistemology was a frequent topic of his writings and his conversations (Clark, 1971, 17).

Reflecting upon his rejection of some of the traditional methods of teaching science and his unorthodox relationship with students, Einstein concluded that he was not cut out for a normal university chair. He resented having to lecture on experimental physics. Lecture cycles did not fit his temperament, as he rarely had well-ordered, well-prepared lecture manuscripts. By the time a particular lecture needed to be given again, he would have lost his previous notes.

Throughout his academic life he struggled for his freedom to think and explore without interruptions. Bertrand Russell asserted that Einstein was lucky that his early academic work was in Europe. If he had taught in America, Russell concluded, he would have been put on so many committees that he would have had no time for original work. As a teacher, he argued for this same sense of freedom and challenge for his students (Clark, 1971, 4, 16–17, 38).

If education is to be of any value at all, Einstein maintained, students must be encouraged to challenge accepted meanings. Students must have the freedom to challenge orthodoxy in every academic area. Teachers must play a questioning, challenging role, as they set up situations in which students can question accepted "fact." Through these challenges we gain the grounding from which we can ask new questions, and through new questions we gain new insight. This insight leads to breakthroughs, the origin of which comes from seeing relationships between concepts that had never been seen before. This questioning, challenging role of teachers is important on many levels, one of the most important of which is that great syntheses are made in individual minds that are liberated from the bonds of orthodoxy.

It is a grave mistake, Einstein asserted, to believe that the student can be prompted to engage in this questioning, challenging role by "coercion and sense of duty." The case is just the opposite, he argued. "I believe that it would be possible to rob even a healthy beast of prey of its voraciousness." If it were possible one could by means of a whip force the beast to eat without interruption even when it was not hungry. The fact that the food to be handed out under such coercion was selected by the master made the destruction of appetite even more likely, Einstein concluded (Einstein, 1949).

The analogy was employed in relationship to what he considered to be established teaching methodology. The worst possible path that schooling can take is to "work with methods of fear, force, and artificial authority." Such techniques destroy the "healthy feelings, the integrity, and self confidence of the pupils." Students emerging from schools that employ such methods rarely have the self-confidence to challenge prevailing opinion (Berger, 1971). Thus, healthy questioning is stifled and the dominance of the capitalist class is perpetuated.

Einstein viewed his role as a teacher in a holistic way, he not only was an academician, but a popularizer and a philosopher-scientist. He considered his role as an educator of the public one of his most important. He devoted great energy to clear prose that was written on a level accessible to the intelligent layman. One of the great tributes to Einstein as a teacher is that the same man who enunciated the most complex and mysterious theory of the nature of the universe was, and remains to this day, one of the easiest to read and most widely read scientists (Clark, 1971, 27–28).

This holism is evident in Einstein's approach to teaching. He expressed the need for teachers to make sure that students leave the school as harmonious personalities, not as specialists. A harmonious personality is far more likely to recognize the need for his or her own personal growth and thus develop new plateaus of motivation in the long run. The stage for lifelong motivation is better set by the development of independent thinking, not by the inculcation of specialized knowledge. A person who has cultivated a knowledge of the fundamentals of his field and has learned independent methods of conceptual processing and working "will surely find his way and besides will be better able to adapt himself to progress and change than the person whose training principally consists in the acquiring of detailed knowledge" (Einstein, 1954). Once a reporter in Boston asked him during an impromptu news conference "what is the speed of sound?" Einstein replied that he didn't know. Reflecting his attitude toward the acquisition of detailed knowledge, he asked the reporter why should he know—it's a fact that you can look up in a reference book."

In addition to his perspectives on the benefits of minimal coercion and the development of independent thinking as opposed to the inculcation of specialized knowledge, Einstein argued that the only rational way to educate is by example. Many educators, he contended, may reach this goal by being an unintentional warning example (Einstein, 1954). There is no exact science that tells us how to carry out this teaching process specifically. Indeed, we may be able to guide young genius about as well as we can guide the wind. But students can, Einstein argued, learn in an inexact way by imitation.

Although Einstein was certainly out of step with the prevailing academic thinking of his time, he serves as not only one of the greatest thinkers but also as one of the great teachers of the twentieth century. As Einstein utilized his talent to present his complex theories with simple illustrations, he himself became an example of what the academician or the teacher could become. He became an example of how the teacher can not only utilize the classroom in creative ways but can also rise about the confines of the classroom and become a public educator in a new sense of the phrase.

HOW SHOULD A SUBJECT BE TAUGHT? The relationship between Einstein and education takes on new meaning in a postmodern context. In this context, learning involves processes of personal, social, and cultural construction of meaning by teachers and students. Teacher educators can seek to understand the processes of construction. A fundamental assumption, from a critical constructivist perspective, however, is that these processes are not under our control. Since teachers and students will make sense of experience in their own unique ways, instruction should be "directly related to the student's perception of relevancy" instead of emphasizing mastery of isolated skills that marginalize conceptual knowledge and attendant processes of problem solving and problem detecting. Heshusius, elaborating on the need for relevancy in instruction, explains this aspect of learning in terms of authenticity:

> Authenticity of the learning and teaching experience becomes of immense importance. By authenticity learning is meant learning for real purposes instead of exercises in learning. And when we make students engage merely in exercises in learning we can be sure that what they really are learning is something else than what we think we are making them learn. It is

important of course to stress that the definition of authenticity cannot be owned by the textbook publisher, or by the programmer of curriculum, for then we are right back into mechanistic formulations and controls: but it must be owned by the students' and teachers' minds and feelings (Heshusius, 1982, 10).

By extension, school subjects, when viewed from a critical constructivist perspective, should be taught so that learning is centered on problem detecting and problem solving activities that allow children to build a solid foundation because what they learn makes sense to them. Problem-centered learning provides opportunities for students to be actively engaged in potential learning opportunities through both "hands on" and "minds on" experiences. We must extend our definition of problem solving beyond that of doing a problem in a workbook, and realize that problem solving is an inherently value-laden activity. While student problem solving is a primary goal of instruction, we must take care to preserve personal ownership over problem solving and problem detecting. Personal ownership of problems occurs at a very early age when young children, in interaction with their environment, learn those teachings that have personal significance. We move further away from the idea of personal ownership in authentic learning situations when we engage in the myth of reductionism. Teachers can provide a learning environment that encourages students to engage in problem solving and problem detecting by ensuring that problems: "are accessible to everyone at the start; invite students to make decisions; encourage 'what if' questions; encourage students to use their own methods; promote discussion and communication; be replete with patterns; lead somewhere; have an element of surprise; be enjoyable; be extendible" (Wheatley, 1991).

In considering how science should be taught, Greg envisioned problem centered learning from a curriculum perspective. He distinguished between the experienced curriculum and the ultimate curriculum in a discussion illustrated in the following excerpt:

> *Greg:* Curriculum is that meshing of everything. How it all interacts is the curriculum. How you play out all those things. But if you ask me what my ultimate curriculum would be, basically it would be students deciding what they want to learn and having a big input into what they want to learn, a lot of negotiation about what's learned. Students being excited about learning. They walk in the classroom and they don't want to leave.
>
> *Team member:* What would your ultimate curriculum be like?
>
> *Greg:* Well, students choosing what they want to learn and basically learning through each other by helping each other. The teacher's role is gathering materials together, giving them some guidance when they get stuck, maybe helping them to use a resource that they're not sure of, helping them out with those kinds of things. A lot of times kids come in and they just sit there like a rock or use that unstructured time to socialize. I think that's why a lot of teach-

ers have them sitting in rows, because the students then see structure and they're supposed to be doing something, rather than just come in and do what they choose. Students would be doing experiments, or doing things like going to a book as a resource or coming up with their own experiments.

Team member: Talk a little about the content as you see how it relates to the curriculum now.

Greg: My ultimate way I would see it as students pick up on a unit or idea, whether it be muscles, hormones, nervous response, and the students would present their findings to the rest of the class. And the rest of the class could either choose to continue their experiments or choose another experiment or project.

Team member: Who gets to choose the content initially?

Greg: Now in my ultimate or the way it is now? Right now, who chooses the content? It depends on where you are. Right now each county says these things should be taught and how it will be taught. So the teacher does that. In my ultimate curriculum the teacher would just choose an area of study but students would choose exactly what they would study within that area.

Team member: So living things would be an example of an area of study?

Greg: An area of study, right. If they want to choose plants and look at how light affects plants, or how fertilizers affect plants, that would be one thing. Or they could choose hormonal response involved versus dissecting and comparative studies between anatomy and physiology and some other organism, if that's what they choose to do. I still think there should be a central area of study, because it makes it a little easier for everybody. It's just for ease, I guess, that you should have these little units. But it also allows students to talk to one another.

Team member: Give me that vision of curriculum again, as you understand it.

Greg: The most important parts, see that's what I'm struggling with, I'm in the middle of that right now. The first thing that comes to mind is what's going to be taught. What the content is. But also how you're going to assess the student learning and what are you going to do with the assessment. But the main thing of the curriculum is the student, the central thing. If you're going to have a central thing it would be the student and off that it would be how to introduce information, how to assess information, how to develop these and other interpersonal skills with the student, all that with the student being the center. And off that would be all those other things like content and processes. . . . . The outcome would be students that decide things like what they're going to learn and how they're going to learn it. And after they've decided how they're going to learn, they decide how they're going to demonstrate what they've learned.

WHAT DOES IT MEAN TO BE A STUDENT?

Students do not arrive at the schoolhouse door already suspended in time; from a critical constructivist perspective they enter classrooms shaped by ideology and culture, which act as a system of meaning and significance. They arrive powerless and oppressed, bringing with them personal beliefs and images of themselves as students. Their community is marked by diversity, in language, race, family experience, gender, ethnicity, religion, economic level, geographic location, all of which influence the construction of meaning. They interpret and make sense of the classroom culture in relation to prior experiences, through a complex process of linking past experiences with the present. Each has a story to tell, a personal journey. Thus, students enter the classroom with worldviews, sets of beliefs that have been culturally validated. An understanding of what it means to be a student in relation to worldview is critical to our interpretation of knowledge. A recognition of students' worldviews suggests a view of knowledge that exists in a cultural context, rather than in isolation; on the basis of this knowledge teachers and students can endeavor to construct emancipatory systems of meaning.

Einstein's experiences as a student provided him with an interest in education and helped shape his viewpoints on the subject throughout his life. The same person who would bring the ideas of curved space, gravity, and time together into a coherent theory experienced frustration and failure during most of his student years. As we trace his personal journey as a student, we can add to our understanding of what it means to be a student.

When he was five, Einstein entered a Catholic school. There were no Jewish schools near the Einstein home and the closest one had high fees. During these early years Einstein had few problems at school. He was an average student and seemed to have no problem being the only Jewish student.

At age ten he enrolled in the Munich Gymnasium. It was here that Einstein's academic troubles began and that he receive the first shock to his intellectual system. He was rather shy and introspective and quite reticent about any stirrings of genius that may have been churning within him. When confronted with demands to submit to the omnipresent Prussian God of authority, Einstein bristled. "The teachers in the elementary school appeared to me like sergeants and in the Gymnasium the teachers were like lieutenants." Einstein at this point became very skeptical of the validity of authoritarianism in education and displayed that attitude in his relationship with his teachers. He treated them with contempt and they repaid him in kind (Clark, 1971, 28, 31, 53).

Not one of his teachers at the gymnasium seems to have recognized his talents. This is not surprising, as the school was almost totally word-oriented and thus not equipped to uncover young Einstein's visually based talents. Rote-based subjects like botany and languages were his nemesis. Einstein seemed to have a tough time processing and dealing with words. His verbal problems, combined with his distrustful attitude, alienated his teachers. He was an enigma, unable to compete on a verbal level with his peers but full of perplexing and difficult to answer questions.

Einstein's classmates dubbed him *Biedermeier,* meaning "honest John," because he just couldn't hide his dislike for the instructors. After one teacher told him that he would never amount to anything, another teacher suggested that he leave school, saying: "Your very presence spoils the respect of the class for me." When he was fifteen, Einstein was forced to leave school because of his poor academic performance. So in 1894, at the age of fifteen, he traveled to Italy to join his parents, who had left Munich a few years before. He had to face his parents without the comfort of a degree (Clark, 1971, 33, 53, 66).

As an unhappy student in Munich, Einstein had learned the value and technique of self-directed study. Through individual reading he achieved abilities far beyond those of his more successful classmates in physics, philosophy, and mathematics. He had become absorbed in Euclidean geometry and within a couple of years after his dismissal from the gymnasium had taught himself calculus. He not only taught himself subject matter but also taught himself to solve problems and to see connections in ostensibly dissimilar phenomena. Formal schooling so far had been a vexing interruption to his contemplations. It had been characterized, from his perspective, by dull, mechanistic methods of teaching. Einstein had made his decision at Munich, he would rather take punishment before he would learn to "gabble by rote."

During his stay in Italy, Einstein decided that mathematics and physics were extremely important to him and he committed himself to a teaching career in these disciplines. The first step in the pursuit of his new goal required entrance into college. He traveled to Zurich to seek admission into the Federal Institute of Technology. His mother had asked that he be allowed to take the entrance exam despite the absence of a secondary degree. The authorities waived the usual requirements and allowed him to take the exam, which he failed because of his deficiencies in languages and botany. The decision was made to send Einstein to the cantonal school at Aarau where he could prepare himself for the entrance exam (Clark, 1971, 1, 33, 44).

THE FOUNDATIONS OF SUCCESS. The school at Aarau offered a fascinating change of academic pace for Einstein. Founded by Johann Pestalozzi, the school was marked by none of the harsh discipline of the Munich Gymnasium. Confronted with teaching grounded in the humanistic legacy of Pestalozzi, Einstein became an enthusiastic student. He flourished in the situation in which his unique holistic and bimodal thinking pattern was rewarded. To the teachers in the verbally oriented Munich Gymnasium Einstein had seemed retarded. To the teachers at Aarau, he was a cocky young man with a special talent. Because of the concern for visual types of learning emphasized at Aarau and other Pestalozzian schools, a unique thinker like Einstein, who suffered from a verbal learning problem, had a chance to succeed. It was at Aarau that his interest in physics was nurtured and allowed to take its own path. Fifty years after leaving the school at Aarau, Einstein confided that Aarau was a happy and pleasant experience for him. It was a place, he said, where students and instructors were united in "responsible and happy work such as cannot be achieved by regimentation, however subtle" (Clark, 1971, 45, 67).

POSTSECONDARY EDUCATION. In the summer of 1896 Einstein left Aarau and successfully passed the entrance examination at the Federal Institute in Zurich. That fall he entered the institute, dedicated to his goal of becoming a teacher of mathematics and physics. Einstein disliked the formality and structure of the school, to the degree that it was structured and formal, which was probably no more than most technical universities of the period.

As a student at the institute, Einstein spent his time at home studying the works of individuals he considered scientific revolutionaries. While he worked on these unauthorized independent studies, his friend Marcel Grossman attended lectures for him, took notes, and kept Einstein briefed on what was happening in class. Einstein's studies of revolutionary thinkers accentuated an already well-developed skepticism. This skepticism was the key to his scientific development, but the bane of his relationships with his professors at Zurich. To them he was one of the minor scholars who might graduate, but who would accomplish little if he did. To the Zurich staff, Einstein was a German pain in the neck. When he told Professor Pernet that he had natural talent in physics, Pernet condescendingly warned him of his limitations. Professor Weber was upset by Einstein's insistence on calling him "Herr Weber" instead of "Herr Professor," and told the young student that he needed to listen more often (Clark, 1971, 59, 61).

Einstein passed his final exams in the summer of 1900 and graduated in August. The coercion of the exams, he recalled, "had such a deterring effect (upon me) that, after I had passed . . . I found the consideration of any scientific problems distasteful to me for an entire year" (Clark, 1971, 62). His friend, Bertrand Russell, interestingly, had the same reaction to his finals: "The attempt to acquire examination technique had led me to think of mathematics as consisting of artful dodges and ingenious devices and as altogether too much like a crossword puzzle. . . . When I emerged from my last mathematics examination I swore that I would never look at mathematics again and sold all my mathematics books" (Clark, *Russell*, 43). The experience turned Russell toward the study of philosophy. The experience turned Einstein toward a passionate pursuit of a new way to define the universe.

BREAKING THE BONDS OF ORTHODOXY. The stratification of learning has been pervasive in our educational systems. It has dominated reductionist teaching practices that are rooted in the culture of standardized testing. As a forerunner of critical postmodernism, Einstein challenged traditional assumptions about schooling that sought to train rather than to educate people. He contributed to the emergence of new paradigms of inquiry which have changed long-held beliefs about teaching and learning.

Einstein's experiences as a teacher and as a learner reveal a different view of knowledge construction. Long before the emergence of new paradigms that emphasize how learners construct rather than absorb knowledge, Einstein was entertaining a holistic view of teaching and learning. His theories, research, and instructional practices were merged with his personal, social, and political values and needs. Indeed, he challenged traditional assumptions about the objectivity of our very ways of knowing. His experiences as a teacher and as a student deepen our conceptual understanding and push us to generate educational alternatives that meet the needs of all students.

Einstein and the Purposes of Schooling

Responding to a request from an organization of science teachers in the summer of 1934, Einstein wrote:

> The most important thing for a teacher to impart to the children is not information and knowledge but rather a longing for information and knowledge and a respect for spiritual values, be they of an artistic, scientific, or a moral kind. To impart knowledge where a playful joy in thinking and curiosity over the facts and results of a school subject have not previously been awakened is directly harmful, for such teaching produces in the pupil a feeling of disgust just as eating when one has lost appetite produces a dislike for food. If, on the other hand, a lively interest once has been successfully stimulated, it will prove active beyond school and will increase the spiritual powers throughout life (Einstein, 1934).

How far we have drifted from Einstein's educational vision. Over the past twenty years conservative critics of education have refuted such perspectives, and have captured the social and educational imagination with their portrayal of a national decline initiated by progressive, process-oriented educational thinkers such as Einstein. Though his educational philosophy is not generally known and he has escaped blame, Einstein could serve as an excellent symbol for all that the right wing believes is wrong with schooling. As they have made the traditional nineteenth-century capitalist dream fashionable again, conservatives present education as a pathway to individual fortune. These critics tell a story of a permissive "liberal" ethic that has precipitated a breakdown of authority, patriotism, and discipline.

In the late 1970s a conservative alliance was formed of business leaders, conservative academicians, and fundamentalist Protestants and Catholics who were newly awakened to their own political power. Ronald Reagan was perfectly suited to unite the coalition. Part right-wing libertarian ideologue, part defender of big business, and part purveyor of fundamentalist pieties, Reagan appealed to all elements of the alliance. Though tensions exist among the allies and the alliance is in no sense monolithic, the conservative reformers have changed the face of modern education. Not only had the liberal reformers put the American economy and way of life at risk, the conservatives argued, they also threatened the sanctity of Western civilization (Kincheloe, 1992; Kincheloe, et al. 1998).

Our awareness of the social context created by the right-wing reforms and the alienation of the postmodern condition can provide the impetus for our vision of educational purpose. It is a social context that Peter McLaren describes as an era of retreat for liberty and democracy. The application of scientific management strategies results in the deskilling (breaking a job into separate components that can be performed by unskilled labor) of teachers and the molding of students to the needs of the corporate hierarchy. Citizenship is linked to the imperative of profit and the retention of the social status quo even when it is at the expense of poor or minority groups. The concerns of emancipation or social transformation are virtually irrelevant in the present conversations about educational purpose (McLaren, 1989, 121).

Yet, as we employ our critical system of meaning we can begin to see the purpose of schooling as more than that of raising test scores and fitting students to corporate needs. As we envision them, schools in a democratic society should exist to help students locate themselves in history, to help them obtain the ability to direct their own lives, to understand the ways that power influences the production of knowledge, and to empower each of them as active agents of democracy. The pedagogy of democratic schools should enable students to develop a system of ethics on which to ground their vision of citizenship and should connect them with the cognitive revolution that inevitably leads to more sophisticated thinking and expanded ways of seeing. Using Einstein as a reference point, this chapter will expand and extend these purposes of schooling.

STARTING WITH STUDENT EXPERIENCE

Why was Einstein so uninterested in his schooling? We believe his disinterest had much to do with the lack of connection between the classes he attended and his personal interests and abilities. He often wrote letters for students who were for one reason or another performing inadequately in school. He sometimes suggested strategies for matching the curriculum to the needs and interests of such students (Einstein, 1952c). Just as in Einstein's time, students today are bored with school but fascinated with certain aspects of the world about them: fashion, friends, cars, TV, rap music, skateboarding, and so on. As these students become increasingly uninvolved in classes that make little sense to them, discourage them, or even insult them, the schools begin to implement sophisticated psychological modification procedures. Such procedures establish rigid school objectives, then monitor and test the disenfranchised student's mastery of the prearranged objectives. The deficiencies of the alienated student become the focus of her or his school life, thus further accelerating a vicious circle of student hostility to education.

Postmodern teachers can and must escape such pedagogical nihilism. Realizing that school has been irrelevant to the disenfranchised student, the teacher must look to the student's personal experience to reverse the drift toward hostility. No student walks through the school doors without a wealth of information, likes and dislikes, values, and untapped abilities. The postmodern educational project begins with the search for this student experience and the use of such experience in the construction of teaching moments. In such schools students learn to write about and to read their own experiences, the things about which they speak and think. Students keep journals, science observation notebooks, and construct their own math story problems.

Albert North Whitehead understood the ways that schools crush the curiosity of students, arguing that most of education involves an obsession with details, with bits and pieces of knowledge. Education of this ilk, he maintained, misses what should be the first step of schooling: the romance of learning. If we are to cultivate this romance we must attend to student interests and student experiences. In this process, we begin to realize the importance of how student subjectivity and student consciousness is produced. As we discussed in Chapter One, the understanding of consciousness construction involves exposing how social values, epistemological assumptions, and dominant views of the world unconsciously shape the beliefs, values, and actions of individuals. Joe Kincheloe has maintained that teachers must research the everyday lives of their students in order to gain the information necessary to build a curriculum based on student experience. In other words, teachers must become life historians of their students, exploring their place in the social hierarchy of their peer group, their romantic relationships, their vocational aspirations, and their relationships with teachers (Kincheloe, 1991, 188; Kincheloe, 1996).

Michelle Gibbs Russell provides specific strategies for understanding student experience. She analyzes the way that dominant views of the world (ideology) construct student consciousness. Teachers begin with an analysis of student memory, she writes, exchanging stories of everyday life, how a student got a funny name, how a student's clothes were ripped, why some students are always late. She explores the dreams students hold for the future and the specific factors that work to interfere with these dreams (Russell, 1983, 273). Postmodern teachers like Russell attempt to understand student stories at a deep level; they work to uncover the tacit infrastructures that shape and direct the plot twists that student stories take. For example, in her work with Helen Keller, Anne Sullivan had to become aware of the tacit assumptions about the roles of language in consciousness that were normally taken for granted. Only by exposing such a tacit infrastructure was she able to connect her curriculum with the unique experience of Keller (Bohm and Peat, 1987, 266–67).

Thus, postmodern teachers who are concerned with student experience develop a double consciousness. Teachers with this double consciousness are aware of the thinking processes of a discipline and the thinking processes of their students. This knowledge begins with an awareness of a discipline and how it has become legitimate. Armed with their knowledge of concrete, formal, and postformal cognition, they begin to think about thinking. It is one thing to have an awareness of the developmental stages of thought; it is something else to connect that knowledge to one's own thinking and the thinking of one's students in a way that allows the rewriting of the curriculum, a rewriting that connects school knowledge to the lived world of students. Such a teaching process would involve a heightened awareness on the part of teacher and students, as leaps from level of thought to another are identified and analyzed. This double consciousness would not allow the thinking process, the cognitive leap, the flash of insight, the moment of creativity to pass unnoticed. Such a double consciousness is not unlike a moment of lucidity in a dream, when the dreamer is aware of both the dream and the fact that he or she is dreaming.

META-AWARENESS: STUDENTS DEVELOPING A SENSE OF DIRECTION

Our double consciousness alerts us to the importance of self-awareness as a purpose of schooling. Einstein inspires our investigation, as he was able to analyze the genesis of his genius, the world's reactions to it, and how it led to his great accomplishments without ever lapsing into a self-indulgent egocentricity. Western thought, especially after Descartes and Bacon, has avoided self-awareness. It was enough to simple accept *cogito, ergo sum* without worrying about the fact that Descartes' statement should have been seen as a command to think rather than as a validation of thinking, a subtle changing of the phrase to *sum, ergo cogito*. Only in the last few decades have Western thinkers drawn guidance from Eastern concerns with inward reflection and meditation and their application to the conditioning of individual consciousness.

Thus, postmodern educators use their double consciousness to reveal the rigid assumptions that not only impede introspection but also block the effort to achieve postformal thinking. This double consciousness, or meta-awareness, allows us to reveal the conditioning process that serves to discourage more sophisticated thinking; it allows teachers and students to discover those areas where they have transcended this social conditioning, where they have broken into the postformal dimension. Such discovery can be applied to other areas of their lives, allowing them to understand more profoundly, to transcend the limitations of commonsense. Indeed, such a process can result in the teachers and students gaining a *raison d'être* for learning, an understanding of their relationship to the world, a sense of direction in the postmodern chaos.

But schools have rarely even thought in terms of such concerns. They see their reasons for existence as twofold: to impart unexamined knowledge and to rank students in conjunction with their concrete ability to memorize and regurgitate such information. Even when formal thinking is encouraged, behavioral strategies are used to manipulate its production. Such manipulative strategies constitute a form of psychic violence that deadens the senses of all involved, that leads to the cognitive illness that is endemic to the postmodern condition. Sometimes in explicit, sometimes in insidious ways, teachers use rewards and punishments as motivators. It is unfair to blame teachers for such strategies, for their professional education often is grounded on a philosophy of behavior modification and positive reinforcement that preaches that a system of rewards and punishments is necessary for standardized test score improvement (Bohm and Peat, 1987, 232). Finding that they are increasingly evaluated on the basis of their students' test scores, teachers are trapped in expertly designed Skinner boxes, behavioral cells that bid the imprisoned teacher to sit still and accept his or her condition.

All of this takes place in a socioeducational context that is portrayed as politically neutral. Teachers are taught *not* to gain a double consciousness, not to examine instructional goals or motivational strategies within a broader social and political context. Educational "training" does not involve analysis of the assumptions about human beings that are embedded in behavioral teaching methods. Henry Giroux labels this uncritical, noncontextual way of teaching as the "pedagogy of the immaculate perception" (Giroux, 1988, 61). Thus, power interests within the larger culture work against the demystification of the so-called neutrality of educational practices. Because social and economic powers construct this "neutral" worldview, it is shielded because of the difficulty of identifying precisely who holds power. As Michel Foucault argued, it is often easier to see who lacks power, than to identify the specific individuals who wield it (Foucault, 1977, 213).

Suffice it to say that in the educational discourse of the latter twentieth century, reformers grounded in decontextualized, outcome-driven, quasibehavioral instructional theory possess the power to represent themselves as neutral experts to teachers and the lay public. Though he was unacquainted with the postmodern analysis of Foucault, Einstein recognized the relationship between power, objectivity, and knowledge:

Many schools depend on the favor of rich people who would never consent to the teaching of truth in sociological matters (Einstein, 1934).

As Antonio Gramsci recognized as he wrote from Mussolini's prisons, as President Havel recognized in the Stalinist prisons in Czechoslovakia, and as the Chinese students recognized after the events in Tianiman Square, those would expose the pseudoneutrality of dominant voices are vulnerable to control and censure (Forgacs, 1988, 348). A new experience, a new vision of reality, a double consciousness provides impetus for individuals to seek a new direction, to escape the hive of conformity, an act which has never been looked upon with favor in schools.

The student search for direction is no simple task in the maze of the postmodern condition. In a way the search for direction is an attempt to restore meaning, an endeavor to resuscitate hope. "Give me something to believe in," the rock band Poison sings to its postmodern, alienated young audience. The Newtonian-Cartesian world viewed the cosmos as a great vacuum filled with atoms that interact only by direct impact. The implications of such a view were devastating to the traditional sense of human belonging and individual connection to the universe. Soon society and people themselves came to be seen as independent and discrete *objects*. Human solidarity was relegated to a lower realm, a relic of a superstitious, premodern age.

The world of interior experience has been erased by Newtonian-Cartesian modernity. The soul, that aspect of humanness where the inner world and outer world meet, cannot be discussed in modern terms even though it is the seat of our most human of characteristics—creativity, intuition, and consciousness. Without soul the search for direction is impossible; indeed, we are reduced to two dimensional characters who are unconnected to our fellow beings or the biosphere (Combs and Holland, 1990, xviii). Schools that reflect the modern fragmentation of meaning not only teach facts in isolation but also teach students in isolation from one another. How can we continue to be surprised when our students express their frustration with the meaninglessness of their school experience? How can we deny the call by postmodern educators for us to pause and consider the purpose, the direction, of educational endeavor?

Despite the great advances of modern physical and educational science, scholars say that they often trust their initial gut reactions more than a scientifically reasoned decision. In many situations, instinct is more reliable than intellect; teacher intuition is more often attuned to the reality of the classroom than many of the scientific studies produced by experts in education. The history of the development of the human mind revolves around the theme of abstraction, the progressive distancing of the mind from the world around it. Contrary to Einstein's passion, modern science was unconcerned with the unity

Einstein and the Purposes of Schooling

of living and nonliving entities. Fragmentation was inevitable (Voorhees and Royce, 1987, 31; Rifkin, 1989, 183).

This double consciousness or meta-awareness begins with the postformal realization that a major portion of cognitive activity has little to do with direct sensation. Indeed, intuition precedes cognition by recognizing the existence of problems, or asymmetries. Einstein, for example, confided that many of his scientific concepts originated in intuitive feelings and sensations (Bohm and Peat, 1987, 262; Courtney, 1988, 46). These intuitive feelings and sensations involve not so much an ability (certainly not a measurable ability) but an awareness of significance or potential significance. When Einstein followed his intuitive feelings, he was simply moving in a direction that allowed him to experience an increased sense of meaning.

One "has an intuition" when a jumble of ostensibly unrelated facts are perceived as parts of a unified and meaningful whole. This ability to uncover meaning is the basis of the artistic imagination, an orientation toward sustained creative perception. Imagination literally means the ability to make mental images, but intuitive artistic imagination involves a sense of direction that allows for the creative production of unique forms, the discernment of new levels of connection. Schools teach a formal cognition that allows individuals to fit new information into categories in order to achieve a preordained final product, usually a generalization. Intuitive meta-awareness, however, is not primarily concerned with categorization but with clarity of perception, clarity of vision. This is what Einstein meant when he described his intuition as a scientist as a sense of direction, as the nonlogical, nonlinear ability to directly perceive an unknown relationship (Voorhees and Royce, 1987, 31–32; Bohm and Peat, 1987, 261; Courtney, 1988, 41).

Einstein's meta-awareness would have accounted for little without the passion he brought to his scientific and humanistic endeavors. The world can become a better place to live, he argued, "only if enough people are bound to principles and ready to suffer for their convictions" (Einstein, 1938). Feminist theory has significantly contributed to our attempt to transcend the cold logic of Newtonian-Cartesian modernism. Madeleine Grumet writes of the importance of passion, feeling, empathy, and the body in the acts of thinking, inquiring, and knowing. Understanding the relationship between commitment and cognition, Grumet and other feminist scholars maintain that as knowers grow passionate about what they know, they develop a deeper relationship with themselves. Such a relationship produces a self-knowledge, a meta-analytical frame of mind that stimulates a synergistic cycle, a cycle that grants them more insight into the issues under consideration.

What emerges from the process is a form of personal knowledge that allows the individual to see the world as more than a modern set of fixed laws. In this context the world is characterized as a process, a set of patterns, a web of dialectical interactions by which the knower's passionate personal participation in events and the emotional, intuitive insight gained from such participation moves us toward a new dimension of cognition, a postformal mode of knowing. Informed by feminist perspectives, postmodern thinkers understand that emotions and passion exert a subversive, disorganizing effect on modern, logocentric ways of seeing. But such disorganization is a major step in the effort to transcend the fragmentation of Newtonian-Cartesian modernism as we attempt to unify our perceptions of ourselves and the cosmos. Passion and emotion are unique human ways of knowing, to deny them is to unnecessarily limit our cognitive ability (Grumet, 1988, 3–15; Belenky, Clinchy, Goldberger, and Tarule, 1986, 140–41; Reinharz, 1979, 242–43; Mahoney and Lyddon, 1988, 216–17).

Teachers who deny the role of passion and emotion in their professional lives not only will limit their own cognitive ability but will fail to motivate their students to either risk participation in the life of the mind or to develop a sense of direction. The cultivation of intuitive meta-awareness cannot follow the dictates of predesigned lesson plans tightly fitted into the time arrangement of school bells. Its development cannot be facilely written into behavioral objectives and then measured by standardized tests. Students acquire a sense of direction, a facility for meta-awareness, very slowly, on their own terms, at their own pace. In schools where test-driven curricula demand the speedy coverage of information, a slow paced effort that encourages students to reflect, take delight, share, and connect will not sell well with those in charge. It will not promote positive public relations by improving standardized test scores. It will not teach thinking.

EINSTEIN AND THE ROLE OF THE TEACHER

Concerned with the role of teachers in school and society, Einstein spoke and wrote often on the topic. Einstein anticipated the deskilling of teachers, and recognized the growing dependency of teachers on their workplace superiors (Einstein, 1952a; Einstein, 1954). Because they are controlled by the overmanagement of the workplace, teachers have less room to be innovative, to teach at the slow pace that encourages meta-awareness. Empirical educational research has "proven" that when the time students spend on a particular subject increases, student standardized test scores increase. Thus, reformers have sought to control teacher work-time to guarantee that they teach directly to specific objectives. Teacher insight into the special needs of their particular classroom has not been taken into account. Concern with producing thoughtful students capable of self-direction has been ignored. Like members of a Third World culture, teachers become victims of power structures and scarce resources; their main interest becomes survival, as time for reflection and analysis of purposes dissolves (McCutcheon, 1981, 188–190; Oldroyd, 1985, 113, 117).

Einstein and the Purposes of Schooling

Though he could not have anticipated the degree of deskilling, the oppressive paperwork, and the muzzling that teachers have endured in recent years, Einstein understood the silencing of teachers by power interests, their isolation, their financial dependence on the economically privileged, their vulnerability to those disdainful of authentic communication and free speech (Plotkin, 1955; Einstein, 1954; Einstein, 1951b). As they take up where Einstein left off, postmodern educators must become students of power. As students of power, they must question why it becomes so difficult to teach about emancipation, meta-awareness, and new ways of seeing.

In the spirit of Henry Giroux's notion of teachers as transformative intellectuals, educators must expand commonsense definitions of power as they search for the ways that certain "apparatuses of power" (e.g., who from the community is invited to speak to students, whose cultures and histories are assumed to be worthy of inclusion in the curriculum, what stories are covered by local newspapers and television and what stories are ignored) portray particular ways of life as legitimate. Returning to Foucault's understanding of power as the ability to determine what constitutes truth, transformative postmodern teachers must begin to deconstruct the "truths" of the school, truths that relegate them to low status and exclude them from the negotiations about their school's purpose. In their professional education and in service acculturation teachers are trained to use a variety of teaching methods. They are rarely taught, however, to criticize these methods. Questions of the implications of these methods for the role of teachers, the power relations within school and society, and the very purposes of school itself, are not asked in the teacher's educational experience. What we have referred to as the attempt to deskill teachers is simply an effort to render educators conceptually and politically illiterate (Giroux, 1988, xxxv, 8, 101).

Postmodern teachers who overcome this form of illiteracy become role models for students in the very process of their struggle and resistance, models of meta-awareness, models of men and women motivated by a passionately held sense of direction. Writing about the attempt to cultivate moral intelligence, Einstein concluded that there is no direct way to accomplish this task:

> One can give a good example by one's own life. One can try to bring about a change in education in our schools so that the supreme value of success is replaced by appreciation of honest work of any kind which improves the well-being of man (Einstein, 1948).

Through their own struggle to understand power relations, the ways that knowledge is produced and made legitimate, and the process by which the curriculum is negotiated and implemented, teachers learn to think and to teach. In understanding the construction of their own consciousness teachers are empowered to help students understand the construction of theirs. Such empowered teachers turn classrooms into what Peter McLaren calls "critical spaces," places where established conventions are subject to question, where the unspeakable can be spoken, where student questions are treasured rather than punished (McLaren 1989, 241). Such classrooms become political sanctuaries where power's unalterable truth is not allowed to terrorize, or to quell our ability to imagine alternatives to what Einstein called "the supreme value of success."

CRITICAL CONSTRUCTIVISM:
THINKING ABOUT TEACHING AND TEACHING ABOUT THINKING

The work of Jean Piaget, combining cognitive psychology and epistemology (the branch of philosophy that studies knowledge, how we come to know), has revolutionized how we understand human learning. Piaget's work, often referred to as constructivism, assumes that there is no knowledge without a knower. The human knower belongs to a particular, ever-changing historical world. The human being as a part of history is a reflexive subject, an entity who is conscious of the constant interaction between humans and their world. This reflexiveness recognizes that all knowledge is a fusion of subject and object. Stated another way, constructivism posits that the knower personally participates in all acts of knowing and of understanding (Lowe, 1982, 163; Gordon, Miller, and Rollock, 1990, 17; Reinharz, 1979, 245).

Viewed from the historical perspective of modernism and postmodernism, constructivism may be seen as the epistemological dimension of the shift to postmodernism, as an epistemological prerequisite for postformal thinking. Einstein's role in the shift is multidimensional. In the first place, one of the main differences between Newtonian and Einsteinian physics involves a change in the observer's perspective. The Newtonian perspective is a God's-eye view of the world, never changing, "out there," always the same regardless of the observer. It takes no account of the relationship of the knower to the known. On the other hand, the Einsteinian perspective is a human's-eye view, in which what you perceive and what I perceive is relative to where we are standing, the conditions of our observation. Thus, the relationship between the knower and the known is very important to Einsteinian physics.

The second dimension of Einstein's role in constructivism's shift to a postmodern epistemology involves his direct interaction with theorists of psychology. In a conversation with Piaget in 1928, Einstein suggested a number of questions that influenced Piaget's subsequent work. Is our intuitive grasp of time primitive or derived? Is it identical with our intuitive grasp of velocity? What bearing do these questions have on the development of the child's conception of time?

As Piaget thought about Einstein's questions it became apparent to him that time and space are not preset categories that are embedded in nature and in the mind of the child. Like other concepts, they develop from earlier "schemes" or previous constructs of representing the world. The child gradually develops an understanding of time from the developmentally more primitive concepts of distance and speed. Einstein had conceived of relativity by "regressing" to a more primitive conception of time. Through Piaget's understanding of Einstein's thought processes in his conceptualization of relativity, Piaget began to theorize the existence of developmental stages and thus the way that the mind constructs its view of reality (Reynolds, 1987, 169–70).

Thus, from Piaget we learn that nothing represents a "neutral" perspective. No truly objective way of seeing exists. Nothing exists before consciousness shapes it into something we can perceive. What appears to us as objective reality is merely what our minds construct, what we are accustomed to seeing. Perception, therefore, is not a passive act of receiving what reality tells us to perceive. For example, physiologists have shown that the physical act of vision dictates the active movement of both the body and the mind (Leshan and Margenau, 1982, 189; Bohm and Peat, 1987, 64).

Anticipating such constructivist tenets, Einstein thought that the discovery of basic physical laws originated in the creativity of the mind rather than simply by induction from experience (Resnick, 1980, 858). Quantum physics pushed the question of constructivism even further as it explored atomic phenomena. Such phenomena can be understood only as links in a chain of processes, at the end of which rests the consciousness of the human observer. The epistemological implications were astounding, what we see at the atomic level depends upon the questions we ask (Frye, 1987, 59).

Einstein and Werner Heisenberg challenged commonsense when they contended that what we see is not what we see but what we perceive. The basic tenet of constructivism reappears, the knowledge that the world yields has to be interpreted by the men and women who are a part of that world (Besag, 1986, 21). Whether we are attempting to understand physics, education, or art, the constructivist principle tacitly remains. Most observers, for example, do not realize that the theory of perspective developed by fifteenth-century artists constituted a scientific convention. It was simply one way of portraying space and held no *absolute* validity. Thus, the structures and phenomena we observe in the physical world are nothing more than creations of our measuring and categorizing mind (Leshan and Margenau, 1982, 189; Frye, 1987, 59).

Think of constructivism this way. A lumberjack, a real estate developer, an artist, a hunter, and a hiker are walking through the forest. Each of them sees and responds to their environment in different ways. To the lumberjack the forest is a source of wood; to the real estate developer it is land to be cleared so that a housing development can be constructed; the artist sees something to paint; to the hunter, the forest is a cover for game; the hiker sees a natural setting to explore. Thus, the backgrounds and expectations of the walkers shape their perceptions. In the same way consider how a classroom is perceived by a class clown, a traditionally good student, a burned out teacher, a standardized test taker, a bureaucratic supervisor, a disgruntled parent, or a nostalgic alumnus. The way our psychosocial disposition shapes how the world is perceived holds extremely important implications for teaching. Each of our students brings a unique disposition into the classroom. Indeed, each teacher carries a unique disposition into the classroom.

On this fact hinges the importance of studying constructivism. Are our psychosocial dispositions beyond our conscious control? Do we simply surrender our perceptions to the determination of our environment, our context? Because individuals are often unable to see the way that their environment shapes their perception (i.e., their consciousness construction), the development of a method for uncovering this process must become a central goal of the educational enterprise. This is where the Frankfurt School's formulation of critical theory enters the realm of constructivism, hence, the etymology of Joe Kincheloe's term critical constructivism.

Critical theory is concerned with extending a human's consciousness of himself or herself as a social being. An individual who gains such a consciousness would understand how her or his political opinions, religious beliefs, gender role, racial self-concept, or educational perspectives had been influenced by the dominant culture. Critical theory thus promotes self-reflection. Individuals come to know themselves by bringing to consciousness the process by which their consciousness was constructed. Action to correct pathological constructions can be negotiated once the self-reflection reveals the psychological, ethical, moral, and political foundations of the pathology.

Once critical theory is applied to constructivism a central question arises. Why do some constructions of reality gain official social approval and reward while others are punished? Such a question takes us back to the question of the influence of power in the construction of our consciousness. Critical constructivism attempts to see through the wall of power, to uncover problems other than those framed by the dominant Newtonian-Cartesian way of seeing, to understand postmodern nonlinearity and chaos with a postformal mode of thinking. Like Einstein's physics, critical constructivist educators attempt to use their understanding of the social construction of reality to rethink and redefine the types of questions we ask about schooling.

A central theme of these rethought and redefined critical constructivist educational questions centers on whose constructions of reality prevail and whose ought to prevail. Michael Young argued over two decades ago that the dominant definitions, the official ways of seeing in schools, are constructed realities that benefit some groups and not others (Young, 1971, 2). The ways that school separates bright from stupid, good citizenship from bad, model behavior from disruptions, are constructions that emanate from those in a position of power to induce less privileged actors to grant their consent to dominant definitions.

Many of the questions we ask about education are not grounded in a critical system of meaning. This system of meaning would serve not only to help understand the genesis of our inquiries but would assist our analysis of the answers we derive. Without this critical theory-grounded system of meaning we are forced to accept the nonproblematic assumptions and constructions of mainstream, modern ways of seeing education. Even when we do attempt to construct a system of meaning to ground our questions, that system may be intellectually immature if we neglect an analysis of the hidden forces of power that shape our logic, anesthetize our ethics, and define what we call a problem. Thus, teachers aware of the tenets of critical constructivism gain the analytical ability to transcend modern constructions of educational reality just as Einstein was able to transcend the modern construction of physical reality. These postmodern teachers begin to remake their world of practice in a way that is cognizant of the deep social structures that have shaped their professional lives.

Critical constructivism allows teachers a critical consciousness, an ability to step back from the world as we are accustomed to perceiving it and to see the ways our perception is constructed through linguistic codes, cultural signs, and embedded power. We would argue that such an ability constitutes a giant step in learning to teach, indeed, in learning to think. Critical constructivism is a theoretically grounded form of world making. We ask penetrating questions. "How did that which has come to be, come to be? Whose interests do particular institutional arrangements serve?" As we remake and rename our world, we are constantly guided by our system of meaning, our emancipatory source of authority (Slaughter, 1989, 264; Schon, 1987, 36).

Often our graduate students who are experienced teachers in elementary, middle, and high schools look at us askance when we speak of critical constructivism, postmodern critique, and emancipation. Their experience in the schools and in colleges of education tells them that such concepts will be treated as communiqués from Uranus if they are brought up in the principals' offices and faculty lounges in their schools. These teachers realize that it is much easier to develop materials for and to "train" teachers in reductionist practices. Such educational reductionism involves the application of a hyperlogical modern approach (some would call it positivism) to the educational act. Reductionists break the process of thinking into discrete steps to be taught sequentially in isolation from one another. Thus, fact acquisition, generalization, synthesis, and application would be taught one step at a time using specific methods, with prearranged outcomes that are measured by standardized assessment instruments.

Such reductionism is so much a part of many of our schools and teacher education programs that many observers do not even recognize its existence. As critical constructivists ponder the purposes of schooling such reductionism is viewed as anathema to efforts to connect student experience to the knowledge of the disciplines in the hope of producing thoughtful and reflective students armed with moral and civic courage. Madeleine Grumet illustrates the tragedy of reductionism in a description of a seventh-grade science classroom she recently observed.

> Take black holes, for instance. I have sat in the back of classrooms where students read aloud from science textbooks describing black holes as if they were pot holes. Only someone steeped in the theory of eternal return could pay attention to that text without terror. Neither text nor teacher acknowledged or questioned the horror of the relentless destruction, the area's cavernous suction that the text described. I looked around the classroom. The only terrified person in it was me. The seventh graders, even those taking notes, seemed isolated from the text, from the world and the universe that it described. Black holes were in the assigned chapter with five questions at the end of it to be done for homework. The questions merely mimicked the chapter prose, so they could be answered without having to even imagine a black hole, let alone worry about one (Grumet, 1995, 18).

In effect, the classroom had become its own black hole. It is obvious from Grumet's description that the passion of Eintein's universe had been destroyed by reductionist teaching. How could such student ever understand Einstein, the physical world, their connection to it, indeed, the life of the mind?

The critical constructionist belief that the whole of a phenomenon is greater than the sum of its parts moves postmodern teachers to resist reductionist efforts to break into parts the various aspects of the learning process. Such aspects would include the stages of understanding, teaching strategies, and the knowledge included in the curriculum. Thus, critical constructivists fight the task analysis fragmentation of learning promoted by the reforms of the reductionists with their lists of "properly" written behavioral objectives, their rigid scope and sequence charts, and their rigidly defined learning procedures of sequential steps for effective instruction.

In lieu of such trivialism, critical constructivist teachers design educational programs that actively involve students in the processes of learning and interpreting new information. Aware of the ways their consciousness has been shaped by their social context, their place (Kincheloe and Pinar, 1991; Steinberg and Kincheloe, 1997; 1998), such teachers encourage students to actively construct meanings for themselves instead of docilely processing the information that confronts them. Critical constructivist teachers

Einstein and the Purposes of Schooling

are far more concerned with their students' cognitive development, their interests, and their involvement with the world around them than with their performance on subskills measured on standardized tests (Poplin, 1988, 411–14). Few teachers ever concerned themselves with young Albert Einstein's interests. If they had, they could not have thought of him, not to mention taught him, in the way they did.

POSTFORMAL THINKING AND THE PURPOSES OF SCHOOLING

Drawing upon our reading of Einstein, our understanding of the postmodern critique, our emancipatory system of meaning, and Kincheloe's concept of critical constructivism, we have a basis from which to reconceptualize the purpose of schooling. Grounded in student experience; aware of the demands of democratic citizenship, including civic courage, cognizant of the ways that the power interests of the dominant culture shape consciousness; dedicated to creation of loving, nurturing, and safe classrooms; and empathetic with the way genius is punished; the postmodern vision of school purpose revolves around teaching students to think in independent, morally responsible, and cognitively sophisticated ways.

With these thoughts in mind, let us expand our previous references to postformal thinking. In no way are we attempting to define genius; neither are we attempting to compose an essential list of what constitutes higher-order thinking. Postformal thinking represents a starting point, a hesitant first step in thinking about thinking that transcends Piagetian formalism. It has an elastic clause. It can always be amended. Thus, the cultivation of postformal thinking is an important purpose of postmodern schooling and involves the following characteristics:

THINKING ABOUT THINKING: EXPLORING THE UNCERTAIN PLAY OF THE IMAGINATION. There is a famous picture of Albert Einstein, eyes wide open and hair radiating like gray kudzu, sticking out his tongue at the camera. It captures Einstein the trickster, the flouter of convention, the class clown, the symbol of the playfulness of the imagination. As he listened to the frolic of his imagination, Einstein took advantage of the inspirations that came from beyond the borders of his conscious mind. His thinking about his own thinking, the contemplation of his self-proclaimed mental pictures without words, his attention to his boyhood science fiction fantasies, allowed him to see beyond the traditional limits of the Newtonian-Cartesian assumptions of his day.

Like William Pinar's notion of *currere* (the Latin root of the word "curriculum," meaning the investigation of the nature of the individual experience of the public), postformal thinking about thinking allows us to move to our own inner world of psychological experience. The effort involves our ability to bring to conscious view our culturally created and therefore limited concept of both reality and self, thus revealing portions of our selves that were previously hidden (Pinar, 1975, 384–85). Drawing upon the parody of postmodernism (the image of Einstein the playful trickster), postformal thinking about thinking transgresses modern convention by exposing its ironic contradictions (Hutcheon, 1988, 22, 37). As Peter McLaren explains the postmodern double reading of the social world, he writes of a teaching disposition that encourages students to think about their own thinking in a postformal manner. Students learn to construct their identities in a way that parodies the rigid conventions of modernism, thus assuming the role of postmodern stand-up comics, and social satirists (McLaren, forthcoming, 7, 30). Thus, by way of this inversion of forms, students disengage themselves from sociointerpersonal norms and dominant cultural expectations. This postformal concern with emancipation via social unearthing moves us beyond the formal level characterized by devotion to linear generalization via proper scientific procedure (Kegan, 1982, 42).

EXPLORING DEEP STRUCTURES: UNCOVERING THE TACIT FORCES, THE HIDDEN ASSUMPTIONS THAT SHAPE. David Bohm, physicist and friend of Einstein, helps us conceptualize this aspect of postformal thinking with his notion of the explicate and implicate orders of reality. The explicate order involves simple patterns and invariants in time, i.e., characteristics of the world that repeat themselves in similar ways and that have recognizable locations in space. Because they are associated with comparatively humble orders of similarities and differences, explicate orders are often what is identified by the categorization and generalization function of formal thought.

The implicate order is a much deeper structure of reality. It is the level at which ostensible separateness vanishes and all things seem to become a part of a larger unified process. Implicate orders are marked by the simultaneous presence of a sequence of many levels of folds with similar dissimilarities existing among them. The totality of these levels of folds cannot be made explicit as a whole. They can be exposed only in the emergence of a series of folds. In contrast to the explicate order (which is an *unfolded* order) where similar differences are all present together and can be described in Newtonian-Cartesian terms, the implicit order has to be studied as a hidden process that is sometimes impenetrable to empirical methods of inquiry (Bohm and Peat, 1987, 174, 187).

Postformal thinking's concern with deep structures is, of course, informed by an understanding of the implicate order. Many have speculated that at higher levels of human consciousness, we often peek at the implicate process. Profound insight in any field of study may involve an apprehension of structures that are not attainable at the explicate order of reality. At these points we transcend commonsense. We cut patterns out of the cosmic fabric (Combs and Holland, 1990, 46). "Artists don't reproduce the visible," Paul Klee wrote, instead they "make things visible" (Leshan and Margenau, 1982, 172). Similarly, Einstein often referred to his physics as based on a process of questioning unconscious assumptions so as to reveal the deep structures of the universe. The theory of relativity itself emerged from his probing of the tacit assumptions underlying classical physics, in particular absolute conceptions of time and space (Reynolds, 1987, 170, 171). As he exposed deep physical structures of the "shape of space," he was at least approaching an implicate order of the physical universe.

Schools are grounded in the explicate order. The dominant culture's conversation not only about education but also the political process, racism, sexism, and social class bias revolves around the explicate order. We come to understand, for example, that the most damaging form of racism is not an overt "George Wallace in 1963" variety, but an institutional racism built into the very structures of our institutions. Critical postmodern theory has taught us that little is as it appears on the surface. When postformal observers search for the deep structures that are there to be uncovered in any classroom, they discover a universe of hidden meanings that are constructed by a variety of sociopolitical forces that many times have little to do with the intended (explicate) meanings of the official curriculum.

ASKING UNIQUE QUESTIONS: PROBLEM FORMULATION. In 1938, Einstein wrote:

> The formulation of a problem is often more important than its solution, which may be merely a matter of mathematical or experimental skill. To raise new questions, new possibilities, to regard old problems from a new angle, requires imagination and marks real advance in science (Quoted in Moore, 1989, 4).

Einstein was concerned with the value of the postformal problem formulation process in physics, but such a process is just as important in teaching. Donald Schon argues that it is ill-advised to reduce the work of teachers to mere problem solving. Such reductionism restricts teaching to the level of formal thinking and captures teachers in a culture of bureaucratic technocracy in which they simply seek solutions to problems that have been defined by their superiors (Schon, 1983, 39–40). If the higher-order cognitive ability of Einstein involved his ability to see problems in the physical universe that no one else had ever seen, then more sophisticated forms of teacher and student thinking may revolve around the ability to see educational problems that no one else has ever seen. The application of such cognition to the reconceptualizing of school purpose moves our educational analysis to a level unimagined by educators trapped within a Newtonian-Cartesian problem solving formalism.

SEEING RELATIONSHIPS BETWEEN OSTENSIBLY DISSIMILAR THINGS. Postformal thinking draws heavily on the concept of metaphor. Metaphoric perception is basic to all scientific and creative thinking and involves the fusion of previously disparate concepts in unanticipated ways. The mutual interrelationships of the components of a metaphor, not the components themselves, are the most important aspects of a metaphor. Indeed, many have argued that relationships, not objects, should be the basis of scientific thinking. Indeed, when we think of the concept of the mind the same thoughts are relevant. We might be better served to think of the mind not in terms of parts but in terms of the connecting pattern, the dance of the interacting parts (Fosnot, 1988, 5; Talbot, 1986, 115).

As she ponders the question of what is basic in education, Madeleine Grumet argues that the concept of relation is fundamental. Ironically, she argues, it is relation that we ignore when asked to enumerate the basics. Education involves introducing a student to modes of being and acting in the world that are new to her or his experience. Grumet concludes that it is the relation, the dance between the student's experience and knowledge that separates education from training or indoctrination (Grumet, 1992).

Postformal thinkers are empowered by their ability to recognize the pattern that connects, the revealing relationship. Einstein's great ability involved such insight. While multitudes saw space and multitudes saw time, virtually no one saw the unusual relationship between them.

CONNECTING LOGIC AND EMOTION: STRETCHING THE BOUNDARIES OF CONSCIOUSNESS. Feminist theory has raised our consciousness concerning the role of emotion in learning and knowing. Feminist constructivists have maintained that emotional intensity precedes cognitive transformation to a new way of seeing. As such, emotions are seen as powerful knowing processes that ground cognition (Mahoney and Lyddon, 1988, 217). For example, Newtonian-Cartesian thinkers are procedural knowers who unemotionally pay allegiance to a system of inquiry; postformal thinkers grounded in feminist constructivism unite logic and emotion, making use of what the emotions can understand that logic cannot. Emotionally committed to their thinking, postformal thinkers tap into a passion for knowing that motivates, that extends, that leads them to a union with that which is to be known. Feminist scholar Barbara DuBois describes passionate scholarship as "science making, [that is] rooted in, animated by and expressive of our values" (Quoted in Belenky, Clinchy, Goldberger, and Tarule, 1986, 140–41).

Einstein serves as a good example of the passionate thinker/scholar. His scientific processes were emotional processes. Problems of thought, he considered emotional problems. Often when he felt he had reached a logical dead end, he would turn to the emotion of his violin. His eldest son reported that playing the violin usually solved his cognitive problems. Einstein saw nothing unusual about this because both physics and music had emotional origins and were connected on a variety of levels (Clark, 1971, 140–41).

SEEING FACTS AS PARTS OF LARGER PROCESSES. Einstein's work has suggested that there is no absolute notion of time and no solid objects. There are only energy fields, interconnecting processes. The theory of relativity saw space not as a domain of nothingness, but as a continuous fabric. Atoms and molecules are simply particular characteristics of this cosmic fabric. Thus, space to Einstein was like a painting, filled with itself. Particular points of the painting, like atoms, contribute to the total experience. When they are removed from the larger process, they take on a different meaning (Frye, 1987, 65; Combs and Holland, 1990, xxiii). Postformal thinkers see facts as more than pieces of information. They see them in relationship to the larger processes of which they are a part.

Return to our discussion of Bohm's implicate order, the level of reality at which separateness vanishes and all things appear to become part of a larger process. Bohm asks us to think of holographic photography to extend the notion of the implicate order. In photography a lens is used to focus light from an entity, so that each part of the entity is reproduced in a section of the photographic plate. In holographic photography, however, a laser light shines through a half-silvered mirror. When the beams unite at the photographic plate they produce a pattern to the viewer that produces the sensation of viewing a three-dimensional object. Contained on every portion of the holographic negative is the whole image that was photographed. Bohm argues that this holographic effect (i.e., that all parts contain the whole) is a very simple version of what is occurring in each region of space all over the universe, and in each part of the brain (Bohm and Peat, 1987, 175; Briggs and Peat, 1984, 110–11).

Language can be thought of in holographic, process-oriented terms. Meaning is enfolded in the structure of language and thus unfolds into human thought, feelings, and activities that have been "discussed," or given words. In the act of communication, this meaning unfolds into the entire community and then to each individual. Thus, in almost a Jungian sense the implicate order of society is enfolded into our consciousness. Drawing upon holography, postformal thinkers cannot think of individuals in isolation from their social context or individuals in isolation from one another. In other words, what is viewed from one angle as society enfolds in what is seen from another angle as individual consciousness. When postformal thinkers look at education, they see it not as something separate but as an expression of the society's implicate order, as a manifestation of the larger social process (Bohm and Peat, 1987, 185).

ETYMOLOGY: THE ORIGINS OF KNOWLEDGE. While it is true that Einstein developed his special theory of relativity in 1905 in isolation from academic institutions, he was not isolated from the knowledge of his predecessors in physics. In order to transcend their work he had to be acutely aware of the origins of the knowledge of his discipline. Scientific work, he wrote, is so connected to the work of one's predecessors "that it appears almost as an impersonal product of his generation" (Clark, 1971, 127). Postformal thinkers recognize the ways the *Zeitgeists* (the spirits of the times) influence knowledge production as they focus our attention on particular problems. In thinking about education, for example, do we attend to questions of equity that emerged from the civil rights movement, questions of gender bias that grew out of the women's movement, or questions of religious fundamentalism that come from the New Right? Indeed, what we know is vulnerable to the ebb and flow of time with its changing concerns, the fluctuating power relations of different periods, and the emotional swings of various eras (Fiske, 1986, 68–71).

At the end of the twentieth century our American culture remains unaware of what Einstein understood decades ago: the implicit rules that guide our generation of knowledge about education are formed by particular worldviews; values; political perspectives; conceptions of race, class, and general relations; and definitions of intelligence (Aronowitz, 1973, 60). Critical theory's exposure of the hidden social assumptions about our knowledge was a crucial turning point in modernism. It marked the end of our innocence. Our loss of innocence was necessary in order to move beyond formal thinking. By studying the etymology of knowledge postformal teachers and students learn about the nature of learning. In the process we accomplish that traditionally neglected but cardinal purpose of schooling, learning to teach ourselves. Without the benefit of postformal etymology, thinking often fails to move beyond the acquisition of second hand, authorized, ready-made facts.

PERCEIVING DIFFERENT FRAMES OF REFERENCE: THE COGNITIVE POWER OF EMPATHY. Einstein set the stage for the postmodern understanding of multiple frames of reference. How is time to be viewed, he asked. As an absolute? From a particular, privileged frame of reference? It depends, he theorized, on the speed of the observer. Thus, the commonsense view of the universe was destroyed. We could no longer be so certain of our observations. Critical postmodernism cannot accept a linear, cause and effect reality, for the complex reality it uncovers demands recognition of multiple causations and the possibility of differing vantage points in the web of the universe. Depending on the context from which a phenomenon emanates or the system of meaning that observers employ to help formulate their questions about it, different realities will be perceived (Lincoln and Guba, 1985, 51; Briggs and Peat, 1989, 153–54; Slaughter, 1989, 262).

Thus, postformal thinkers look at events from a variety of perspectives. Postformal teachers will realize that the models of teaching they have been taught, the definitions of research with which they have been supplied, the angle from which they have been instructed to view intelligence all represent a particular vantage point in the web of reality. In their postformal attempt to move beyond the tyranny of these Newtonian-Cartesian "privileged" perspectives, they begin to ask about other ways of seeing educational phenomena.

Critical constructivist postformal thinkers like liberation theologians in Latin America make no apology for beginning a cognitive process by attempting to understand the perspective of the oppressed (Welch, 1985, 31). The way to find an alternative view to the mainstream perspective, they argue, is to understand an institution from the vantage point of those who have suffered the most as the result of its existence. These subjugated knowledges allow postformal thinkers to gain the cognitive power of empathy. Such a power enables postformal thinkers to take a picture of reality from different angles. The intersection of these angles allows for a form of analysis that moves beyond the isolated, fragmented analysis of modernity. Whereas modernist photographs are two-dimensional prints, postmodern, postformal photographs are three-dimensional holographs. Understanding derived from the perspective of the excluded allows for an appreciation of both the nature of justice and the invisibility of the process of oppression, knowledge that is lost on less sophisticated observers.

CONTEXTUALIZATION—ATTENDING TO THE SETTING. Joe Kincheloe and William Pinar have developed a curriculum theory of place in which geographical setting and the way it informs human action become very important to the educator's attempt to understand the purpose of school (Kincheloe and Pinar, 1991). The development of a context in which an observation can assume its full meaning is a key element in the construction of a postformal mode of thinking. For example, a listener who lacks adequate context to understand the "order" of music will judge an avant garde composition as meaningless. When Europeans first heard African music, they attempted to assess it in the terms of another musical form. Unable to appreciate the context that gave meaning to the African music, the Europeans did not hear the intentions of the composers and performers with their subtle rhythms and haunting melodies. They heard primitive noise (Bohm and Peat, 1987, 130).

Once again Newtonian-Cartesian modernism fails to convey a valuable perspective about the world of thinking and teaching, as it fails in its reductionism to account for context. In modern empirical research so-called scientific controls contribute to a more perfect isolation of the context that is being investigated. Attention to circumstances surrounding the object of inquiry must be temporarily suspended. This suspension of attention is based on the assumption that these extraneous circumstances will remain static long enough to allow the study to be validated. Of course, these extraneous circumstances never remain static. They are constantly interacting and shaping. To exclude them is to distort reality (Longstreet, 1982, 136).

Like African or European music, every classroom possesses a context all its own. A postformal teacher or observer understands that the meaning of classroom events depends upon what has happened previously, the prior negotiation of meanings, representations, codes, and conventions. When a supervisor or administrator walks into a class without this knowledge, he or she cannot expect to understand everything that is occurring. Thus, Newtonian-Cartesian empirical researchers or evaluators often make judgments based on fragmented information that is not placed in context by deeper understanding. In the same way, students learn information for standardized tests that is stripped of context and robbed of connection to the world of lived experience, to anything that would endow it with significance. As Einstein realized in his schooling, decontextualized learning becomes a rote-based exercise in futility. Einstein simply couldn't understand how students remain as interested as they do.

UNDERSTANDING THE INTERACTION OF PARTICULARITY AND GENERALIZATION, FORMALITY VIS-À-VIS POSTFORMALITY. A troubling aspect of the theory of postformality involves the question: when is it that we move from formal to postformal thinking? Grounded in the Newtonian-Cartesian world of science, formality emphasizes the production of generalizations. The constructivist teacher's concern with particularity, the unique experience of each learner, seems rather unscientific to the modernist scientist. To the constructivist teacher the scientism, the obsession with generalization of the modern thinker is not very helpful in the everyday world of the classroom. Formal generalization does not account for the novel, the unexpected, the particular.

Postformal thinking moves beyond a simple concern with generalization. In the process, however, it transcends the desire to know only the unique. Piaget is helpful in this context. We want to *assimilate* in the Piagetian sense of the term. We want to understand the commonalties of particular categories. This act of assimilation, of seeking these commonalties, is a search for generalization. But assimilation without Piaget's notion of accommodation never moves beyond lower cognitive levels. Accommodation involves the reshaping of cognitive structures to accommodate unique aspects of what is being perceived in new contexts. Stated another way, through our knowledge of a variety of comparable contexts we begin to understand their similarities and differences, we learn from our comparisons of different contexts. As we accommodate as critical constructivist, postformal teachers we come to understand the unique and particular aspects of our classrooms, aspects that allow us to connect the unique experiences of our students to the world at large.

Uniqueness and particularity are flies in the Newtonian-Cartesian ointment. The realm of the particular complicates the attempt to produce generalized laws that can be applied to the effort to predict and thus control human behavior. What is good for one citizen is good for all, at least for citizens in that particular classification, that generalization. In the same manner what is good for one student is good for all, the justification of standardization.

We return to Kincheloe and Pinar's notion of place to ground postformalism's transcendence of mere generalization or mere particularity. Place, as social theory, brings the particular into focus, but in a way that grounds it contextually in a larger understanding of the social forces that shape it. Thus, we make use of general understandings but not to the point where we only study groups of things rather than single entities. When the particular is treated as a sample of a species or a type its essence is lost. It is not itself. It is a mere representative. Viewed in this way the particular has no proper name; it is alienated and anonymous. Children in schools are only types with certain learning styles, certain class and racial backgrounds, certain percentile performances, they are not individuals (Kincheloe and Pinar, 1991). Postformal thinkers see beyond this tendency of modern science.

DECONSTRUCTION: SEEING THE WORLD AS A TEXT TO BE READ. In our discussion of deconstruction in Chapter One, we asserted that it can be described as the extension of Einsteinian relativity into new dimensions of reality. Beginning with this idea, let us extend our discussion of deconstruction to the cognitive terrain of postformal thinking. The postformal thinker reads between the lines of a text, whether the text be, as with Einstein, physical reality, or for a teacher, the classroom. Thus, a text is more than printed material, as it involves any aspect of reality that contains encoded meaning to be deconstructed (Whiteson, 1986, 419, 425; Scholes, 1982, X, 14).

Reading a social text involves the development of the capacity for self-criticism of the historically constituted nature of one's consciousness. Thus, deconstruction of text becomes a subversive activity that allows us to read the lived world in a new way. Our new reading frees us from the official interpretations of the dominant codes. Employing such deconstructive analysis, postformal teachers begin to see schools as arenas where power interests compete over control of representations of the world. To sustain their privilege the dominant must regulate representation. Thus, they must encode the world in forms that support their own interests. For example, the military must convey representations of an evil world full of constant threats to our continued national survival. The military, the government, and the news media were all too eager to have us accept Saddam Hussein as the new Hitler with a dangerous military capability. Conveniently forgetting that the U.S. government had armed him, the same power elites were just as eager to have us believe Hussein was vanquished when we wanted to stop the war. The military wishes us to believe that each sunrise brings with it the possibility of a *Red Dawn* with alien paratroopers landing in midwestern hamlets, that "liberals" in the land want to cut defense expenditures even if it means making us vulnerable to foreign tyrants. By successfully representing the world in these ways, the military establishment can retain its huge budgets and its power in policy setting.

Understanding the process of representation allows postformal teachers to understand the ways that the consciousness of their students is constructed. We read our students as living texts with their life histories, their stories, and their enthusiastic digressions. The postformal teacher as deconstructionist views these stories and the way they are told as texts full of signs and codes. A central act of critical postmodern teaching involves helping students restructure their own stories in light of an understanding of the way power shapes our self-representations. These narratives of meta awareness are comfortable to the students themselves and are manifestations of the students' discovery of their own voices. Einstein the student was not so lucky, his voice was deemed irrelevant.

SEEING CONCRETE AND FORMAL THINKING AS IMPORTANT ASPECTS OF ANY COGNITIVE PROCESS: LEARNING THE APPROPRIATE USE OF CONCRETE AND FORMAL THINKING. In order to formulate his various theories about the universe it was necessary for Einstein to perform a plethora of concrete and formal thinking activities. In no way did the development of the theory of relativity involve only what we have described as postformal thinking. Obviously, on a concrete level he had to use systems of classification. On a formal level he had to make specific generalizations about certain information he uncovered.

Every act of thinking we have described as postformal involves concrete, formal, and postformal dimensions. Granted, our comments here may seem obvious; however, they are presented with the technocratic nature of contemporary schooling in mind. This technocratic impulse tends to hyperrationalize the new ideas it encounters, in the process reducing a process such as the cultivation of postformal thinking to a set of discrete and measurable steps. By its very nature, postformal thinking does not lend itself to such a process. The benefits of such thinking are lost if it is reduced to a sequential set of standardized operations that can be committed to a teacher's or a student's memory. Different questions will imply different types of thinking. No set of steps to a postformal thinking can exist because they are always evolving, always contingent on context.

NONLINEAR HOLISM: TRANSCENDING SIMPLISTIC NOTIONS OF CAUSE AND EFFECT. While the formal operational orientation functions on the basis of the Cartesian assumption of linear causality, the postformal perspective assumes reciprocity and holism (Van Hesteran, 1986, 214; Kramer, 1983, 92–94). Holism implies that a phenomenon can't be understood by reducing it to smaller units, only by understanding it as an integrated whole. It is the opposite of reductionism. For example, in film the value and significance of a particular image is lost when it is viewed in isolation. When it is perceived in relationship to the rest of the film's images it is understood as part of an organic whole. The film is the totality, not a succession of discrete image (Talbot, 1987, 95; Bohm and Peat, 1987, 189).

This returns us again to David Bohm's conception of implicate order. The implicate order of a film, or a piece of music, or a painting is constantly unfolding from an original perception in the mind of the artist. If one were to see the last three minutes of *Godfather II*, one could have little understanding of the forces that cause Michael Corleone to order the murder of his brother Fredo. One must see the hours of preceding film to understand how Michael Corleone comes to justify the murder of his own brother. William Faulkner stated that the entire history of the Compsons and the novel *The Sound and the Fury* came from his mental picture of a little girl with muddy drawers in a tree peering into a house. More traditional conceptions of the creative process use a machine model, implying that the whole emerges out of an accumulation of detail, the whole is built out of a set of pieces. Again looking at *The Sound and the Fury*, it could be argued that the suicide of Quentin Compson some fifty years after Pickett's charge at Gettysburg was as tied to that event and its ordained failure as much as his suicide was tied to his sister's eventual involvement with a Nazi officer. Thus, another separation of formal and postformal thinking emerges, the creative unfolding represents a postformal act and the sequential accumulation of detail represents a formal act. In any creative act, we would argue, an implicate order emerges as an expression of the creator's whole life, his or her *Lebenswelt*. The formal attempt to separate this holism into parts misses the essence of the creative process and the attempt to teach based on this formalist, linear assumption will contribute little to the cultivation of creativity (Bohm and Peat, 1987, 157).

Thus, creativity originates in the holistic depths of an implicate order. Such an order does not operate in a Newtonian universe of absolute, linear time. Events happen simultaneously rather than in a particular order of succession. When Einstein or Mozart or da Vinci saw whole structures of physics, music, or art in a single flash of insight, they grasped the implicate order, the overall structure of a set of relationships all at once. In such a moment modern linearity is subverted and Newtonian time is scrambled, an understanding that Einstein reached not only in a special relativity sense but also in our cognitive sense (Reynolds, 1987, 171).

Such a holistic understanding carries with it several social consequences as modern hierarchic conceptions of order give way to postmodern heterodoxies. As with linear, absolute, Newtonian time, modern formality saw an inherent order in the physical and the social world. The Newtonian-Cartesian way of seeing was comfortable with natural orders, such as the man as head of the household, psychologist Carl Brigham's hierarchy of the intelligence of ethnic groups, the order of civilized and uncivilized cultures, etc. In the nonlinear postmodern world such orders began to lose their ability to justify themselves; the hourglass was turned on its side.

UNCOVERING VARIOUS LEVELS OF CONNECTION BETWEEN MIND AND ECOSYSTEM: REVEALING LARGER PATTERNS OF LIFE FORCES. As the result of a dinner conversation with Einstein, Carl Jung theorized his notion of synchronicity, the meaningful connection between causally unconnected events. Postformal thinkers understand Peter McLaren's conception of the realm of "impossible possibility" in which teaching begins to search for connections between causally unconnected phenomenon (McLaren, forthcoming, 9). It is in this way that we begin to transcend our current disposition of being in the world, our acceptance of boredom, alienation, and injustice. In a way we become the science fiction writers of education, imagining what is admittedly not yet possible; but because of the fact that we can conceive of it, like science fiction writers who imagined trips to the moon, it becomes possible.

Postformalism is life-affirming as it transcends modernism's disdain of life, its devaluation of the spiritual. In its postmodern deconstructive manner, postformalism contests the "meaning of life," that is, the actual definition of life. In the process of deconstruction it begins the task of reshaping on multiple, possible, contradictory levels of the definition of living. Transcending Newtonian-Cartesian fragmentation, postformal thinkers understand that life may have less to do with the parts of a living thing than with patterns of information, the "no thing" of the *relations* between parts, the "dance" of a living process, i.e. life as synchronicity.

Postmodernism is the consummate boundary crosser, ignoring the no-trespassing signs posted at modernism's property line of certainty. It is possible that postmodernism will lead us across the boundary that divides living and nonliving. Those characteristics that modernism defined as basic to life are present in many phenomena in the universe, from subatomic particles to weather to seahorses. Because all life on the planet is so multidimensionally entwined, it is extremely hard to separate life from nonlife. Indeed, some scientists have already begun to argue that the best definition of life is the entire Earth. Seen from this perspective, modernism's lack of concern with ecological balance is suicidal on many levels (Talbot, 1986, 53, 130, 146, 180).

The only definition left for life in the postmodern world is not some secret substance or life force, but a pattern of information. This elevates the recognition of the relationships from the cognitive to the spiritual realm, for it is the relationships that is us. The same is true for consciousness; sensitive intelligence is present wherever an entity can tune in to the woven fabric of cosmic information, the implicate order of the universe. Thus, from this definition the ecosystem is conscious—the "no thing" of perceived pattern is the very basis of life and mind. Postformal thinkers thus become ambassadors to the domain of the pattern. The cognitive revolutions that Einstein initiated are starting to succeed, the old regime is beginning to crumble. Possibility is infinite as we watch the guardians of the old order, the schools, defect to the postmodern insurrection (Kincheloe, 1998, Kincheloe, et al. 1999).

Rolling the Epistemological Dice

"God does not play dice with the world," Einstein said early in his career, referring to the idea of orderly and knowable universe (Clark, 1971, 38). The quote represents Einstein's epistemological position and his hope that despite his work, despite his unintended weakening of modern science, knowing in an assured way was still possible. Einstein's wish could not come true; with his work the postmodern breakdown of the logical ordering of reason, the subverting of objectivity took root (Hutcheon, 1988, 74–75). Though he kept denying it, Einstein pushed us toward uncertainty. Einstein is a transitional figure, a subversive member of the old regime, a reluctant vanguard of the new.

EPISTEMOLOGICAL HISTORY:
FROM PYTHAGORAS TO EINSTEIN TO CRITICAL POSTMODERNISM

Creative innovation in physical and mathematical science traditionally has influenced society's epistemological perspective. In the ancient world the mathematical advances of the Pythagoreans made possible the development of rational deductive systems for numbers and geometrical figures. Later, Plato described the nature of mathematical knowledge with his theory of ideas (or forms) that were precise, eternal objects of rational insight. Newton formulated modern "classical mechanics" that led to a certain knowledge of the physical world grounded in the mathematics of motion. Kant theorized a mathematical science of nature, arguing that space and time are a priori forms of sensibility, while substance and causality are a priori forms of understanding. When Einstein's relativity and quantum theory are thrown into the context, we can see that our way of knowing is affected (Schlipp, 1949, 357–58). This chapter will analyze that effect and its implications for education.

Knowledge has traditionally been viewed as objective. We all sought an ultimate truth. Aristotle maintained that through empirical deduction we could arrive at truth, conveniently ignoring the fact that he was the one dealing the cards from a stacked deck. (As in all games of chance, make sure you cut the cards.) Universal laws could be derived by working from the general to the particular:

All men are mortal. Socrates is a man. Therefore, Socrates is mortal (Courtney, 1988, 5).

But in the last century these ancient ways of knowing have collapsed. Many have accepted the idea that there are a variety of ways of knowing. Two particular epistemological events in the early part of the twentieth century set the stage for the collapse.

First, Bertrand Russell disrupted Aristotelian certainty by contending that the "All men are mortal" syllogism was simply a sentence. He substituted the sentence, "The King of France is bald." Russell argued that this sentence made no sense for two important reasons: 1) there was no current King of France; and 2) no King of France had been bald. Taking up where Russell left off, Ludwig Wittgenstein maintained that knowledge is gained in context. Employing the phrase criteria in context, Wittgenstein posited that knowing emerges in the relationship between: 1) using criteria that are rational; *but* are 2) in a specific context (Best, 1974, 17). This means that we use criteria that are rational for us (these criteria could differ between different individuals) and relate them to a particular context (Courtney, 1988, 5). Wittgenstein understood the concept of the stacked card deck.

The second event, of course, was Einstein's theory of relativity and its destruction of the Newtonian-Cartesian notion that life and the cosmos worked like a machine. Emerging from the epistemological ashes of the mechanistic universe was Heisenberg's theory of indeterminacy, that the observer cannot be removed from the experiment. (Heisenberg also understood the need to cut the cards.) Quantum physics is based on this principle. From an epistemological perspective, classic objectivity does not exist; accuracy is possible only from a particular vantage point and a specific context. Indeed, what we know is merely our point of view. If our knowledge is to be logical, it must use rational criteria that are grounded in a particular context. Based on this understanding, Michael Polanyi's theory of personal knowledge emerged.

Polanyi argued that scientific inquiry was similar to artistic creation. It was grounded not in empirical proof but upon personal belief. Reflecting Heisenberg's theory of indeterminacy, Polanyi contended that we all have a personal attitude, a unique relationship to what we know. But modern science is detached, he argued, and views its purpose as the production of objective knowledge. Such an epistemological purpose is misguided and holds dramatic implications for education. Polanyi was an avowed opponent of the founders of experimental psychology, psychologists who have shaped the nature of modern schooling. John Watson and B. F. Skinner took their epistemological models from what they considered to be the most objective and perfect science, physics. Unfortunately, the physics to which Watson and Skinner turned was Newtonian, not Einsteinian. Despite the fact that Einstein destroyed the objectivist, mechanistic orientation of physics, the behavioral experimenters latched on to the old paradigm in their conceptualization of psychology. Knowing is not an objective process, Polanyi concluded; it is more "an intellectual commitment" (Courtney, 1988, 5–7).

Polanyi's work was a very important force in the attempt to understand epistemology in light of the Einsteinian challenge. His conception of personal knowledge not only challenged the Newtonian-Cartesian separation of the knower and the known, but also set the stage for the critical postmodern concept of knower participation in knowing. Slowly it became apparent that Newtonian-Cartesian epistemology contributed to an alienation from, and a depersonalization of, society. As we look around us at the beginning of the twentieth-first century, we see a human environment polluted by individuals who empirically measure progress in short term profits, and government bureaucrats who measure progress more and more by their success in forcing individuals into conformity. The behaviorism endemic to the epistemology has had no problem with the manipulation of individuals for desired ends. The educational system grounded in this way of seeing has molded students to foster efficiency and economic productivity at the expense of social concern, self-knowledge, meta-awareness, and creativity (Mahoney and Lyddon, 1988, 192).

Teaching, unlike the classification of different acids, is not a constant and predictable activity. It always occurs in a world of uncertainty. Thus, the definition of what knowledge teachers should possess is also uncertain. The question of how to teach teachers what to do in these conditions of uncertainty is even more elusive. But, guided by the Newtonian-Cartesian epistemology, schools of education were constructed so that the uncertainty of professional practice was scientifically eliminated and replaced with verifiable empirical knowledge about the act of teaching. The uniqueness of particular teaching situations was dismissed by educational scientists, whose clients demanded official knowledge. Challenges to the Newtonian-Cartesian view of knowledge produced too much anxiety. Science in the modern world has not existed to raise doubts. It was born to provide answers. Viewed in a larger historical context, the science of modernism replaced the religion of premodernism. The scientific method was substituted for church liturgy. Like religion, science sought the certainty of rules, orders, and structures to relieve the anxiety of not *knowing* (Schon, 1987, 11–13, 171).

The Newtonian-Cartesian quest for epistemological certainty assumed that the world was neat and tidy. In much the same way, Luther, Calvin, and Wesley produced religions that were neat and tidy. Knowledge could be produced far more easily if knowers were identical, unbiased, and infallible instruments of perception. From the epistemological perspective we could all see the world from the "correct" vantage point. Since we all operate from a similar place in the web of reality, what use is there for an analysis of the construction of our individual consciousness? The question of why we see the world as we do is irrelevant in the Newtonian-Cartesian landscape. The objectivist tradition provides a shelter in which to hide from the deeply personal dimensions that inhabit all human actions and interactions; personal issues, which, if they were freed from the Newtonian-Cartesian box, might well force an uncomfortable element of self-revelation. Drawing on Polanyi's conception of personal knowledge, postmodern thinkers seek insight into how their own and other people's assumptions about the world are constructed. Educators who do not understand themselves clearly will misconstrue the intentions and actions of others (Shweder and Fiske, 1986, 1–2).

Thus, because of the post-Einsteinian world's breakdown of belief in a mechanistic cosmos, educators find themselves in a world characterized by an epistemological crisis. Social scientists and educators are faced with difficult questions for which they have no answer: What is the correct pathway to knowledge? What criteria do we use to produce knowledge? and What constitutes knowledge? As social and educational analysts have become more aware of the social and individual construction of knowledge, they have come to realize that knowledge produced by inquiry is quite specific to the method that is used.

For example, a statistician and a critical educator will analyze a particular intelligence test differently. To the critical educator the test discloses a tacit set of unexplored social, cultural, and racial assumptions about not only the nature of intelligence but what knowledge is valued by the dominant society. To the statistician the test is valuable measuring instrument whose rank ordering of individuals or social groups relative to their intelligence is either quite similar or dissimilar to other intelligence tests; for the statistician tests the *thing*, not the *test taker*. Depending on the observer's vantage point, the test is seen differently. Indeed, the epistemological crisis deepened because of the fact that the two observers of the intelligence test cannot even talk to one another.

Einstein's challenge to the discipline of physics helped set off a chain reaction of events that has caused what Jurgen Habermas has labeled the dissolution of epistemology. After the birth of scientific thinking during the Enlightenment, modern inquirers ignored the study of the context that shapes the way we define knowledge. Within the modern worldview, epistemology dissolved into a circumscribed analysis of proper research techniques. Any concern with the role of the knower faded away. Epistemology could not ask contextual questions about the assumptions behind knowledge or the cultural roles of science because empirical scientific knowledge was the only form of knowledge that was recognized as legitimate. No form of knowledge existed independent of science that would allow scientists to reflect on their methods and personal assumptions. The dissolution of epistemology involved the facing of the critical dimension of the study of knowledge.

The critical epistemology that emerged from the Frankfurt School values the understanding of the philosophical, historical, cultural, and political contexts in which knowledge is produced. At the same time an understanding of such contextualization is deemed to be important for professionals of all stripes. The act of reading, thus, is revolutionized by the application of critical epistemology, as the reader is aware of the context in which she or he reads and is able to uncover new dimensions of textual meaning: Where did the text originate? To whom is it addressed? For what purposes was it produced? What values does it promote? Who benefits as a result of its entry into the consciousness of its readers? Critical theory exposed the tacit dimensions of knowledge. No longer was knowledge as chaste and innocent as the Newtonian-Cartesian modernists portrayed it (Franker, 1986, 353–54; Howe, 1985, 14; Held, 1980, 254, 259; Eisner, 1983, 23).

Feminist theory is the quintessential example of a critical epistemology. Feminist scholars begin with the assumption that knower and known are always historically situated. Thus, feminist epistemology, or women's ways of knowing, transforms modern views of knowledge, forcing scientists and teachers to envision new relationships between the knower and the known. Knowledge is viewed from a postmodern perspective that attacks the modern deference to authority and science as power.

The androcentric conception of a neutral, objective, hierarchical nonreciprocal interaction between knower and known is transcended by the feminist attempt to reconnect the knower and known. As a result of this reconnecting, feminist theory allows the knower to prohibit science from blinding her or him intentionally, thus restricting what science can "see" in schools. Because they have exposed what can be ascertained from the mundane and the banal, feminist educators have reopened a whole new area to inquiry. These scholars have uncovered the existence of silences and omissions where modern educators had perceived only "what was there." Because they applied their own experience to the act of perceiving, women scholars were able to expose such omissions. Thus, they hitched knower to known (Fee, 1982, 383; Mies, 1982, 120–21; Belenky, Clinchy, Goldberger, and Tarule, 1986, 19, 134).

Modern knowers, feminist epistemologists maintained, erased the self, "out reasoned" their intuitions and inner voices, and ended up with nonspiritual objectivist perceptions of society and education. Using Newtonian-Cartesian definitions, modern knowers saw objectivist perceptions as certain and scientific; feminist, self-grounded understandings were inferior, impressionistic, and simply journalistic. Not only were the feminist perceptions unscientific, unverified intuitions, but they were emotion-based and value-laden. The feminists became the first to realize that modern knowledge had released itself from any social or ethical responsibility. Objectivity in the Newtonian-Cartesian sense implied ideological passivity and an unquestioned acceptance of a privileged socioeconomic position. Modern objectivity demanded a separation of logic and feeling. Indeed, feeling was labeled an inferior form of human consciousness, thus providing a rationalization for those knowers who rely on logic to oppress those consciousness associated with emotion or feeling. Feminist theories have maintained that the hierarchy of logic above emotion is one of the tacit structures historically used by men to dominate women (Reinharz, 1979, 242; Fee, 1982, 384–85).

Feminist epistemology is an important facet of the cultural move from modernism to postmodernism. Challenging the notion of the superiority of male-centered Western culture, feminist theory exposed the particularity of the allegedly universal truths that ground Eurocentric society (Giroux, 1991, 23–24). In this context feminist epistemology led Western thinkers to reconsider the value of non-Western epistemologies that in the past had been demeaned or ignored. Afrocentric and Native American ways of knowing are very similar to the anti-Cartesian perspectives of Polanyi. Although we wish to avoid a simplistic romanticization of indigenous ways of knowing, we can learn from these "primitive" epistemologies and their refusal to separate reality. In these "primitive" epistemologies, or subjugated knowledges, reality has never been separated into spiritual and material parts. Self-knowledge serves as a grounding for all knowledge in most African and Native American epistemologies. Interpersonal relations and group solidarity, as well as respect for the individual, are viewed as important, and diunitary logic has moved these cultures to treasure the unity of spirit and matter, individual and world (Semali and Kincheloe, 1999). The Eurocentric Newtonian-Cartesian worldview and these indigenous ways of knowing come into direct conflict over epistemological issues of mind and body, humans and nature, self and other, spirit and matter, and knower and known. These conflicts have had serious historical consequences. Thus, that which traditionally has been viewed by Western scholars as primitive becomes, from the perspective of postmodern critical constructivist epistemology, a valuable source of insight in the attempt to define a more just and equitable form of knowledge (Myers, 1987, 73–75; Nyang and Vandi, 1980, 245).

Rolling the Epistemological Dice

Through our synthesis of the Einsteinian epistemological challenge, feminist notions of knowing, and indigenous peoples' subjugated knowledge, we ground our attempt to envisage a theory of knowledge that is capable of confronting a postmodern cosmos. From this critical postmodern vantage point we gain the ability to question the so-called "knowledge base" of the social sciences and education. Our critique allows us to formulate new ways of knowing and alternative strategies of inquiry in our work as educators. We have entered a new social and educational dimension, a terrain of uncertainty where the Newtonian-Cartesian rules do not always apply, where the separation of mind and matter is not simply assumed, where multiple ways of knowing are sought and valued (Poster, 1989, 30).

As we begin our epistemological journey into this postmodern realm, we come to realize that the voice of authority, of rational *man*, is no longer a universal voice. Such a realization allows us to begin the task of deconstructing the assumptions of Newtonian-Cartesian logic and the "common sense" of the schools. It allows us to see inside the way that traditional science fabricates an imaginary world. Like any story, science is composed. Indeed, like a story, it is a language game. As we come to ask who made the rules of the game, we see that the "truth" of the Western tradition is another narrative that often has served to erase or at least ignore the stories, cultural traditions, and ways of knowing of those who, because of race, class, gender, and economics, constitute the "other." Thus, the Western patriarchy and ethnocentrism, so vehemently denied by defenders of the faith, are coaxed from the shadows. We see the ways that school knowledge privileges the Western canon and in the name of objectivism protects Western society and tradition from a genealogical analysis of its historical formation and from social criticism in general.

A critical postmodern epistemology not only exposes the shadow values, assumptions, and forms of prevailing notions of social and school knowledge, it also produces new concepts of knowledge. New meanings, new ways of knowing emerge from the breakdown of traditional assumptions about schooling. We begin to see forms of study that were ignored and knowledge that was unrepresented in the old school. Based on these epistemological understandings, postmodern educators maintain that learning begins only when the knowledge of school is grounded in the tacit knowledge that students bring to the classroom. Thus, knowledge of media, music, and popular culture is treated as a legitimate form of knowledge by critical postmodern educators.

This is very different from the curriculum necessitated by a Newtonian-Cartesian epistemology, a curriculum that simply transmits the isolated knowledge of the disciplines. The critical postmodern teacher attempts to integrate the knowledge of the disciplines in the context created by a set of projects chosen in consultation with students. Many commentators have simplified and distorted the spirit of the critical postmodern school by charging that it merely substitutes the study of popular culture for the study of traditional disciplines. Schools that are based on a postmodern epistemology demand that knowledge meet the test of a reconceptualized notion of relevance. This critical notion of relevance *does not imply a rejection of tradition* but does demand a standard for deciding what is included in the curriculum. At this point the teacher attempts to convince students that these reconceptualized knowledges are valuable. They give students the ability to learn what they want to know. The Great Tradition, the Western canon, is not taught as a *self-evident* source of superior knowledge. As with any other knowledge, students and teacher use their critical epistemology to determine the origins and question the assumptions of a literary work, a historical viewpoint, or an approach to science or math (Giroux, 1991, 24; Giroux and Aronowitz, 1991, 15–16).

EINSTEIN'S CLASSICAL INTENTIONS

Despite the epistemological avalanche triggered by his work, Einstein remained true to many goals of classical (or modern) science. Like Newton before him, Einstein believed that reality corresponds to physical laws. These laws, he maintained, are objective and exist separately from any particular knower or observer. Although his theory of relativity told us that different observers see different events, it still operated in the confines of a Newtonian-Cartesian epistemology. Einstein thought it brought us closer to understanding the objective laws of the cosmos (Peat, 1990, 680).

Nothing nonphysical causes anything, Einstein concluded. His cosmic reverence required no nonphysical structure of reality. Indeed, his awe involved speculation about the order and harmony that was omnipresent in physical reality (Morrison, 1987, 54). Thus, physical reality for Einstein clung to a Newtonian absolutism in that if the inquirer's mode of inquiry was properly scientific, laws would be forever immutable. *This* from the harbinger of the postmodern age, from the father of relativity? The irony was not lost on Einstein; he himself suggested that special relativity should have been known to the world as the theory of invariance (Jaki, 1987, 10).

Ever the ambiguous, amphibious one, half in the modern water, half on the strange postmodern land, Einstein clung to a Newtonian-Cartesian belief in a reality "out there," independent of how we decide to study it. The universe was still rational, predictable, and ruled by tangible, predetermined, and universal laws (Jaki, 1987, 10; Penrose, 1991, 37; Burich, 1987, 23). If one detects a hint of determinism in Einstein's epistemology, he or she is probably correct. Indeed, he argued that everything was determined by larger forces over which humans exert no control. Insects, stars, vegetables, and humans all dance to a mysterious tune played by an invisible piper (Burich, 1987, 230).

Rolling the Epistemological Dice

While it is true that, after the theory of relativity, time and space could not be viewed in the same way, Einstein never attempted to destroy absolutism when he maintained that no single frame of reference was privileged. To Einstein, this simply meant that all natural laws must retain their freedom from any *particular* vantage point so that absolute laws that are valid in every situation and every observation can be formulated. Such a formulation saves our epistemological souls, protecting us from the chaos, the "hell" of a relativistic pluralism of reality constructs based on every observer's experience.

Sustained by his "faith" in the rationality of the universe, Einstein in one sense attempted to free science from its egocentric and anthropomorphic blinders (i.e., its observer relativism; its dependence on different frames of reference) as he moved to a higher objectivity with his principle of invariance. In retrospect it is easy to see that his definition of rationality remained within the boundaries of the Newtonian-Cartesian way of seeing (Burich, 1987, 22). Theoretical physics would eventually force us to consider a variety of ways of seeing, an alternative set of geometries that were rational in the classical sense (Gangadean, 1987, 89–90). However, though committed to an absolutist science, Einstein opened the door to the stranger of epistemological pluralism. This mysterious stranger proceeded to ignite a revolution that in the late twentieth century is still burning, just not beginning to singe the hair of the "laity." As it links up with the subversive spirit of postmodernism, the epistemological world as we know it will be destroyed by fire.

QUANTUM PHYSICS—THE REAL EPISTEMOLOGICAL OUTLAW

Einstein reluctantly developed perhaps the most unfortunate label in the history of physics, relativity. Maybe sameness or invariance would have been more appropriate descriptions. To Einstein, the theory of special relativity only gave the *appearance* of a cosmos in which all observations are relative (Jaki, 1987, 9; Morrison, 1987, 52). Thus, relativity in the context of epistemology is not the most radical aspect of Einstein's work. The symbol of relativity is more important to epistemology than its reality.

Quantum physics, the study of matter at the subatomic level, developed by Max Planck and extended by Einstein, disallowed a conception of reality that was consistent with the common sense of the everyday world. Among other disquieting characteristics they found that subatomic particles have a wavelike nature, meaning that it is inaccurate to speak of them as existing in a particular place. When a bullet is shot from a gun, for example, Newtonian physics and common sense tell us that we can measure both the bullet's speed and its location to chart its trajectory. The news from quantum physics was that we can't do this with subatomic particles such as electrons. Trajectory, thus, cannot be conceptualized in the quantum realm. Physicist John Wheeler characterizes subatomic particles as great smoky dragons whose heads and tails we can find, but whose bodies are lost in a thick fog (Talbot, 1986, 17). What is more amazing at the quantum level is that depending on what types of questions we ask about the dragons, we get entirely different answers, completely different pictures of what they look like. This realization led Werner Heisenberg to his theory of indeterminacy, the idea that the inquirer is an inseparable part of the inquiry that laid the epistemological foundation for quantum physics. Heisenberg argued that classic objectivity does not exist. Accuracy is possible only from a particular vantage point (Courtney, 1988, 5).

The amazing implications of quantum physics forced quantum physicists, Niels Bohr in particular, to develop a formal reconceptualized epistemology. Their Copenhagen interpretation, or quantum epistemology, theorized what could be known about the subatomic microcosm. Connecting observer to the observed, Bohr and his colleagues refused to talk about atoms and electrons, that was not what they were observing. Thus, quantum epistemology delved into the irrational in nature. We must accept the irrational, the Copenhagen physicists argued, for when we try to ignore it and build rational pictures or models of the quantum world, the classical ideas of Newtonian physics slip in to distort it. What then is quantum reality? Bohr said that there is no quantum world, only an "abstract quantum mechanical description" (Peat, 1990, 64–65).

EINSTEIN, THE GUARDIAN OF EPISTEMOLOGICAL TRADITION?
Although he was responsible for some of the initial ideas that led to quantum physics, Einstein considered the Copenhagen description to be epistemological defeatism. Drawing upon his classical Newtonian roots, Einstein posited that if quantum physics doesn't grant us a realistic perspective on events at the subatomic realm, no matter how strange it might be, then the theory is insufficient. Using the logic of modernism, Einstein thus rejected quantum physics as a theoretically inadequate description of submicroscopic phenomena. Employing his frequently used dice metaphor, Einstein wrote in 1926:

> The theory produces a good deal but hardly brings us any closer to the secret of the Old One.
> I am at all events convinced that He does not play dice (Quoted in Penrose, 1991, 37).

In addition to his problems with the realism of the quantum description, Einstein also was offended by quantum theory's subjectivity. There must be something yet undiscovered in the subatomic world to account for our observation of it, he maintained. Acting in his role as guardian of tradition, Einstein was not ready to let Bohr and his quantum colleagues pull the epistemological carpet out from under him. O. B. Hardison Jr. described Einstein's guardian role as more like that of a chess player than that of a

Rolling the Epistemological Dice

craps shooter; he never accepted that an objective world of time and space did not exist at the quantum level (Hardison, 1989, 49).

Uncomfortable in his new role of the caretaker, the guardian, Einstein argued that eventually a discovery would uncover a more comforting and classical level of reality, an objective description of location and trajectory. He wrote:

> Even the great initial success of the quantum theory does not make me believe... although I am well aware that our younger colleagues interpret this as a consequence of senility. No doubt the day will come when we will see whose instinctive attitude was the correct one (Quoted in Talbot, 1986, 27).

For the rest of his life Einstein attempted to disapprove quantum physics. In the minds of most avant-garde physicists his attack was grounded on one fatal flaw. Without question, he assumed the existence of a physical and objective reality (Talbot, 1986, 27).

Einstein never strayed from his firm belief in scientific objectivity. Scientific objectivity, as Einstein conceived it, set forth a reality that: 1) is permanent despite any individual's inability or refusal to recognize it; 2) is material, physical, and external to the human mind; 3) is ordered by invariant universal laws. Thus, Einstein was grounded in a traditional epistemological realism, instead of a naïve realism, since the truths of the physical world were not merely derived from sensory experience but were formulated as constructions of the scientific imagination. The fact that the imagination was utilized, however, did not disturb Einstein's equation of objectivity with the constancy of physical *laws*, not physical *observations*. For example, an observer on a speeding train may describe the path of a falling basketball in terms of a parabola; an observer on the ground describes the path as a straight line. To Einstein the realist, these differences in description were irrelevant as long as the physical law expressed as a differential equation remained the same for both observers (Morrison, 1987, 52–53).

THE INTERSECTION OF AVANT GARDE PHYSICS WITH POSTMODERNISM

Einstein remains an ever-paradoxical figure. Firmly grounded in traditional epistemology, his work and spirit laid the foundation for dramatic changes in the way we consider knowing. Many of the dramatic changes in late twentieth-century physics have emanated from the mind of David Bohm. Born to the generation that followed Einstein, Bohm came to know him in the last year of Einstein's life. A series of conversations with Einstein at Princeton in the early 1950s alerted Bohm to the possibilities of a physics beyond the quantum. Drawing upon a foundation constructed by his deep understanding of quantum theory, Einstein's insights, and his own insightful creativity, Bohm developed a series of theories that have pushed physics to a new dimension at the same time that they have expanded our social and epistemological imaginations (Peat, 1990, 146–48). While many have contributed to the avant-garde physics of the late twentieth century, we will focus upon Bohm's work as representative of the cutting edge of the discipline. The following ten points offer a beginning for those interested in the educational implications of the conjunction of physics and postmodernism.

THE UNIVERSE AS AN UNDIVIDED WHOLE: NATURE CANNOT BE ANALYZED AS IF IT WERE A CONGLOMERATION OF PARTS. Bohm argues that although science uses the language of holism, science has in practice studied the physical world as if the fragments explored under microscopes and accelerated in particle chambers were actual reality. Drawing on the ideas that would form the basis of his notion of implicate order, Bohm called for an examination of reality that sought the enfolded connections among events. Bohm's ideas thus emphasized the flux and flow, the stages of events; not simply the event itself (Bohm and Peat, 1987, 197–98; Briggs and Peat, 1984, 98).

Postmodernism, like Bohm's physics, has decried the fragmentation of Newtonian-Cartesian epistemology. Human and social experience has been reduced, postmodernists argue, to discrete and arbitrary pieces that are separated from the combination of forces that provided the human experience its distinction in the first place (Britzman, 1991, 35). Newtonian-Cartesian love, for example, involves a raised heartbeat, a specific percentage increase in hormonal secretion, and a behavioral expectation of positive reciprocation. Modern curriculum is removed from the social realities that grant significance to the knowledge to be "mastered." Indeed, modern schools see society as one cog of a larger machine that is to be studied. Postmodernists see human beings and society as interconnected aspects of a broader framework, an implicate order, that reveals itself when the evolutionary possibility of humanity is entertained (Oliver and Gershman, 1989, 30).

TRANSCENDENCE OF DOMINANT, CERTIFIED WAYS OF SEEING: SCIENTISTS AND EDUCATORS AS COGNITIVE CARTOGRAPHERS. Bohm has maintained that to take wholeness seriously is to give up all that is familiar and comfortable about our understanding of the physical world. In other words, Bohm is asking us to step through the postquantum looking glass to the other side of the mirror. For example, Bohm and others have recognized that quantum systems are related in a manner that insults the traditional explanations of Newtonian-Cartesian physics. At the subatomic level, processes are connected in ways that have nothing to do with commonsense conceptions of fields, pushes, pulls, waves, particles, or direct or indirect correlations. Dominant ways of seeing have nothing to do with such disconcerting quantum processes. For example, correlations between particles in different locations are often instantaneous and do not require intercommunication. Labeled nonlocality, such interactions (or non-interactions) are irrational from a Newtonian-Cartesian perspective. The time has come for a deconstruction and redefinition of the term "rational" (Bohm and Peat, 1984, 99; Peat, 1990, 130). The process of redefinition may bring us to a level of understanding of physical reality that opens doors only imagined by science fiction writers.

Drawing upon the postmodern analysis of Frederick Jameson, Henry Giroux and Stanley Aronowitz take the idea of transcending familiar ways of seeing into the social and educational realism. The postmodern critique alerts us to the dominant ways in which social reality is "mapped" and thus gives us the power to formulate new cognitive maps that take into account the unique conditions created by new electronic and informational technologies. In many ways the socioeducational space created and occupied by television, mass advertising, computer technology, music videos, video games, and the like is as uncomfortable and as unfamiliar as the microspace "described" by quantum physics. The postmodern "creation of new constellations of forms," that is, the rewriting of our lives and the ways that we represent ourselves is similar to the attempt of avant garde physics to rewrite our understanding of physical reality (Aronowitz and Giroux, 1991, 60–61).

THEORY CONSTRUCTION AS MEANS TO INSIGHT, NOT AS BEGETTER OF ABSOLUTE KNOWLEDGE AND TRUTH: THE DEVELOPMENT OF A POST-EPISTEMOLOGICAL SCIENCE. Bohm is quite concerned about producing insights into the physical world. An insight, he argues, is not a rigid truth but an act of perception, a new angle on the "wholeness." An insight might involve a poet's ability to connect individuals to an empathetic flash about the taste of sorrow, not a definitive treatise on the topic. Knowledge of sorrow is transitory. Each time we experience it we find ourselves in new circumstances. The taste in the new context is slightly different and we slowly understand the feeling in subtly different ways.

Advantages can be gained from giving up the traditional epistemological quest for final knowledge. The post-epistemological scientific world emphasizes the delicate, ever-shifting nature of relationships between physical objects; the undivided nature of reality, not the individual pieces of our existence. Seen from a Newtonian-Cartesian perspective, the heart is undoubtedly not the brain on one level; but on another, more subtle, plane, there is no way to separate the function of the two organs. Indeed, to separate them is to lose *insight* into the genesis of heart function and disease (Briggs and Peat, 1984, 97–98).

Jean-François Lyotard maintains that the postmodern world is an environment in flux, a social cosmos where the epistemological certainties of the past have been destroyed by technical and scientific innovation (Lyotard, 1984, 80). Thus, individuals must steer their own courses and develop their own insights without the guidance of validated benchmarks, unquestionable philosophical assumptions, or universal definitions of reason. Knowledge is constantly changing in the postmodern world as the pace of social change in general accelerates to a dangerous speed. Newtonian-Cartesian modernism attempted to control the changes by stepping outside of history, developing permanent fixtures of truth, and using them to produce discursive closure, in an end to history and an end to conversation (Hutcheon, 1988, 101). Postmodernism operates from within history, knowing that present circumstances will change (probably tomorrow), and that history cannot be escaped. Postmodern educators, thus, understand that no curriculum is final, no canon sacrosanct. There is always tomorrow in the postmodern world.

STRETCHING BEYOND MECHANISTIC WAYS OF SEEING: THE COMING COLLAPSE OF THE NEWTONIAN-CARTESIAN WORLD. Most scientists continue to practice their craft as if the mechanistic worldview had never been questioned. They do not see that agent provocateur, quantum physics, already has performed its subversive task with aplomb; it has sown the seeds of ruination for Newtonian-Cartesian mechanistic fragmentation. Quantum physics showed that the concept of separate atomic particles cannot be maintained and previously validated fragmented of reality have lost their definition as discrete entities that exist in time and space. As the result of quantum analysis, physicists' pictures of individual subatomic particles have blurred into post-impressionistic portraits of ill-defined clouds (Briggs and Peat, 1984, 100–01).

The Newtonian-Cartesian master narratives and mechanistic ways of seeing are also crumbling in the social sciences, humanities, and education. In Western philosophy post-structural, critical, and feminist perspectives have raised challenges to tradition via questions of ethics and justice. Critical theory is, in a sense, the quantum physics of social theory because it reframes our postmodern picture of fragmented social and educational reality. Foucault, Derrida, Lyotard, Habermas, and Baudrillard have successfully challenged the empiricist assumptions (the metanarratives) of science and other cultural systems. As they challenged the epistemological authority of consensus, they exposed the illusion of consensus. They tapped into the ways of seeing of the marginalized and the dispossessed from the subjugated perspectives of those groups. They found the importance of the master narratives: that social reality and educational practice are structured by discourses (what can be said about particular subjects, who can say it, and who must listen), and that the discourses are shaped by the master narratives as well (Hutcheon, 1988, 6–7; Giroux and Aronowitz, 1991, 19).

THE INSEPARABILITY OF OBSERVER AND OBSERVED. After quantum theory, the assumption that the observer and that which he or she observes constitute discrete parts of the universe cannot be supported (Briggs and Peat, 1984, 99). Of courses, the questions we ask about quantum reality shape the picture of the subatomic cosmos that we paint. Our location in the web of reality, our vantage point, influences our questions.

Thus, to remove the knower from the object of study is to distort the process of knowing.

Postmodernism is grounded in this constructivist conception of the inseparability of the knower and the known, it transforms the "givers" of modernism into the "constructions" of postmodernism. Thus, while reality may exist, it is molded by the discourses, concepts, and categories of human interpretation. Many have taken such an assertion to mean that the world is meaningless. Why should social scientists and educators even attempt to perform their tasks? Postmodernists respond that constructivism does not imply meaninglessness, it only implies that any meaning that remains to be found is created by us ourselves (Hutcheon, 1988, 43, 146). Such an understanding holds dramatic implications for the ways that we inquire and teach. It grants us a critical distance that allows us to uncover that which was hidden by the assumptions of certainty, the ironies, the ambiguities, the intentions that shape what we have become.

THE INSEPARABILITY OF WHOLE AND PART: ABANDONING THE IDEA OF A RIGID BODY FOR THE NOTION OF "WORLD TUBE." To Bohm, structures of reality are parts of larger flowing movements, like a vortex in a stream. Einstein initiated the concept with his idea that there are no Newtonian rigid bodies existing absolutely in space and time, only relative ones. In the place of rigid bodies, Einstein introduced the idea of a world tube or the history of a region of space. Einstein's world tube rejects the notion of the particle as smallest unit of physical analysis and implies that matter was best conceived as a process, as an interaction of whole and part. Indeed, where does the river end and the vortex begin? Of course, there is no way to tell because physical reality is an infinitely complex, rationally unanalyzable continuous process (Bohm and Peat, 1987, 72: Briggs and Peat, 1984, 62, 101).

In the same way that avant-garde physics subverts the notion of the unified or rigid particle as the smallest coherent unit of analysis in the physical universe, postmodernism subverts modernism's notion of the free, coherent, transcendent, unified individual (or subject). The idea of a free, coherent individual is grounded in an acceptance of a rational, self-determining consciousness that is free from any type of consciousness-construction. Postmodernism contends that human subjects gain their "subjectivity," their meaning in the world, through their social relations. Thus, the human subject is shaped by multiple and contradictory forces. The self is no longer a simple warehouse for consciousness. It is a site of the ambiguous pushing and pulling of a multitude of influences. As with a vortex, it is hard to determine where human consciousness ends and social and discursive acts begin.

THE INSTABILITY OF LANGUAGE: SCIENTIFIC LANGUAGE IS THE PROGENY OF THE NEWTONIAN-CARTESIAN WORLD. We must talk, David Bohm argues, but we must remember that our words are never about absolute things. At our best we express insights. At our worst, we communicate illusions. Quantum theory, for example, undercuts our complacency about the meaning of words such as "path." It is not that the electron's path is uncertain. It is the linguistic use of path in this context that doesn't work. Echoing Wittgenstein, Niels Bohr often reminded his colleagues that reality is just a word in the particular word game of science. Drawing upon Bohm's theory of enfolded order, we can see that all science is grounded in a language that is designed only to describe the explicate order. Thus, language is a prisoner of the Newtonian-Cartesian wardens. What we can conceptualize is significantly limited by the failure of language to keep up with new dimensions of reality (Briggs and Peat, 1984, 103; Peat, 1990, 45, 69, 157).

A central tenet of postmodernism involves its description of the instability of language. Frames of reference seem to be a matter of systems of description or discursive rules rather than of that which is being described. Language, thus, does not possess a fixed and absolute correspondence to reality. The individual's construction of meaning, as a result, is freed from the confines of traditional usage by this postmodern understanding. We are empowered to see that the meanings that are considered most legitimate are significantly determined by power groups who exert influence over the economic and cultural workings of a culture (Hutcheon, 1988, 145; Aronowitz and Giroux, 1991, 92–93). Indeed, one of the tragedies of any absolutist, feminist, or other essentializing school of thought, is that having accepted the need to free language and thinking from its Newtonian-Cartesian constraints, some wish to immediately place a new set of constrictive meanings upon society.

THE WHOLENESS OF THE UNIVERSE CANNOT BE CAPTURED BY ONE GRANT THEORY: THERE IS ALWAYS ANOTHER VANTAGE POINT FROM WHICH TO QUESTION REALITY. Each time in the history of science we arrive at a point at which a particular paradigm fails to provide consciousness-expanding, meaningful answers, we have reached an epistemological watershed. In effect what happens during this period of dissonance is that we discover a deeper wholeness to the cosmos than we had ever before anticipated. The holistic nature of reality extends far deeper than our maps, theories, or equations ever portrayed it. Martin Heidegger once provided an insightful example that attempted to illustrate the difficulty of finding one description that captures the wholeness of reality. Comparing truth to a drinking glass, Heidegger explained that as one rotates the glass to see one particular aspect, another aspect is concealed. The glass, he concluded, can never be positioned in a manner that allows one to see the whole glass. Whatever one sees of the glass, however, contains its wholeness within it. From a previously unconsidered angle we may see another dimension of the wholeness (Briggs and Peat, 1984, 103).

"Let us declare war on totality; let us be witnesses to the unpresentable," Lyotard wrote, in an attempt to reflect the postmodern notion, that wholeness cannot be captured by one grand theory (Lyotard, 1984, 82). Within the socio-educational domain, postmodernism rejects attempts to delineate an essential transhistorical human nature, a fixed theory of intelligence or ossified stages of cognitive development, or the *correct* human goals that must be pursued. Typically, such totalities wrap themselves in the banner of objectivity and scientific disinterest, thus freeing themselves from a distasteful debate. The postmodern attack on totality is offered in the attempt to deflate an authoritarian epistemological machismo, replacing it with a diversity of perspectives and voices. The stories of the subjugated that emerge from particular historical struggles offer new perspectives on the wholeness of society, perspectives that allow us to see Heidegger's glass from new angles (Aronowitz and Giroux, 1991, 67–70).

THE INABILITY OF OLD ORTHODOXIES TO NAME THE CHANGES THAT ARE PROPELLING US INTO THE TWENTY-FIRST CENTURY. Newtonian-Cartesian physics assumes that we live in a world in which the scale of size and energy is taken for granted. The quantum world in Newtonian terms is an irrational land of mystery, a funhouse of mirrors, where objects instantly transform themselves from particles into waves, entities "walk" through two doors at once, and "distant relatives" use the telephone whenever communication is needed. The Mad Hatter and Door Mouse reign supreme. Physicists have been baffled by the action of subatomic particles and their ability to maintain a "nonlocal" connection that has nothing to do with space or time. Newtonian-Cartesian concepts have little relevance for such a terrain (Peat, 1990, 132; Kincheloe, 1998; Kincheloe, et al. 1999).

The postmodern condition that is marked by a media-propelled landscape of consumerism is a cosmos markedly different from the world into which the modern physical and social scientific disciplines were born. In the postmodern world, political and consumer discourses merge into a grammar of manipulative images. Postmodern critiques assume that such unprecedented conditions cannot be understood within the framework of modernism (Hutcheon, 1988, 205, 210). One of the few chances we have to escape the torturous possibility of falling deeper into the pit of mindless consumerism and objectivism is to understand the postmodern analysis of power relations within texts, codes, and cultural signs, indeed, within curricula and school definitions of success. Like Newtonian-Cartesian scientists, the attempts of traditional liberals and conservatives to explain the power relations of the postmodern world are inadequate. Indeed, postmodern epistemology gives us a chance to go beyond, to explain what has traditionally eluded us: to explain the construction of the conscious operation of power, the ways that our schools unwittingly promote particular views of reality and self (Kincheloe, Steinberg, and Gresson, 1996).

The Nature of Genius

In considering the genius of Edgar Allan Poe, poet and literary critic James Russell Lowell observed:

> "There comes Poe with his raven like Barnaby Rudge,
> Three-fifths of him genius, and two-fifths sheer fudge."
> (Oxford, Lowell, 319:8)

Lowell's attempt to understand the dimensions of Poe's genius left him floundering: he could quantify but not define why or how Poe accomplished great literary works. As they have bantered the word "genius" about, generations of critics and philosophers have attempted to reduce, qualify, and model the roles and requirements of genius. In our attempt to understand the "stigma of genius," it is essential to discover not what genius *is*, but what genius is *not*. As Lowell defined his own role: "A wise scepticism is the first attribute of a good critic" (Oxford, Lowell, 319:16), Lowell acknowledged the deconstructive act of scepticism. It is within the mandate of deconstruction that we discuss the natures of genius.

In Chapter One we introduced the postmodern notion of deconstruction. As our method of interpretation, we immersed ourselves into the world of genius, its origin, its progression, and its existence in a modern world. As we "read the world" of genius, understand the forces that shape it, ask questions of its nature, and seek not to define, but to discover the hidden dimensions of genius, we are able to uncover the layers of "sheer fudge" as components of the nature of genius. As our philosophical strategy, we examine genius from its etymological construction to transformations in the notions of genius. The "text" of genius begins with myth and breadth, yet "ends" in the modern era as a narrow, reduced shadow of itself.

ETYMOLOGICALLY SPEAKING . . .

Ancient Greeks acknowledged the genius spirit within each human, and divided the concept of genius into the divinely inspired entity and the "mad" or demonic entity. "As an act of demigods, genius came from inspiration; the source of this inspiration was the gods and to be inspired was to personify a mystical power" (Albert, 1975, 140). Plato conjectured that genius contained elements of madness and along with that madness, actual possession. Socrates defined the madness as the *daemon* that inhabited a man and created his genius.

The Roman genius, the "begetter," was the spirit of paternal ancestry; the genius was believed to reside within all men. The female counterpart to genius was the *juno*, she who lived within all women. Each Roman had a personal genius or *juno* that served the citizen as sources of inspiration and talent. "Official prayers were addressed to the Genius of Rome, whether masculine or feminine, whether god or goddess" (Walker, 1983, 339). The Arabic *djinni* or *genie* was similar to the Roman entity and granted wishes or gifts to the person who contained the personal *djinni*.

Ancient mythology defined genius as either divinely inspired, or as a component of madness. (Even today, these "characteristics" of genius are considered to be part of the grand definition of genius. It is interesting to note that even in the modern logical and scientific genius, there are still connections to divine inspiration, for example, the concept of giftedness; Where do these gifts come from? Who inspired them? Who "gave" them to the gifted? Why doesn't everyone have these gifts? Who selects the gifted? The entire notion of gifted implies a present of some sort.)

After the Classical Age, the only notion of genius that remained was patriarchal. Genius was looked upon as a type of muse (feminine in nature) that inspired the male. The Middle Ages ushered in a genius that did not create, but was merely able to duplicate and imitate previous creations, a convenient reinforcement of the Church's desire to suppress original thinking.

The rebirth of the classical age, the Renaissance, brought a new concept of genius. A genius was a *man* who created new visions, through art, literature, science, and other media, and who was acknowledged by the world. Creativity became an important "ingredient" of genius, and distinct characteristics, such as *pazzia* (madness) and/or melancholy were identified with those that attained the title of genius. "Applied to great men, however, the term [*pazzia*] referred to qualities associated with the melancholic tem-

The Nature of Genius

perament, such as eccentricity, sensitivity, moodiness, and solitariness. These were far from negative qualities. Emulating these manifestations of melancholic behavior was turned into a fad in sixteenth century Europe" (Becker, 1978, 24).

Coupled with the spiritual and mystical origins of genius, the Enlightenment added to its definition: "It is around the start of the eighteenth century that the term genius began to acquire its modern meaning. In the sense that it was used to denote a mysterious quality, a creative energy, that certain individuals were assessed as possessing. However, it was not until the middle of the eighteenth century that the name of genius became applied not just to the quality, but to the individuals manifesting this" (Becker, 1978, 24). Explanations of the rational and genius followed, and distinct characteristics combined in a "recipe" to set apart the genius from the "normal man." Newtonian-Cartesian models of genius were extensively detailed and many parts have been preserved and used throughout the centuries; words and definitions vary, but the rational, scientific notion of genius remains part of the popular consciousness. Categorization and reductionism have eviscerated genius and we are left with taxonomies that must be followed to properly call an individual a "genius." The deconstruction of modern notions of genius leaves one keenly aware that "rules and models destroy genius and art" (Oxford, Hazlitt, 243:28).

The idea of madness, melancholy, and mystery as components of genius relaxed in the wake of the Romantic era. Genius in the arts and genius in science were separately recognized and visions of creative surges and inspiration came into focus. Emerson's "Method of Nature" claimed that "When Nature has work to be done, she creates a genius to do it" (Oxford, Emerson, 208:3). Up until this point, genius had been attributed largely to the rational intellectual, and many artists had been placed in a secondary category because they possessed particular talents. The Romantics validated the artist as a genius. While Kant theorized that genius was really a label for the artist only, Gerard viewed genius with a broader perspective and noted that genius was based in "the faculty of invention," by means of which a man is qualified for making new discoveries in science, or for producing original works of art (Gerard, 1966, 74–74). Imagination became a primary component of genius and the rational was supplanted in favor of imagination and the self. "The man of genius, reconstituted in the Romantic vision, became the embodiment of this new spirit and was enthusiastically hailed as the Erlosungskraft, or force of redemption and the guiding light of the age. Underscoring this consecration of genius was a sense of the inexplicable, the mystical" (Becker, 1978, 27).

The late-nineteenth-century and early-twentieth-century origins of genius became more precise and were categorized into two main areas: the genetic and the social-psychological constructs of genius. As a cousin to Charles Darwin, Francis Galton came by his notions of genetic genius naturally. Galton was the first scholar to consider that individuals were intrinsically different and that investigation into their differences had merit (Clark, 1983, 13). In his mid-nineteenth-century study, *Hereditary Genius*, Galton contended that genius was basically biological in origin (a pleasant reinforcement, no doubt, to Galton, given his brilliant cousin); he saw the inheritance of genius as genetically inspired. Intelligence and personality were basically genetic talents. Freud agreed with the initial contention that the biological roots of the family have everything to do with genius; however, he differed in his interpretation and placed the emphasis on the family as a sociopsychological influence. Freud saw that personality and motivation were directly influenced by the degree of genius, which was a direct offshoot of the family. As scientifically rooted as both Galton and Freud appear to be, it is important to note that the idea of the genetic origins of genius still attributes a human being's quality of genius to luck and chance and where one just "happens" to be born and to whom. We can find the origins of both luck and chance with the notion of the demi-god and the divine nature of genius (Albert, 1975, 140–42).

Genius has been defined and redefined for the past three millennia, yet in the attempts to reduce genius to a "thing" that inspires or inhabits *man*, we seem no closer to understanding the nature(s) of genius. Once again, the failure of scientific rationality is manifest. The myths from antiquity to the hyperrationalities of the modern age have not helped us to discover genius or to teach children. Let us hope that by discovering what genius is not, we will be able to work individually with students to encourage their individual djinni. Thus can the tyrannies of certain, "verified" notions of genius be overcome.

ASSUMPTIONS ABOUT MODERNIST CONCEPTS OF GENIUS

Our deconstruction of genius reveals four tacit assumptions about the definition of genius, its role, and its identification:

1) Attempts to define genius (like perceptions of intelligence, student performance, and school quality) are reductionistic;
2) The characteristics of genius are categorizable;
3) Genius is socially constructed; and
4) Genius is a male attribute.

1. Attempts to Define Genius Are Reductionistic

Scholars and psychologists of the twentieth century have produced many models, tables, and taxonomies to define genius. There is an inherent need to label and define all components of being human. A lack of concrete definition leads to an ambiguity with which

The Nature of Genius

governments, schools, and the public are unable to cope. Parents worry about missing genius in their children, and there is a desire to compare one's child with her or his peers. To attach the label of genius to offspring has become desireable, another way of "one-upping" the Joneses:

> My younger brother and his wife are both schoolteachers, and they have a 10-year-old son who was born when they were in their 40s. They drill this boy endlessly, and he has never, ever been away from them. They take him everywhere: meetings, dances, even adult parties. They tried very hard to enroll him into the school's gifted program, and he was finally accepted when he entered third grade. Now they're saying that this child is a "true genius" and the true geniuses are only born of older parents. Is this true? At what age do they develop their genius?
>
> P.S.: I don't have children of my own and feel sorry for this child. He talks and acts like a little old man.
>
> Anonymous, Albuquerque, New Mexico
> (*Atlanta Constitution*, *Parade Magazine*, Sept. 15, 1991)

Experts, scholars, and teachers also rely on definitions that inherently contain a finite depth. Using postmodern analysis, we see that the assumptions and definitions of Cartesian logic can be laid bare by the ways that the structure of traditional science constructs imaginary worlds. Like a novel, experts "write" definitions and classifications of children through specific testing and the creation of models. Parents and teachers rely on these definitions of genius to label and place children "where they belong." Through deconstruction we see not where "gifted" children are placed but where other children are not placed.

"Experts" on genius, those that have constructed the modern realm of genius, have reduced genius to a game of rules constructed by language, test scores, and isolation of the notion of genius from the "whole" vision of a child. As we turn to an emancipatory system of meaning grounded in deconstruction, we can temper our own system of meanings of genius with a dose of postmodern self-analysis and epistemological humility. Again, we turn to our postformal way of thinking.

Joe Kincheloe discusses the reductionism of thinking through the disconnection of the knower and the known. He asserts that the separation of the knower and the known grounds the Newtonian-Cartesian world. "Cartesian reductionism asserts that all aspects of complex phenomena can be best appreciated by reducing them to their constituent parts and then piecing these elements together according to causal laws" (Kincheloe, 1991, 27). By this separation and alienation from the whole view of genius, experts are able to use only an explicate concept of genius, thus eliminating the meaning, significance, and application of the "whole picture" of genius.

Formal thinking such as Piaget's also implies an acceptance of the Newtonian-Cartesian mechanistic world view of genius, a view trapped within a cause and effect, hypothetical deductive system of reasoning. Unconcerned with questions of power relations and the way they structure our constructions of genius, formal operational definitions of genius accept an objectified, depoliticized way of seeing how genius works. Such a perspective disallows conceptions of genius that fall outside the "acceptable" and conventional ways of being intelligent.

Reductionism is common in the study of teaching and education. Mainstream teacher-education texts discuss the formation and inception of the public school in the nineteenth century, attributing much of the system to Horace Mann, "the father of the American school." The historical significance of the public school is grounded in the movement by Mann to establish the highest expansion of democracy within the school: the idea that every citizen will be given a chance to make something of him or herself through the public system (Johnson, Collins, Dupuis, and Johansen, 1988, 284; Ornstein, Levine, 1989, 174; Madaus, Kellaghan, and Schwab, 1989, 46–48; Walker, Kozma, and Green, 1981, 56–60). However, when we historically contextualize the founding of public schooling and consider social and political variables that directly influenced the inception of the public school, we see a considerably different picture.

Horace Mann and the common school crusaders in Massachusetts founded the first system of state-supported public schools in the United States in the 1840s. Drawing upon the traditional Yankee worship of the work ethic and a harmonious social order, Mann's schools have come to represent in the traditional mythology the supreme expression of American democratic values. But the Massachusetts of the 1840s was a quite different socioeconomic world of the seventeenth- and eighteenth-century Puritan societies that gave birth to the traditional Yankee ethics. The industrial revolution had changed that world forever. The values of social harmony and hard work were coopted, perverted, and utilized over the subsequent decades to discipline future workers who might become frustrated with prevailing wages, work conditions, and the benefits. Ideals of social harmony and the work ethic were taught to children in schools as part of an attempt to forestall labor unrest and to prevent strikes and demands for economic justice. When we view the creation of the public schools through contextualized frames, we come to understand how the implicate meanings attached to public schools alter the construction of consciousness.

Our lives are filled with reductionistic constructions. The media facilitate our tunnelled visions. An article reported through the Knight Ridder News Service advises us that:

> If your marriage breaks up, Philadelphia divorce lawyer Neil H. Stein says the cause likely will be one of these: disagreements about child rearing, traumatic health or financial problems,

resentment over who is doing more, sexual incompatibility or extra-marital affairs, lack of money and conflicts over expenses, religious differences, addiction and/or recovery, disputes about relatives, employment-related conflicts, or failure to grow together. (September 17, 1991)

Sounds as if he just about covered everything, doesn't it? However, Stein has reduced the breakdown of the whole of marriage into separate and shallow parts. Somehow his confidence with fitting the ills of a marriage into one sentence doesn't indicate an understanding of the implicate order of the marriage. Why is it that we seem so quick and eager to accept lists and concepts from "experts"? Without a postmodern desire to deconstruct reality, we allow our subjectivities to be manipulated by special interests that each have their own tacit agendas.

The educational experience of Albert Einstein illustrates how reductionism and the classification of students serves to negate many forms of genius. Einstein's early life in schools was plagued by his inability to be articulate and to develop language skills. Because of his ineptness in verbal communication and poor performance in standardized procedures of schooling, Einstein was classified as a slow learner. James Gallagher asks of Einstein: "Could he get into a first-rate college today?" (Gallagher, 1975, 46). Based on his performance in public school, it is unlikely that any of today's universities would be anxious to accept him. Because of Einstein's "failure" in one area, he was reduced to a category that determined his scholastic future. The use of standardized testing, or even "enlightened" creativity assessments and rigid taxonomies of genius limits us to a prescribed definition of genius. "In the instrumental rationality of much educational research the attempt to translate such intricate relationships into numbers often renders the data meaningless in the eyes of practitioners. Until researchers free themselves from the oppressive culture of positivism their research will remain irrelevant to teacher practice" (Kincheloe, 1991, 101).

Because it emphasizes certainty and prediction, formal thinking organizes verified facts into a theory or classification model. The facts that do not fit into the theory are eliminated, and the developed theory is the one that best eliminates contradictions in knowledge. Thus, formal thought operates on the assumption that of the resolution of contradiction is a critical objective (if it doesn't fit into the predefined "box," shave off those "contradictions" until it does). School and standardized testmakers, assuming that formal operational thought represents the highest level of human cognition, focus their efforts on its cultivation and measurement. Students and teachers who move beyond formality are often unrewarded and sometimes even punished.

Reduction of genius serves to decontextualize the whole of genius and to limit us as to how we work with students and construct our educational system. Even those theoreticians who give a liberal interpretation to educational constructs of genius and intelligence still fall into a chasm of decontextualization. Positivism, generated by Newtonian-Cartesian modernity, infiltrates the consciousness of both the conservative and liberal expert. "The failure of late twentieth century liberalism is directly connected to its inability to understand the underside of scientific hyper-rationality" (Kincheloe, 1991, 65). Liberal scholarship serves to give false security to educators who sincerely want to "do the right thing" and who traditionally reject using only standardized tests. "The broadly diffused liberal position on moral philosophy and educational ethics is the chief inheritor of the dual Enlightenment project of linking reason to freedom and linking social progress to the increasing development of scientific rationality" (Giroux, 1988, 53). The concept of "abstract rationality" still serves to reduce and limit our perceptions of reality. Giroux suggests that Kohlberg, though cognizant of moral and social constructs, still limits his definitions of human beings by not considering power relations. Kohlberg's androcentric moral reasoning is securely based in the Newtonian-Cartesian tradition.

Genius in a postformal context does not imply an attempt to redefine or to "rewrite" genius. Instead, it initiates a reflective and contextualized dialogue that is always concerned with the expansion of the natures of genius. Our perceptions of genius are not closed, limited, or reduced. Rather, they are elastic in nature, ever changing and redefining themselves. If educators stopped trying to reduce genius by defining it, an Albert (or Alberta) Einstein would be welcome in any university.

2. *The Characteristics of Genius Are Categorizable*
I (Joe Kincheloe) recall an experience from eighth grade when I sat on wooden bleachers and watched the home football team in a tense and close game against our rivals. Several rows in front of me sat a fifth grader, Andy, a low achiever, a slow learner, a student who had never had any luck with school. Many of his teachers felt Andy was close to being mentally handicapped, as he was unable to understand how to complete even simple scholastic tasks. The game was in its final quarter and our team had a third down and fifteen yards to go. The quarterback had been sacked continually and it seemed impossible for the team to get beyond our opponents' defense. Andy had been quietly engrossed in the entire game. Before the next play, I remember being startled by Andy suddenly jumping up and shouting: "Screen pass!"

I was astounded at the call that Andy made. Of course! It seemed perfectly obvious that if the quarterback was getting sacked, then using a screen pass was the obvious offense. The key to a screen pass is to let the defensive line and linebackers rush the quarterback unimpeded; as they approach the quarterback, a receiver runs past the charging defensive players, gathers a set of blockers, and if successful, catches the pass with only the defensive backfield to elude.

The Nature of Genius

I always think of Andy when I consider genius and giftedness. In order to understand the importance of performing a screen pass at that time, one would have to possess a high level of cognitive thinking processes. In order to identify that this strategic call was the perfect solution, he or she would have to be aware of the history of football, the intricate details of the structure of the game, and the rules of the game, and possess the ability to see through the mass of players on the field and to predict which play would allow the home team to break the impasse. When calling a screen pass, Andy had to understand the importance of adjusting to what was happening on the field at all times and the strategy behind each play. The body of input, the discovery of patterns, and the suggesting of solutions to an unstructured problem, is, at the very least, evidence of formal problem-solving abilities. Yet Andy was categorized as "slow." I don't know whatever happened to Andy. I would like to think that he overcame the labels and the incorrect attitudes toward him. But I am enough of a realist to expect that the labels already placed on him as a ten-year-old have governed his life ever since.

Twentieth-century psychologists, sociologists, and educators have constructed many models and "recipes" for genius and giftedness. Using identifiable characteristics, researchers suggest ways to test and classify genius. Preoccupation with identification has saturated the literature from the 1920s to the present. Through deconstruction we are able to understand the significance of placing genius and possible attributes into categories. As we discuss the popular models for the identification and teaching of genius, we do not look for answers, but ask questions. These questions can empower us to consider new, informed actions in the teaching of children.

IQ TESTING

At the beginning of the twentieth century, the French government commissioned Alfred Binet to develop a special curriculum for students who were considered to be "slow learners." Binet was interested in identifying individual differences in intelligence (Clark, 1983, 13). In 1921, Lewis Terman divised an intelligence scale at Stanford University. He wrote:

> It is safe to predict, that in the near future intelligence tests will bring tens of thousands of... high grade defectives under the surveillance and protection of society. This will ultimately result in curtailing the reproduction of feeble-mindedness and in the elimination of an enormous amount of crime, pauperism, and industrial inefficiency (Terman, 1916, 6–7).

In a study that continued well over forty years, the progress of fifteen hundred California children was followed. Terman described the research:

> I was a senior in psychology at Indiana University and was asked to prepare two reports for a seminar, one on mental deficiency and one on genius. The reading of those two reports opened

up a new world to me, the world of Galton, Binet and their contemporaries. By the time I reached my last graduate year, I decided to find out for myself how precocious children differ from the mentally backward, and accordingly chose as my doctoral dissertation an experimental study of the intellectual processes of fourteen boys, seven of them picked as the brightest and seven as the dullest in a large city school.... The experiment contributed little or nothing to science, but it contributed a lot to my future thinking.... My dream was realized in the spring of 1921 when I obtained a generous grant from the Commonwealth Fund of New York City for the purpose of locating a thousand subjects of IQ 140 or higher (Terman, 1954, 222–23).

The use of the Stanford-Binet Intelligence Scale, based on the research of both Terman and Binet, is still the most popular test used to identify intelligence. This scale was designed to measure general intelligence and ability:

A person's score on intelligence tests is usually given as an Intelligence Quotient (IQ). In developing the intelligence test, variations in test performance caused by age differences were taken into account. This adjustment led to the idea of IQ, which is computed by the mental age divided by the chronological age times 100. Standardized on the general population, the test developed with an average IQ at any age set at 100. The middle 50 percent of the population falls between 90 and 110 IQ. On the Stanford-Binet, an IQ of 132 reflects the beginning of the upper 2 percent of the population, and a score of 68 IQ reaches the top of the lower 2 percent (Clark, 1983, 11).

IQ tests do not calculate variables of race, socioeconomic class, or gender. Intelligence testing does not measure intelligence, instead it indicates an aptitude for certain types of concrete thinking. The tests are misused in their attempt to categorize children through intelligence. One might muse that the Puritans would have loved IQ testing, as they are excellent tests to discover who would be able to be "vocationally fit" in a system that discourages individual thinking and initiative. Little criticism and virtually no deconstruction of the popular test of intelligence quotient has been found in mainstream teacher education and gifted and talented students. Terman's studies were instrumental in contradicting previous stereotypes of genius. His studies utilized children who were predominantly male Caucasians from a specific area in California. Following is a summary of the general characteristics of the group:

1. The average member of our group is a slightly better physical specimen than the average child....
2. For the fields of subject matter covered in our tests, the superiority of gifted over unselected children was greater in reading, language, usage, arithmetical reasoning, science, literature, and the arts. In arithmetical computation, spelling and fac-

tual information about history and civics, the superiority of the gifted was somewhat less marked....
3. The interests of gifted children are many-sided and spontaneous, they learn to read easily and read more and better books than the average child. At the same time, they make numerous collections, cultivate many kinds of hobbies, and acquire far more knowledge of plays and games than the average child...
4. As compared with unselected children, they are less inclined to boast or overstate their knowledge; they are more trustworthy when under temptation to cheat; their character preferences and social attitudes are more wholesome, and they score higher in a test of emotional stability...
5. The deviation of the gifted subjects from the generality is in the upward direction for nearly all traits. There is no law of compensation whereby the intellectual superiority of the gifted tends to be offset by inferiorities along nonintellectual lines (Gallagher, 1975, 34).

Without belaboring the obvious, let's silently deconstruct and question some words and phrases:

- slightly better?
- average child?
- many sided and spontaneous?
- better books?
- less inclined to boast?
- more trustworthy? more wholesome?

"The time is probably not far distant when intelligence tests will become a recognized and widely used instrument for determining vocational fitness.... When thousands of children who have been tested by the Binet scale have been followed out into the industrial world, and their success in various occupations noted, we shall know fairly definitely... the minimum 'intelligence quotient' necessary for success in each leading occupation" (Terman, 1916, 7).

As I (Joe Kincheloe) grew up in the Appalachian Mountains, most of my (Joe Kincheloe) young friends came from poor families. My friend Larry's father was a woodcutter and his mother stayed at home. When I visited his small house, I noticed that there were no books or magazines and Larry's family never received a newspaper. This presented a stark contrast to my own home, with its daily paper, *Newsweek*, *The New Republic*, *U.S. News and World Report*, and a room with bookshelves to the ceiling that we called the "library." Larry was brilliant. He showed me how to "read" the forest (how to not get lost on a hike); to avoid poison ivy and poison oak; how to identify what was edible and what was not. He unsuccessfully tried to teach me how to work on a car (or at least to identify parts of the engine). All of these skills were learned from his father, who, because of his poverty often collected food from the forest and could not afford the luxury of a mechanic for his ancient Ford pickup truck.

Larry was the teacher, the genius. I was the plodding student, the slow learner. By the second week of the first grade, our roles were reversed. Sitting across from me, Larry would whisper in reference to the teacher's assignment: "What's she talking about?" It was obvious (to me), the teacher's expectations, her words, were identical to those of my parents. Larry didn't have those words. When I was confronted with a school assignment that I didn't understand, I could turn to the expertise of my college-educated parents. Larry's parents finished the sixth grade. If I had a problem at school, my parents understood the social conventions of the institution. Having experienced only failure in their schooling, Larry's parents were reluctant to approach the teachers. Without my advantages, Larry was deemed stupid. I was gifted. Larry was never "successful" in the school system.

STRUCTURE OF INTELLECT

During World War II, many young men were tested for their abilities to become fighter pilots. After a large amount of draftees passed the standardized IQ tests with average IQs of 120, they were unable to complete pilot training; consequently, the government hired J.P. Guilford to design an appropriate testing model to identify those that would have an aptitude to learn the intricacies of how to fly. Guilford developed his Structure of Intellect (SOI) based on the analysis of specific abilities of intellect. Using a 120-celled cube as a model, he divided intellectual performance into three main areas:

1. *Operation:*   Cognition (discovering or recognizing data)
Memory (retaining new information)
Divergent production (generating logical alternatives from given information)
Convergent production (generating logical conclusions with emphasis on best response)
Evaluation (comparing data to make judgments)

2. *Content:*   Figural (concrete forms)
Symbolic (letters, numbers, musical notes, etc.)
Semantic (concepts or ideas)
Behavioral (information involving human interaction)

3. *Product:*   Units (individual units of information)
Classes (items grouped by common properties)
Relations (connections between items of information)
Systems (organized aggregates of information)
Transformations (changes or modification of existing information)
Implications (expected or predicted connections between items of information)

The use of this model and the test for pilot training was considered appropriate when one considers that pilot "creativity" would include the ability to evaluate and act in certain situations without a predetermined result (creative problem solving). However, Guilford's model (developed with the needs of the armed services in mind) is now used in many current gifted/talented programs and rarely is applied to the "normal" or "average" classroom. Abraham Tannenbaum assessed several measurement programs, among them Guilford's model. He questions the validity of the model due to the fact that ". . . these instruments have little or nothing to do with creative productivity or performance. In other words, it is naive to assume that divergent thinking encompasses the complex processes of creativity" (Tannenbaum, 1983, 273). In fact, Tannenbaum points out that Guilford even questioned the validity of using SOI for testing, as creativity in individuals is never regulated and one must be aware of the "instability" of the testing. The fact that Guilford measures "separate, unrelated" functions totally negates the possibility of "subsets" that could exist (Tannenbaum, 1983, 273). Once again, as in IQ testing, instruments that are developed for one particular measurement have been misappropriated for another measurement.

Guilford discusses genius in *The Nature of Human Intelligence* where he points out that a genius excels over others because he or she possesses a wealth of stored information (Renzulli, 1977, 11). That information can be found in cells of the 120 Structure of Intellect cube. Which cube would Larry fit into? Andy? Without subsets, the probability of Larry or Andy testing out as a genius through Guilford's model is remote.

One can easily obtain a well-produced and heavily publicized set of brochures marketing the SOI by SQI Systems, a division of M & M Systems. The use of this package promises to "reduce the failure rate in school (or on the job) from the high percentage it now is (50–70% illiteracy rate in the United States) to a comparably low percentage" (Meeker, 1981). The literature states that SOI is "scientific," that it "provides a system for developing 90 kinds of intelligence" and that SOI "helps people to reach their potential." SOI maintains that inabilities in learning are categorizable and once the area that is having difficulty is identified then that area can be "trained." The Guilford Model of the

Structure of Intellect can be presented to schools by Dr. Mary Meeker and Dr. Robert Meeker. The in service lasts two days; fees are $800 per day, plus expenses (fall 1991 prices). Each participant must purchase a workshop packet at $175; this packet includes enough literature to enable one to start on testing with the SOI. Page four of the brochure asks the question, What makes SOI so different?

    The answers: SOI derives from theory.
             SOI is practical.
             SOI is cost effective.

  It is frightening that programs such as the SOI are instituted at a substantial cost to a school system and are used to evaluate students in a categorized and inappropriate manner. The final statement that "SOI is cost effective" reinforces the concept of a student as worker, as automaton, "just program him or her correctly, and the student will do the right thing." Guilford developed a model fifty years ago to determine creativity and intellect in airplane pilots, and schools are now using the same model via the SOI program to define and discover genius in children.

POPULAR TAXONOMIES AND MODELS

There are many ways to measure characteristics of genius. Many of the techniques focus on diagrams or models to illustrate levels of intelligence and to formulate teaching techniques to address the various levels.

  Benjamin Bloom is well known for *Bloom's Taxonomy* (1956), in which six distinct levels of cognitive thinking are presented. Teacher education is largely based on this taxonomy and there are few who are unable to remember memorizing its definitions for knowledge, comprehension, application, analysis, synthesis, and evaluation. Bloom's work encourages teachers to structure teaching around isolated levels of thinking as well as isolated qualities of intelligence. Many children are overlooked by testing that relies heavily on Bloom's theories. Teachers spend hours poring over lesson-plan drafts, trying to squeeze in levels of performance that can be evaluated using *Bloom's Taxonomy*. (Many colleges of education market notepads with Bloom's six categories printed in little boxes with spaces in which the teacher can fit appropriate parts of the lesson plan, thus preventing too much emphasis in one area.)

  Other ways to identify intelligence and genius can be found in Joseph Renzulli's *Enrichment Triad* (1977) and in the *Torrance Test for Creativity* (1975). While these instruments are more elastic in their approach toward working with children, they focus mainly on the identified gifted child. Many programs that incorporate Renzulli or Torrance have excellent programs that teach exciting and stimulating ways to learn... however, they teach the segment of the school's population that previously has been iden-

The Nature of Genius 109

tified as gifted. Consequently, quantitative and standardized exams, usually the Stanford-Binet, are used to classify a child as gifted and then he or she has the "privilege" of being in the QUEST, CHALLENGE, ENRICHMENT, or GIFTED/TALENTED program.

Our (Shirley Steinberg and Joe Kincheloe's) son Chaim came home from third grade bubbling about a new game called "Spontaneous" that he learned in the QUEST program: "It stresses creativity through creative answering. We are asked a question like: What if all the water in the world turned to gasoline? We have one minute to think of answers and two minutes to go around the table and give as many answers as our group can (by taking turns). When the time is up, we get points: three points for the most creative answer, and one point for a common type of answer. The judge gives out the points. It is fun! I love it!" Do the kids in your regular class play the game? "Only the kids in QUEST play it." Do you think kids not in QUEST could play the game? "If they were divided in small groups, of course they could."

Of course, it is great that Chaim has such a fun time in class and his mind is allowed to wander down paths of fantasy. As parents, it is difficult to criticize a program that your child loves. However, as teachers, we wonder who is not in the program. The screening process for the QUEST program is described in a handout to parents:

> Identification of students for the gifted and talented program is based on state-mandated criteria which include the student's performance on aptitude/ability, performance on a test of academic achievement, and the student's classroom performance. A total of 90 points must be accrued through this process for a student to qualify under state guidelines for service in the program the gifted and talented. However, some underachieving students whose grades may not reflect their giftedness may qualify if their aptitude test scores are at or above the 96 percentile (Central Elementary School Letter, September 17, 1991).

The next year Chaim took the aptitude/ability test and "failed" miserably; he had been ill and had been up late the night before. His teacher noted his poor performance and he was retested; not every child's performance is observed by his or her teacher and retested; not every child takes tests well; not every child has genius or giftedness that will score highly on standardized tests. Larry and Andy would have loved playing "Spontaneous," but they could have never tested well enough to be given the chance.

Programs that are developed to stream out certain children who test "well" are elitist and negate the mandate of public schooling. If one is able to "make" the program, he or she is "pulled out" of regular programming and given opportunities for field trips, computer-based learning, special fine arts projects, and other "nonregular" curricula. Many parents spend time at schools insisting their child be placed in gifted and talented programs. What about the child who does not have an advocate to insist that he or she be included in alternative programming? What child does not deserve this "special" treatment? (Kincheloe, 1999)

3. Genius Is Socially Constructed

Education and educational research have been dominated by the Newtonian-Cartesian paradigm, and, within this structure, by "power elites." When we recall the founding of American public schools, we see that the power structures represented by business and government play a critical, although tacit, role in education. Although dominant power interests are being served, those in the margins are neglected. Paulo Freire refers to the education of the marginalized as the *Pedagogy of the Oppressed* (Freire, 1972). As critical educators, as deconstructionists, we must be acutely aware of the importance of addressing the needs of the subjugated, and of constructing a counterpraxis that will enable them to emancipate themselves. School screening for genius or gifted intelligences, narrow testing procedures, more often than not are culturally and gender biased. When we deconstruct perceptions of genius, intelligence testing, and "gifted" education we realize that we must look at the tacit manifestations of power that influence our thinking.

Educators in antiquity also used definitions that were socially constructed. Aristotle was convinced that a genius must be taken by an inhuman frenzy: "there is no great genius without madness," he said (Albert, 1975, 140). Was this definition of genius rooted in the fact that when one goes beyond the norm and creates something from a different perspective, this unexplainable creation may be accompanied by excitement and fervor, a type of possession or madness, or merely by enthusiasm generated by talent? Observations by the Greek philosophers, grounded in their own constructions of reality, attributed genius to madness. In much the same way, many of today's educational researchers define genius through the perceptions of today's society. By these definitions, the vocal, the power elites, define what qualities it is socially acceptable to call genius.

Robert Albert (1975) "defines" genius through past and present social construction. He presumes to give genius a behavioral definition; each quality attributed to genius is based on the social and economic perceptions surrounding the genius. Albert asserts that "Undiscovered genius is one common misconception" (Albert, 1974, 141); implying that unless the consenting public agrees in some collective manner that genius exists, it does not exist. Let us turn to the genius of fine art.

The nineteenth-century Romantic Era in art was followed by Realism. Both movements were embraced by the art public and fueled by the art critics who were part of the art establishment; art was a solid economic venture. In the latter part of the century, the Realist movement was replaced by a new group of artists who did not insist on painting literal interpretations of subjects. Ushered in by Claude Monet, Edgar Degas, Édouard

Manet, Auguste Renoir, Paul Cézanne, and others, art became a collage of light, movement, and color. The Age of Impressionism was born. Thought of by the Parisian public and art critics as an insult to true art, impressionism was perceived originally as a mess of unfinished sketches and "color so raw that it hurt their eyes" (Janson and Janson, 1996, 128). New artists were forbidden to exhibit in the Salon des Beaux Arts and the impressionists eventually organized their own exhibits, which were scorned and ignored by the "educated" and wealthy French.

Adolphe William Bouguereau was considered to be France's greatest living artist, a true genius. Bouguereau was nothing more than an excellent draftsperson, able to render a perfect imitation of any painting; he thought of himself as the keeper of the classic style that imitated without passion; copies of Ingres, David, and Raphael. However, none of us seem to remember his work today. The consciousness of the people in the late nineteenth century was constructed by the social definitions of art. The power elite owned the galleries and backed many artists, and it was not in their interest to allow this "upstart" movement into the art scene. Consequently, impressionists were not considered to be geniuses; rather, they were merely palette packing painters who splattered their ideas on cheap backgrounds and peddled them in the streets.

Within thirty years, the same Parisian elite would realize the economic potential of the impressionists and adjust their market to accept them. But, as always, those in power in the art world were still controlling matters.

The definitions of genius that resulted from Galton and Freud have several common elements that Robert Albert listed in his attempt to define genius. According to Albert, a genius must have a "*deep-seated, strongly persistent personality*," which continues to develop over a long period of time. Works of genius must continue over a *good length of time*, as well. A genius must create or organize "*acts leading to reputation or eminence*," that is, the genius must be noted by the public and by experts. Recognition of genius is essential to its being labeled as genius. *Productivity* is essential in Albert's definition of genius; the production of "great" bodies of work also add to the definition of genius. Productivity by a genius must be referred to often by other "noted" participants in a field and must be cited in their research (Albert, 1974, 140–50). Many other definitions of genius resemble Albert's socially constructed postulates.

One questions just how long a "good length of time" is, and who is rating the persistence, personality, and output of the "genius." What is considered eminence? Who are the experts and the public that defines this eminence? Who will tally the productivity of the genius? What will be excluded? Included? Who will review the genius' book, painting, or research project? Who is funding the review? Who is funding the genius? Who is threatened by the new creations or discoveries of the genius? If one is not recognized during her or his lifetime, do they become "retroactive" geniuses when they are discovered? Is genius like an old wine that must ferment and mellow before becoming palatable? Whose interests are being served in defining genius?

Prior to 1948, William Faulkner was reduced to writing film scripts because of the disdain for his novels shown by the critics, the publishing houses, and the public. Yet within five years of Malcolm Cowley's publication of *The Faulkner Reader*, Faulkner received the Nobel Prize for Literature, and his writing became acknowledged as the work of a genius. Power defined and recognized his genius, and then the public acknowledged that genius.

Endorsements from the media, "experts," and the government define genius and ways to market evaluations of genius. Many in service workshops and test designs have cropped up in the last two decades. Gifted and talented programs employ gurus to bring "genius detection" programs to a school system. This serves two functions: it plays up to the desire of parents to have their children defined as geniuses, and justifies a school's claim that it serves the "special needs" of its students. Selection of these gurus can depend on identification by those in power:

> Dr. Renzulli has used his own empirical research and observation of gifted students and their teachers to point out directions for enriching educational activities. His approach is that of a teacher trainer, registering concerns about activities for gifted and presenting an enrichment model that can be used as a guide in developing defensible programs for gifted that are indeed qualitatively different.
>
> This book should make the most difference where it counts, with teachers, and gifted students in the classrooms. In summary, Dr. Renzulli's text is a first step toward a much needed technology for developing gifted education.
>
> > Dorothy A. Sisk, Director
> > Office of Gifted and Talented
> > U.S. Office of Education
> > Department of Health, Education and Welfare
> > Washington, D.C.
> > (Renzulli, 1977)
>
> (The Enrichment Triad Model: A Guide for Defensible Programs for the Gifted and Talented by Joseph S. Renzulli is available for $15.50, paperback, 88 pages. Workshops on the Enrichment Triad are $800 per day plus expenses from members of Dr. Renzulli's staff)

It is not difficult to imagine the reasons for a program's success if the program's director is able to lasso a governmental endorsement for publications and workshops. It appears that at the prices indicated, Dr. Renzulli and his staff are definitely "enriched."

The Nature of Genius

4. Genius Is a Male Attribute

"Today I want you to call out names of people who come immediately to your mind that you would consider geniuses. Don't worry about raising your hand, just begin calling out and we will record the names on the board."

> Beethoven! Mozart! Napoleon! Faulkner! Bach! Einstein! Van Gogh!
> DaVinci! Michelangelo! Kennedy! Edison! Patton! Schwartzkopf! Brahms!
> The Russian Composer, what was his name? Hemingway!
> We need more painters! Degas! Picasso!
> Hey, you guys, what about Martin Luthur King? Freud!
> Steinbeck! Leonard Bernstein, wasn't he a genius?
> Wait a minute, we haven't even named a woman! You're right!
> How about Virginia Woolf? Thomas Wolfe! Tom Wolfe!
> We need more women! Wasn't there a woman painter?
> Has a woman written any famous music?
> Come on, there must be someone! Margaret Thatcher!!!!

(This is a transcript from an Introduction to Education course for new majors in Education. There were thirty-three women and four men, three African American students and thirty-four Caucasian students.)

The fact of the assumption that genius is a male (and usually Caucasian) attribute is evidence that our consciousness is constructed. The ancient Roman *juno* was absorbed by the genius and the only remaining female inspiration came through the muse, who was basically created to enhance the man and give him power. Women are historically considered nurturers, the "powers behind the throne." Men have dominated and defined our culture. Women have supported it.

In research about intelligence and genius, Caucasian males are the dominant sample. Terman's studies (1951) were comprised largely of middle-class, Caucasian males. The mention of gender and its effects on his study were minimized:

> The achievement of the group at midlife is best illustrated by the case histories of the 800 men, since only a minority of the women have gone out for professional careers. By 1950, when the men had an average age of 40 years, they had published 67 books.... They had published more than 1400 scientific, technical, and professional articles; over 200 short stories, novelettes, and plays, and 236 miscellaneous articles on a great variety of subjects. They had also authored more than 150 patents... (Terman and Oden, 1951, 33–34).

I (Shirley Steinberg) remember being in fourth grade. I was so anxious to answer every question. I loved school, and I loved to read and ask questions. Sometimes I was so excited about the lesson, I would hold up my hand and wave it madly. Once in a while,

I would even call out the answer! My teacher would continually tell me to calm down, but I didn't feel like calming down. She told me that I wasn't acting "lady like." My report card showed a "U" for citizenship, and the comment space had the word "egocentric" written on it. I noticed that the boys never got in trouble for calling out answers; actually, she usually smiled and answered them or extended their comments. Kids in the class made fun of me and called me a "big mouth." The boys could talk out of turn, jump around, and act really silly, but they hardly ever got in trouble.

The same things happened to me in fifth and sixth grade. By the time I got to junior high, I knew not to interrupt and would wait patiently to answer a question. But then the kids teased me for being a "smart aleck" and my only friends were the few girls who still answered questions. It was so important to be popular in junior high. I was never popular; I just kept raising my hand.

Feminist theory has alerted us in the last decades to the minimalization of women in studies of genius. Ever the afterthought, women have traditionally been measured by male researchers who used male subjects. In the feminist insurrection, not only is the androcentric myth of genius challenged, but history has begun to be rewritten in order to resurrect the long-buried juno. Because of the advent of feminist critique, no longer can the litany of genius exclude subjugated talents and subjugated definitions of intelligence. Needs of the marginalized must be addressed. The history of genius and the perception of genius must be rewritten to include both genders, all races, and classes.

Gertrude Stein Charlie Parker Toni Morrison Alice Walker Scott Joplin Confucius Buddha Simone de Beauvoir Mary Cassatt Mary Shelley Harriet Tubman Josephine Baker Billie Holliday George Eliot Georgia O'Keefe George Sand Lillian Hellman Elizabeth I Joni Mitchell Adrienne Rich Felix Mendelssohn's sister... what's her name? Marie Curie Sappho Gloria Steinem Hannah Arendt James Joyce Maya Angelou Margaret Atwood Judy Chicago Margot Fontaine Vanessa Bell Sarah Bernhardt Sandra Bernhard Catherine the Great Ann Sullivan Helen Keller Scherazade Madonna Albert Einstein's "second" wife???

Einstein's Unique Thinking Style

The traditional mechanistic application of and view of knowledge as an abstract machine, a processor of symbols, permeates western thought and has been prevalent in many of the curricular reforms of the 1980s and 1990s. Scientist Stephen Hawking describes a view of knowledge that symbolizes much of the rote memorization found in today's classrooms:

> I think a human being is like a computer, but a bit more complicated than the computers we have today. I don't think anyone would suggest that computers have an immortal soul (Hawking, 1989, 5).

Science educators, concerned with what science students can and should be learning, have looked to a more constructivist notion of how knowledge evolves. They have come to realize that learning is more than the rote absorption of knowledge, more than the construction of abstract understandings through our mental operations. Students do not enter school as a blank slate. They are "products of particular sociocultural environments and historical epochs, and they come to school embodying constructions of society and self based upon their own ongoing sociocultural experiences" (O'Loughlin, 1991, 27).

Constructivism serves as a progressive pedagogy in education and has its roots in the structuralism of Piaget's developmental theory. Piaget asserted that "the structure of the mind is the source of our understanding of the world" (Venn and Walkerdine, 1977, 73). However, his notion of the adaptive function of cognition was conceptualized in terms of a biological process. Piagetian theory has been linked with constructivism, and four principles of constructivism have emerged:

> Knowledge consists of past constructions; constructions come about through assimilation and accommodation; learning is an organic process of invention, rather than a mechanical process of accumulation, and learning occurs through reflection and resolution of cognitive conflict and thus serves to negate earlier, incomplete levels of understanding (Fosnot, 1989, 19–20).

However, "constructivism can mean different things to different people" since, from a constructivist perspective, there are multiple ways of knowing (Wheatley, 1991, 9). A more critical approach to constructivism suggests that some of the tenets of Piagetian theory are problematic. Some scholars have expressed concern about the individualism that is inherently associated with the abstract formalism of Piagetian theory, an individualism that reeks of modernism's view of subjectivity that can be formed outside of cultural context:

> ...the individualist approach reduces reality to the acts of the individual's constitution; objects of reality are seen as products of individual cognitive operations rather than as products of social and historical constitution (Sampson, 1981, 731).

For some researchers and theorists the emphasis on logico-mathematical problem solving and abstract reasoning in Piagetian theory has been problematic, particularly when it is viewed as a sanction for a technical type of knowledge that "causes men and women to become a tool of technology" (Buck Morss, 1975, 41).

Constructivism has also been described as nonmechanistic and nonreductionist, in contrast to existing paradigms (Hesusius, 1982). As a set of values and beliefs, constructivism was built on particular assumptions that are understood not merely in terms of opposition to old principles. Poplin has emphasized the danger of defining a constructivist paradigm only in opposition to a reductionist paradigm. As we consider the potential role of constructivist epistemology in education reform, we can gain insight by reflecting on Einstein as a knower and on the unique aspects of his thinking style.

Albert Einstein's thinking style was unique. He followed his own inclinations and blazed a new cognitive path for those interested in genius and in education. As with other great scientists, Einstein was fascinated by the way people think, the way discoveries are made, and the source of creativity. He passionately wanted to understand his own thinking patterns and the nature of scientific imagination in general. He often tried to explain his unique thinking style, concluding that it was "rather vague" and nonlogical (Hoffinan, 1972). If Einstein himself had so much trouble understanding his own patterns of thought, then those who try and have tried to analyze his thought patterns will also encounter difficulty. As a result there is no realistic hope of precisely copying his thought patterns, nor should we try. If Einstein has taught us anything, it is that the road to genius has many different routes. With this in mind the examination of Einstein's unique thinking style is not undertaken with a goal of literally recapitulating his method, but to gain insight into the possible way that genius operates (Kincheloe, et al. 1999)

One of the most basic of manifestations of Einstein's genius was his talent for perceiving old things in new ways. Einstein made the strange seem familiar and the familiar seem strange, and in this way he consistently posed challenges to conventional wisdom (Sagan, 1978). In this sense, Einstein ultimately constructed knowledge outside of the accepted paradigms of his time and approached phenomena in new ways. The Pythagorean proof was a harbinger of things to come, for Einstein would apply his ability to see unity in ostensible dissimilarity to increasingly complex problems. Indeed, he would apply his style to the nature of the universe itself. As Gerald Holton has contended, genius finds itself not in solutions to kale problems, but in the attempt to solve eternal problems.

THOUGHT HAS A GESTALT NATURE

It is easy to throw the word genius around in a discussion of Einstein, but it is harder to trace the origins of his thinking patterns. Words or language, as we write or speak them, he said, do not seem to play any role in the way I think. When Max Wertheimer, one of the founders of Gestalt psychology, questioned Einstein about the nature of his thoughts, Einstein told him that his thinking did not seem to emerge in any verbal formulation. When he constructed his early proof of the Pythagorean theorem he immediately recognized its obvious truth from mere visual inspection. His first reaction was that the theorem needed no proof because it was obvious to him that the acute angle determines the sides. Einstein's thinking had gestalt properties in the sense that "concepts have an overall structure that goes beyond merely putting together conceptual building blocks by general rules (Lakoff, 1987, xiv).

The recognition of the truth of the Pythagorean theorem is a good example of Einstein's thought. "I rarely think in words at all," he told Max Wertheimer. "A thought comes, and I may try to express it in words afterwards" (Patten, 1973, 17). He said that the physical entities that serve as the pieces with which thought is constructed are "certain signs and more or less clear images which can be 'voluntarily' reproduced and combined." There is, he continued, a definite connection between these pieces with which thought is constructed and relevant logical concepts. At this point Einstein brought in his omnipresent desire to achieve unity. The need to achieve unity or "to arrive finally at logically connected concepts" is the emotional foundation on which his free play with concepts rested. This "combinatory play" with concepts, from Einstein's perspective, seemed to be the most important feature of productive thought. This must take place before the unity of concepts can be expressed in words that are signs that can be communicated to others (Einstein, 1959).

THOUGHT IS EMBODIED

Not only does most of our thinking go on without words or signs but most of it occurs unconsciously. If this were not the case, he asked, "how... should it happen that we 'wonder' quite spontaneously about some experience" (Einstein, 1970, 9). The young Einstein displayed great talent for nonverbal activities, including not only his visual recognition of mathematical principles but also an ability to complete jigsaw puzzles, build with prefabricated blocks, and construct colossal playing-card houses. He spent hours on them, sometimes building houses fourteen stories high. Not only did such activity require patience and precision but it also necessitated a talent for spatial relations, balance, and symmetry. The unconscious development of these talents went on completely without words and caused Einstein to "wonder quite spontaneously" about perceived imbalances or asymmetries in the natural world (Patten, 1973). Gerald Holton contends that to Einstein the objects of the imagination were real, visual materials. Much like the shapes of a jigsaw puzzle or the symmetry of a card house, Einstein could playfully reproduce or combine these visual mental objects in order to achieve a new synthesis or a new understanding of an old problem. Einstein's unique thinking style was embodied in the experience of constructing card houses and completing jigsaw puzzles, in the sense that "conceptual systems grow out of bodily experience and make sense in terms of it; moreover, this core of our conceptual systems is directly grounded in perception, body movement and experience of a physical and social character" (Lakoff, 1987, xiv).

The ability to visualize provided the foundation that took him to thought patterns that transcended experience. This thought is essential to the understanding of Einstein's physics. The axiomatic foundation of theoretical physics cannot be inferred from experience, he argued, but is essentially a free invention of the human mind. Indeed, physics deals with finding connections between sensory experiences. Our understanding of physical objects is gained by arbitrarily assigning concepts to repeatedly occurring complexes of sense impressions. While our conceptions of bodily objects are uninhabited creations of the human mind, Einstein maintained that they owe their meaning to the totality of sense experiences with which they are coordinated and with which they possess an intuitive connection (Rosenthal-Schneider, 1970). In order for him to approach the physical unity in an intelligent manner it was necessary to engage in such transcendent thought patterns. When he examined logically the concepts that emerged from thoughts and verbal expressions, he concluded that they all come from free creations of thought that cannot be inductively extrapolated from sense experiences (Schlipp, 1944).

THOUGHT IS IMAGINATIVE

Nothing illustrates more clearly Einstein's development of concepts from free creations of thought than his thought experiments. He imagined himself pursuing a beam of light and in the process imagined what he would see. It was through this thought experiment, he realized later, that "the germ of the Special Relativity Theory was contained" (Holton, 1979, 159). In another thought experiment that was designed to reconcile the special theory of relativity with gravitation, he imagined a man falling from the roof of a house. Through this thought experiment Einstein realized that during the fall there existed no gravitational field for the man. Once he understood this fact, Einstein was able to extend relativity to coordinate systems that moved nonuniformly relative to one another.

Through the use of thought experiments, Einstein freely selected the axiomatic bases of his theories. However, he claimed, the freedom was limited. It was not like the freedom of a fiction writer, but more like that of an individual who wants to solve a complicated puzzle:

> He may suggest any word as a solution, but there is probably only one which really solves the puzzle in all its parts. That nature... has the character of such a well designed puzzle is a faith which is, however, to a certain extent encouraged by the successes of science up to date (Rosenthal-Schneider, 1970, 140).

Einstein's thought experiments illustrate the imaginative nature of thought: "concepts which are not directly grounded in experience employ metaphor, metonymy, and mental imagery, all of which go beyond the literal mirroring, or representation, of external reality" (Lakoff, 1987, xiv).

THOUGHT IS ECOLOGICAL

This is not to say that Einstein's theories were reached without logical precedents. While free play of concepts was essential to his solutions to the puzzles of the universe and to his insight into the unity of concepts, the concepts were not encountered in an intellectual vacuum. Einstein stated that analytical discussions of the work of David Hume and Ernst Mach influenced him both directly and indirectly in his attempt to understand and reconstruct the nature of absolute space and time as he worked on his theory of relativity. The interplay between his thought experiments and his basic understanding of the historical development of physical thought allowed him to challenge the assumptions of science that had existed for centuries. Concepts that have contributed to a logical explanation of natural phenomena sometimes gain such an authority over us that we forget their earthly genesis and consider them to be intractable. We must understand their development and reconstruct them in light of new discoveries and the insights provided by new thought experiments. Here Einstein was adding a historical dimension to his unique creative thought, a historical dimension that fits neatly into the postformal notion of etymology. He viewed historical thinking as an instrument, a tool that could be used to define physical concepts more precisely and thus to further the development of physical science. It was this historical thinking that introduced him to the world of conflicting ideas and the intellectual growth that would come out of that world. This historical dimension gave an ecological structure to Einstein's thinking, the interplay between his thought experiments and his understanding of the historical development of physical thought contributed to the overall structure of his conceptual system.

THE ROLE OF DISSONANCE IN THOUGHT

Einstein's sense of wonder was engaged when an experience came into conflict with a concept that was already established in his mind. The resulting dissonance moved him to search for resolution and thus evoked great imaginative powers within him. Whenever a conflict was experienced, it set the magical thought world into action, and the development of this thought world was, Einstein wrote, in a way "a continuous flight from wonder" (Einstein, 1970, 9).

Einstein realized that all of science has been moved by conflict. Some historians of science almost set up a Hegelian dialectic, a "dialectical scientism," to explain the rocky road to scientific progress. Gerald Holton argues that scientists of genius are those who sense the strains of conflict and who possess an inner need to deal with antithetical ideas. Indeed, the very essence of Einstein's genius revolved around his sensitivity to conflict. The search for explanations for dissonance can be found throughout the history of science. The dissonance encountered by Henri Becquerel with the discovery of radiation is an example:

> Becquerel was fascinated by Röntgen's discovery of X-rays and wondered if the natural luminescence, or glow, of certain minerals might also be accompanied by similar X-ray emission. He took a thin crust of a uranium crystal and placed it on a photographic plate wrapped in lightproof paper. The whole wrapping was exposed to sunlight for several hours. When developed, an outline of the crystals showed up on the photographic plate. Subsequently, in a similar experiment he found that where some uranium crystals had been left in a dark drawer, unexposed to light, together with a photographic plate, they left even a stronger outline on the developed plate! At that moment he must have been very surprised and could have exclaimed: "Hey! There is a discrepancy here!" He became so interested in this phenomenon that during the following years he became totally engrossed in his work.

Einstein's Unique Thinking Style

The cognitive dissonance upon which Einstein thrived has since provided the basis for a frequently used instruction strategy in science classrooms, the discrepant event. The discrepant event, also known as "Disconformation of Expectancy" or "Conceptual Conflict," occurs when a learner is faced with a situation that is in conflict with what is expected. "The doubt, perplexity, contradiction and incongruity result in arousal of conflict and a need for the learner to resolve the dissonance" (Liem, 1989, xxxii). Piaget (1974) maintained that dissonance was an essential first step in learning. Dissonance is also evident when constructivists describe the value of introduction "perturbations" into any type of learning experience.

EINSTEIN'S BIMODAL THOUGHT

Einstein was a bimodal thinker, meaning that he brought the power of his logic and his intuition (what some refer to as "left-brain" and "right-brain" thinking) together to produce a powerful creative synergism. When such a synergism was applied to physics, it gave us the theory of relativity, revolutionized twentieth-century science, and pushed the world toward the postmodern era.

The relationship between this bimodal characteristic and Einstein's thinking style and scientific work can be documented. He constantly sought to resolve what others perceived as disharmony, to bring together, to synthesize, to find commonality where it was not thought to exist. In the 1905 paper on relativity entitled "On the Electrodynamics of Moving Bodies," he did not use the term relativity. In fact, he did not use the term until 1911, years after other physicists had referred to his work in that way. Einstein referred to the theoretical basis of his work as Invarianten Theorie until social pressure forced him in 1911 to change. In the first sentence of the 1905 paper he wrote: "It is known that Maxwell's electrodynamics, as usually understood at the present time, when applied to moving bodies, lead to *asymmetries* which do not appear to be inherent in the phenomena." Einstein's emphasis is on the confrontation of the asymmetry when electrodynamics are applied to moving bodies. Relativity may in a sense be a misleading term in this context; invariance of physical laws may better express his impulse. When Einstein "relativized" the asymmetries, he was providing one simple explanation for ostensibly dissimilar phenomena.

Gerald Holton explains the Einsteinian search for invariance of physical laws in the following way. In his 1905 relativity paper Einstein created a thought experiment that involved inducing a current in a conductor. To determine the level of current of a moving conductor with respect to an unmoving magnet, one must employ a specific kind of equation. When one attempts to calculate the level of current with an unmoving conductor while the magnet moves, a different kind of equation must be used. The current that is produced is identical in both cases, thus the phenomenon is *symmetrical*. The method for calculating the current, however, was *asymmetrical*. Later in the paper Einstein "relativized" the problem by providing one equation that could find the correct current in both cases. This is the essence of relativity: the use of one method to reconcile apparently asymmetrical phenomena.

We have come to recognize this aspect of relativity only through hindsight. Relativity is simply another aspect of symmetry. Einstein sought to point out the inherent symmetry of the four-dimensional continuum of time and space. In the process, he became the first to describe correctly the homogeneity of this four-dimensional medium. This, of course, was a manifestation of his search for unity, but it goes beyond merely that. It reveals a style of thinking that not only recognizes conflict, but finds in the conflict new questions that were never before considered. In Einstein's three great and very different papers of 1905, this style of thinking is manifested. All three began by pointing out previously unperceived asymmetries. The more orthodox beginning usually involved the recognition of a puzzle that was posed by inexplicable data from experiments. In all three papers Einstein discarded the asymmetries by proving them to be unnecessary; they had emerged, he argued, from too narrow a scientific focus. Because he concerned himself with asymmetry while holding unity as his goal, Einstein was able to bring a new perspective to these problems—he was able to break out of what Thomas Kuhn called "normal science" and initiate the breakdown of the Newtonian paradigm.

ASYMMETRY IN EINSTEIN'S PERSONAL LIFE

Not only was Einstein's scientific work marked by a concern with asymmetry, but his life itself was characterized by apparent asymmetries and polarities. These personality traits that many observers perceived to be in conflict with one another were not, however, seen that way by Einstein. This difference of perception may offer insight into the nature of Einstein's unique thinking style. He saw beyond the superficial appearance of conflict not only in science but in his personal life as well. When his contemporaries and his biographers saw a conflict between his image as the oldest and most sagacious of men and his utterly uncontrived childlike traits, he saw none. He frequently referred to his use of childlike curiosity and his ability to see the world through the eyes of a child as a key to understanding his way of thinking. Relativity emerged from a mindset that asked questions about space and time that only children would want to know.

Many perceived a conflict between the Einstein who could concentrate for years on one problem of physics and the Einstein who was always open to personal requests for help or personal involvement in humanitarian causes. Observers found it hard to believe that one who was connected intimately with the nature of cosmology and the secrets of the universe would also be presupposed to deal with the "merely personal." His steadfast search for unity regardless of the dominant trends and his unwavering faithfulness to a well-defined personal identity revealed by his disdain for external authority whether it was scientific, political, or even sartorial, seemed to many to be in conflict with his openness to humanistic appeals.

Einstein saw no conflict in these behaviors, believing in fact that they were born of the same spirit. The physicist cannot limit himself to thinking within the confines of physics, for the search for truth knows no disciplinary limits. If we are to be valuable human beings, he argued, we must be moved by a search for the truth and a desire to contribute to the welfare of the community. To be valuable contributors we must bind our lives to the promotion of the well-being of others, and the best way to do this is to achieve liberation from the self. In this liberation from self the apparent conflict between dedication to intense cosmological speculation and the humanistic impulse is resolved. Both activities emerge from an orientation that is not egocentric, a reverence for truth and justice and a recognition of their inseparability. Both the search for cosmological truth and humanistic endeavor are, in the childlike eyes of Einstein, manifestations of good citizenship. It is not the fruits of scientific research that elevate humans and enrich their natures, he argued, but the urge to understand that lifts humans out of self-centeredness and creates humanity's most sophisticated expression, social consciousness (Einstein, 1959).

Others saw a conflict between Einstein the "grand public personage" with all his wit, charm, and even charisma, and Einstein the loner, the solitary child, the bookworm, the aloof observer of human affairs. Once we understand his emphasis on the transcendence of self, we may no longer view the public and private Einstein as being in conflict. "I live in that solitude which is painful in youth, but delicious in the years of maturity," he wrote. In his youth he had not succeeded in his quest to conquer selfish orientations; by manhood, he had. He did not demand the approval or validation of others to motivate his search for truth; he did not work for extrinsic reward. It was this inner-directed orientation that moved him to say: "My passionate sense of social justice and social responsibility has always contrasted oddly with my pronounced lack of need for direct contact with other human beings and human communities." He could fight for humanistic causes, but he did not need human plaudits to sustain his drive (Holton, 1971–1972, 97). Thus, the public and private Einstein could coexist without any need for a shift in his holistic orientation, both sides were manifestations of a gregarious personality with a desire to ponder the nature of things in solitude.

A conflict was often seen between Einstein the liberal agnostic and Einstein the man with a strong sense of religion. To see these two positions as polarities is to rob Einstein of his holistic approach. He possessed what he considered to be the religious orientation of a scientific man. A scientific religion, he argued, is quite different from the religion of a naïve man. For the naively religious, God is a being who deals out rewards and punishments. We seek his rewards and fear his punishments in much the same way that a child reacts to an authoritarian father. It is this form of religion that Einstein rejected; and it is because of this rejection that the term agnostic is used in connection with Einstein.

There is no conflict between the Einstein who rejected an egocentric religion of personal rewards and punishments and the Einstein who considered himself to be deeply religious. The rationally religious person is possessed by a sense of universal causation, he contended. Einstein's religious feeling took the form of "a rapturous amazement at the harmony of natural law, which reveals an intelligence of such superiority that, compared with it, all the systematic thinking and acting of human beings is utterly insignificant reflection." The rationally religious person uses this feeling of awe as a "guiding principle of his life and work." Einstein's religious thought cannot be separated from his omnipresent attempt to transcend the self, as he argued that this feeling of awe must be used to free mankind from the "shackles of selfish desire." When people sense the awesome intelligence behind the universe and use the feeling to help transcend the bonds of selfishness, Einstein maintained that they approach that spirit which has possessed the religious geniuses of the ages (Einstein, 1959, 49–50). The final step in the process is the use of the cosmic reverence to initiate moral action, acts of love toward one's fellow human beings. This higher spirituality can take place, he concluded, when religion has been purified of the elements of superstition. Thus, Einstein's religious thought was very logical and consistent, marked not by conflict but by continuity.

Conflicts with his scientific work have been pointed out, including the opposing perceptions of Einstein as a scientific revolutionary and a scientific conservative and the possible conflict between Einstein the unified field theorist and Einstein the quantum theorist. The debate over Einstein the revolutionary or Einstein the conservative can be settled by the conclusion that he was both. His ability to ask new questions may have shattered the foundations of physics and moved the discipline in revolutionary new directions; but throughout his life Einstein was concerned with the continuity of physical scientific thought and its historical evolution over the centuries. As to the field and the quantum, it must be remembered that Einstein's main objective was to explain unity. His work on quantum theory, while admittedly confusing the easy attempt to understand the unity, took place within the context of his broader search for unity.

The perceived polarity that possibly grants the clearest insight into Einstein the holistic, bimodal thinker was the view of Einstein as the representative of rationality and Einstein the intuitive scientist. Observers were confused by the apparent conflict between a style of thought characterized by the clarity of its logical construction and the intuitive side of that same style. Einstein's intuitive mind was marked by an aesthetic sense of sci-

Einstein's Unique Thinking Style

ence, a call for science to transcend the search for merely *logical* bridges from experience to theory, and great inferential leaps from possibility to principle. It is here at the logic-intuition polarity that modern split-brain theory can help clarify the nature of Einstein's unique thinking. It is at this point that Einstein can be viewed as the quintessential bimodal thinker and that insight into the nature of creative genius can be gleaned. The logic-intuition dichotomy is false; indeed, Einstein's logic and intuition synergistically merged to form the necessary pieces of one of the great minds of the century. The merger reminds us of the universal human potential for postformal thought and the possibilities for the cultivation of such thinking styles in ourselves and others. It reminds us of the value of the interaction between Newtonian-Cartesian linearity and postmodern simultaneity.

HOW WE SEE THE BRAIN: CURRENT HEMISPHERICAL RESEARCH

Only a few scientific discoveries in the twentieth century have created as much interest as the research into the different functions of the asymmetrical halves of the human brain. Few scientific discoveries have been as distorted by popularization as has hemispherical research. Instead of making the general public's view of the way the human brain works a sophisticated one, the popularizers of these research findings have often confused and muddled perceptions by presenting hemispherical brain functions as a list of discreet responsibilities. For example, the right hemisphere controls music. It has been claimed that the brains of scientists are oriented toward the left hemispherically; the brains of artists toward the right. American Indians, some have told us, have a right-brain culture; Western Europeans have a left-brain culture. The distinctions go on and on with their assumptions, generalizations, oversimplifications, and thus distortions of the complexity of the relationship between the hemispheres.

There is, of course, some truth in the popular distinctions, but caution is essential. The basic anatomical functions of speech and language are centered in the left hemisphere. Indeed, research consistently indicates that an injury to the left side of the brain is far more likely to destroy the capacity for speech than an equally severe injury to the right side. The reason for this seems to be that the left hemisphere is more anatomically specialized for specific information-processing skills. The right hemisphere is apparently more diffusely organized and as a result injuries to this side will not result in the restriction of a specific information-processing skill. This diffuse organization benefits space-orientation skills which require the processing of many simultaneous inputs at one time, a characteristic fundamental to the workings of the right hemisphere (Ornstein, 1977).

The basic concept of neural bimodality centers on the idea that brain hemispheres receive incoming stimuli in tandem. There is no way to separate what we say, when we say it, or our purpose for saying it into the specific function of one hemisphere, especially if the brain is holographic in structure. Thus, it is misleading to assert that the process of speech is the function of the left hemisphere. The anatomical mechanical process of speech is controlled exclusively by the left hemisphere. The content is not. This seems to be a point at which much of the confusion about hemispherical function resides. All intellectual skills are complex webs of interactions between the hemispheres. The point is not that each hemisphere controls a specific function exclusively, but that *together* the hemispheres contribute to the totality of that function, be it speech, art, writing, or music. Admittedly, this sounds quite obvious. But there is an importance in recognizing this interactive role of the hemispheres that is quite relevant educationally.

The popularizers of neural bimodality have called for educational innovations that demonstrate an awareness of brain function. Sometimes the calls for reform do not take this hemispherical interactiveness into account, as they propose activities to improve only right hemispherical skills. Often these activities are designed to take place in special lessons taught in isolation from the rest of the curriculum. It is naïve to assume that we can educate one half of the brain at a time. Educators must constantly think of the interactive characteristic of brain function. At the very time that writing, reading, and arithmetic are being taught, educators must also orient students to the different modes of thought representative of each hemisphere. To break hemispherical skills into components and teach them as components is to lose the very integrative characteristic that grants humans their special perception.

The debate on brain hemispheriality continued through the 1980s but began to fade by the 1990s. Researchers focused on the influence of semantics in relation to different hemispheric processes, producing educational innovations (Stacks and Sellers, 1986, pp. 266–85). Foremost among these was the whole-language movement. Indeed, it was suggested that "the emergence of whole language teaching methods at the demise of traditional methods may be related to the incompatibility of traditional methods with the dual nature of the brain's organization" (Danes and Mollica, 1988, p. 86). At the turn of the millennium, postformalists look back at the insights and excesses of such reforms and use both to rethink theories of cognition and the education they support.

A FEMINIST RECONCEPTUALIZATION OF COGNITION

> Talking of poetry, hauling the books
> arm-full to the table where the heads
> bend or gaze upward, listening,

reading aloud, talking of consonants,
elision caught in the how, oblivious
of why
                   (from *In a Classroom* by Adrienne Rich)

    Much of Einstein's early school life was frustrating for the inquisitive boy who spent much of his time asking why, only to be countered by teachers who asked how. Soon after children enter the halls of the public school, they quickly learn how to answer questions without inquiring further. "Playing the game" has become a pastime in the schools, the workplace, and even the home. A "smart" child knows when to be quiet and how to answer appropriately. Children who have difficulty with schooling many times do not "know" the rules of the learning game. Successful children are often those who must become secret knowers, who view the world of learning from a protected shell that allows them to answer publicly with the appropriate response and to know privately that something is seriously wrong with how they are being educated.

    The Enlightenment taught Western peoples a way of thinking based on logic and reason. The great thinkers of the period laid the foundation for the modern age of rationality, which left no doubt as to the right and wrong answers to any question. Reductionistic attempts to define cognition in the age of postmodernity have led many of us down the simplistic path of "left" and "right" brain thinking. Armed with shallow definitions, educators have pounced at the chance to define both students and themselves in essentialist little boxes with qualified characteristics. How often have we, as teachers, heard the following or variations?

"I hate math and love art, so I know that I am right-brained."

"She is impossible to teach; her right-brain dominates. She hasn't a clue about science and math."

"Native Americans are totally right-brained, they are incapable of being logical."

"Men's left-brain thinking leaves no room for emotion or intuition."

"Black students should be encouraged in the arts and sports; they're right-brained."

    Girls are told that they aren't expected to do well in science and math. Even if they have visionary parents and belong to visionary school systems, subjects that are traditionally considered "male" are taught in ways consistent with the rational and the logical. Many boys feel awkward about learning with emotions and intuition and pronounce it too feminine or girlish, an attitude reinforced by society. Because of the attempts of educators to categorize children, both genders are denied the opportunity to develop cognition beyond the expected mode of formal thinking. In essence, our flirtation with split-brain theory has inhibited intellectual growth.

Many books and in-service workshops have been created to train teachers how to combine both the "left" and "right" brain. People who are concerned about overdevelopment of one side are taught exercises and games in order to work on the other side. Under the auspices of creating a *whole* through *two* parts, each "side" of the brain is examined independently and the *correct* method applied. One can imagine a circle with two distinct halves, the purpose of "whole brain" thinking is to *attach* both halves to become *one* circle. In the modernistic way of the rational, science and reason are used as a "method" to combine both "sides."

Models of cognitive growth (see Chapter Five) are developed in order to teach "to" certain parts of the brain. In an attempt to define genius, Philip M. Powell created a continuum on which he analyzed three types of genius, (1) the analytic, (2) the synthetic, and (3) the integrated (Powell, 1987, 96–100). Even though Powell acknowledges the existence of both modalities and the importance of their development, he is restricted through his own definitions into classifying genius throughout history into one of the three categories. In his positivistic attempt to discuss genius, he drives each "type" of genius into its own personal garage, complete with oversimplified tools of the trade.

Powell steers toward integration of both modalities at times, but his combining of the logical and the rational limits him to another category that evades postformal thought. He is determined to list "parts" of the whole on a graph and then categorize thinkers into each column. This reductionism traps us into a labeling syndrome. One merely replaces "right" with "synthetic" and "left" with "analytic" to end up with the same split brain theory that is popularized through quasipsychological/educational literature. Through Eurocentric eyes, Powell designates Immanuel Kant as the quintessential analytic genius, Einstein as the synthetic genius, and da Vinci as an integrated genius. He suggests that we develop new methods to measure intelligence by directing our testing methods to the three main areas. Thus, students can be classified by the results of their tests (a new system of segregation). Powell's discussion of genius is bogged in the mire of positivistic definitions and a last-ditch attempt to hold on to the modern, the rational.

Since our evolution into a postmodern era, feminist theory has given breadth and redefinition to the nature of thinking. No longer are we destined to define our ways of knowing and learning through narrow descriptors that invite generalization, that answer only the *how*, and ignore the *why*. With an understanding of different ways of seeing *why* and applying *how* in order to expand our knowledge, we are introduced to a kaleidoscope of meanings by means of a synthesis of both the logic-based and intuition-based modalities. Thus, we are attempting to free the discourse of cognition from the reductionistic handcuffs that have held genius in bondage for decades.

With the inclusion of non-Western methods of thinking, ways that for half a millennium have too often been subjugated by the colonialism and suppression of the Western world, we are able to view cognition not as "an act,"... but as a continual cycle of connection in bimodality. Indeed, the postformal notion of uniting emotional and rational ways of knowing embraces the synergistic yin-yang of hemispherical bimodality. Instead of recreating a patriarchal discourse based on establishing hierarchies, feminist and other ways of knowing embrace knowledge as a conduit that connects the knower and the known.

In *Pedagogy of the Oppressed*, Paulo Freire discusses the "banking" technique of teaching. He describes the act of teaching as a system of deposits and withdrawals, with teachers holding and dispensing items from the bank of knowledge. There is no connection between the student, the teacher, and the knowledge. As easily as one picks up stones from a gravel pit, a child picks up individual pieces of knowledge. Any connection between the child and what she or he learns is by chance, and the "amount" of what is known is established by objective testing procedures.

Feminist pedagogy engulfs the teacher and student as knowers in a continual effort to link what is known to their lives. Instead of a quantifiable set of "pebbles," the gravel pit can be expanded to a never-ending meteor shower of what has been, what is, and what can become. Answers are neither right nor wrong, but a series of observations or solutions that apply to many sets of questions. The process of learning is explored and the product becomes a partner, not the ultimate goal.

Instead of choosing the "left" side of the brain as the logical, and the "right" side as the intuitive, both knower and known embellish what attributes are needed to synthesize knowledge. Using a combination of the narrative (usually attributed to the "feminine") and the theoretical ("masculine"), learning continues in a discourse of bimodality. Before it acknowledged the intuitive parts of thinking, modern learning could only carry the student so far; thinking "skills" stop at the formal level.

Because of the "knowledge of connection" (Pagano, 1990, 13), feminist theory does not fear that the act of learning can include, and even be intimate with, ambiguity. Patriarchal or modernist ways of knowing restrict the learner to the fragmentation of information and an insistence on determining the answer. Ambiguity is inconceivable, imagination is squelched, and the discourse of learning is closed. When a state of disconnection occurs, modernist teachers neatly resolve all contradictions and leave no end untied. Albert Einstein was confronted by the scientific method throughout his schooling and found it impossible to function "successfully." Until he left the school system and dabbled with the possibility of possibilities and the relativities of relativity, he was a dysfunctional student, disconnected from knowledge, from his teachers and from his world.

Women's Ways of Knowing: The Development of Self, Voice, and Mind traces the language and moods that are attributed to knowing. In order to integrate both the logical and the intuitive, we consider even our words of learning. Patriarchal discourse makes use of "either/or," instead of a language of possibility; "should, ought" instead of insisting on "change." The new language of learning looks at "growth." One discusses knowledge using "we" instead of "they." The authoritarian separation that insists on the objective, the dualistic nature of modern thinking—*the right* or *the wrong way*—can be replaced by a multiplicity of knowing: accepting the subjective, *the possible* (Belenky, Clinchy, Goldberger, and Tarule, 1986).

Patriarchal methodology deals with the verbalism, rhyme scheme, alliteration, and literary techniques of a poem. Yet, when looking at poetry with a feminist critique (setting aside patriarchal limits), the student can consider the emotion evoked, the multiple meanings implied, and where the poem stands in relationship to both the poet and the reader. Neither approach to teaching poetry is effective without assistance from the other. When considering the entire "world" of a poem, students' knowledge is expanded by an understanding of the importance of rhyme or literary device within a wider text of meaning that enables them to read the whole poem. The modernist way of knowing gives way to an inclusive and intuitive way of knowing that acknowledges the technical as well as the emotional. Pagano believes that feminist pedagogy includes a deep reading of a story that is both empowering and liberating (Pagano, 1990, xviii). She contends that the use of the emotional in pedagogy joins with the theoretical to give a connection with the student and the knowledge.

When interpreting a poem, it is vital that the connection of bimodality sets up the leap to postformal thinking by understanding that all interpretations are not equally valid. A postmodern approach to understanding a poem will be grounded in both theory and in intuitive and emotional ways of knowing. An overinterpretation (using only the intuition of the reader) can also be disconnecting (Belenky, Clinchy, Goldberger, Tarule, 1986). As it evolves into a democratic, inclusive way of learning, feminist pedagogy seeks to avoid changing from one dogma to another. Our bridge to postformal thought is built with many types of materials and an undetermined number of plans.

DEVELOPMENT OF BIMODAL THOUGHT: EINSTEIN'S EARLY YEARS

Einstein combined the intuitive power associated with the right hemisphere of the brain with the logic associated with the left side to produce a dynamic form of bimodal thought.

Einstein's Unique Thinking Style

The special power that the logic-intuition synergism granted Einstein facilitates comprehension of his genius and helps reconcile the apparent polarities in his life and his intellectual approach. The various manifestations of Einstein's hemispherical synergy are worthy of study by all individuals interested in the educational process and the development of postformal thinking.

Why did Einstein develop this bimodal ability? How did he come to integrate a powerful intuitive hemisphere with a superior logical hemisphere? Any definite answer to those questions is certainly impossible, but researchers have speculated about the origin and nature of Einstein's bimodal character. For example, Bernard Patten has postulated that not unlike many other people Einstein may have been able to cultivate his nondominant "right" hemisphere beyond normal levels because of a "left" hemisphere dysfunction in early childhood.

Patten argues that the "left" hemisphere problem that manifested itself in poor schoolwork, deficient and delayed language skills, and even misbehavior initiated a compensation in "right" hemisphere-based intuitive development. Einstein, Patten continued, was able to achieve tremendous mental capabilities by circumventing his poorly developed verbal abilities and developing a unique way of learning and thinking. The examination of Einstein's childhood reveals some interesting support for Paten's thesis. Einstein did not learn to talk until the age of three, and his sister Maja reported that a difficulty with speech continued into the middle years of his childhood. He searched for words with great difficulty, she said, and moved his lips to repeat every spoken sentence, a practice he did not abandon until age seven. Of course, schoolwork went poorly for the young Einstein, and he displayed weakness in most academic disciplines, especially arithmetic and foreign languages. His failures were not the result of not trying, however, for he worked hard with his homework assignments, often completing them incorrectly.

His behavior was often bad in his early and middle childhood, and sometimes expressed itself in violence. Many violent episodes of Einstein's youth are on record, including throwing a chair at his violin teacher, hurling a bowling ball at his sister, Maja, and attempting "to knock a hole in (Maja's) head" with a trowel. Aggressive behavior is often characteristic of children with learning problems, and this could have been the case with Einstein.

While the behavioral problems certainly disappeared as Einstein grew into a most gentle and sensitive adult, the legacy of his verbal problems persisted. Helen Dukas, his secretary for years, deemed him a weak speller, and Einstein himself often referred to his problem with language. My poor memory for words, he said, has presented me with problems that seemed sometimes impossible to overcome (Hoffman, 1972). On another occasion he confided, "When I read I hear the words. Writing is difficult, and I communicate this way very badly" (Quoted in Patten, 1973, 16).

Einstein's verbal problems were not unique, as an examination of the backgrounds of other eminent people demonstrates. Lloyd J. Thompson has collected pieces of educational biography about a number of famous and creative people who shared such dysfunctions, including Thomas Edison, Harvey Cushing, Auguste Rodin, George Patton, and Woodrow Wilson. All of these men (no similar research has taken place with women) had some degree of what was diagnosed as "reading, spelling, or writing retardation" in their youth (Thompson, 1971, 39). Like Einstein and countless other individuals, these accomplished and creative men may have benefited from an early logic-based dysfunction that forced them to use the abilities of their intuition, abilities that are often neglected by many people. As they entered adulthood and their slowly developing rational capacity matured, the great mental power resulting from the synergistic combination of the two modes of thinking began to assert itself.

Einstein, in company with these historical figures, has been posthumously labeled "learning disabled." According to current legal definitions, the learning disability label is applicable when a student demonstrates a significant discrepancy between academic achievement and intellectual ability in one or more of the following areas: oral expression, listening comprehension, written expression, basic reading skills, reading comprehension, mathematics calculation, mathematics reasoning, or spelling. Documentation must support that the discrepancy is not primarily the result of a visual or hearing impairment, mental retardation, emotional disturbance, or environmental, cultural, or economic disadvantage. Adelman and Adelman have suggested that the posthumous diagnosis of "learning disabled" is based on unsatisfactory evidence; that perhaps other explanations exist for the identified problems of Einstein and other prominent individuals.

A constructivist view of learning does not lend itself to the "identification of specific subgroups of students for special services or instruction, such as learning disabilities" (Poplin, 1988, 402). Unfortunately, in the context of a reductionist educational environment, children who do not "fit" the school are frequently categorized as special, remedial, or even gifted. A rethinking of the purpose of schooling should include insight into the need to fit the school to the child, rather than the conventional idea of fitting the child to the school. This can only be accomplished through the realization that the "political, economic, and social structures in which we are acting are also enmeshed in the web of reductionism" (Schon, 1973). The reflection and personal experiences necessary to prompt new meanings and transform old ones are subjugated when reductionistic curriculum, segmented school days, teacher specialization, and the categorization of students are valued, both explicitly and implicitly, within the educational community.

It is not surprising that Einstein experienced difficulty in learning environments that emphasized reductionist principles of rote memory and mechanical learning. These learning experiences prompted him to comment:

> It is, in fact, nothing short of a miracle that the modern methods of instruction have not entirely strangled the holy curiosity of inquiry; for this delicate little plant, aside from stimulation, stands mostly in need of freedom; without this it goes to wreck and ruin without fail. It is a very grave mistake to think that the enjoyment of seeing and searching can be prompted by means of coercion and a sense of duty (Quoted in Goertzel and Goertzel, 1962, 253).

While all students, including those labeled "learning disabled" come to school with rich background experiences and knowledge, the problem is magnified when the prevalent paradigm in schools is reductionism. It is ironic that many postformal thinkers were stigmatized by schools that labeled them learning disabled. Like countless others, Einstein was a victim of this manifestation of the modern cognitive illness.

BIMODAL THINKING: IMPLICATIONS FOR EDUCATORS

The implications of patterns of human development are very important for all educators. Logic-based dysfunction and/or the timing of rational maturation may be crucial determinants of early school performance and thus, oftentimes, all subsequent academic performance. Definitions of intelligence are intimately tied to early verbal abilities in modern schooling, and verbal ability is at least to some degree dependent upon rational maturation. As early as 1937, Samuel T. Orton recognized the possibility of a logic-based maturation connection in his book, *Reading, Writing and Speech Problems in Children*. Interestingly, Orton postulated that many of the defects in language function come from an abnormality in the process of "establishing unilateral brain superiority." Though he preceded split-brain research by twenty-five years, Orton was referring especially to problems caused by a slow development in logic-based functioning. He went on to contend that such disorders could be remedied by specific training if we could diagnose them and design the proper training for each case. Without increased knowledge of rational mode dysfunction the possibility of achieving Orton's goal is far more likely. The "natural remediation process" employed by Einstein and countless other creative geniuses grants insight into the remediation of other students and individuals who are labeled as slow or are punished in some way for an unusual pace of rational maturation, or, as Orton thought of it, an abnormality in the process of "establishing unilateral brain superiority."

The data seems to demonstrate that rational maturation dysfunction has an impact on early school performance, especially when school success is so dependent on verbal ability. Students in Einstein's time as well as today are judged on the basis of their verbal skills, and that judgment is made very early in lower grades. Rarely are students rewarded for nonverbal talents such as the ability to construct card houses, a skill that Einstein developed into an art form as a small child. Schools, too often, are not aware of the need to reward intuitive-mode abilities and even more infrequently are they prepared to take obvious intuitive talent and find ways to connect it with rational development. Thus, the possible postformal synergism is lost and potential creative genius goes untapped.

At the same time that schools often withhold rewards, and hence future academic success, on the basis of slow rational development, there is a danger worthy of consideration for those children who *do* experience early development of logic-based verbal skills. Does easy verbal facility indicate a rational mode dominance that can cause a child to depend on logic to the neglect of intuition? If this exaggerated dependence takes place then, does the achievement of bimodal thought become far more difficult for the child who learns verbal skills early? Interestingly, it is this child who is often the superior pupil, who finds school to be a comfortable atmosphere, and who may define himself or herself in terms of school success. It is this child who is labeled a formal thinker and often finds it very difficult to move to what has been described as postformal thinking. It is this child who is less prone to misbehavior, who is often the favorite of the teachers, who completes assignments to the letter of the instructions, but often exhibits little ability or interest in bold creative plunges or in challenges to the prevailing way of accomplishing a task.

Examples of this type of student abound. Take the music student who at an early age learns to read music well and proceeds through musical training successfully, acquiring new technical skills each year. While there are many exceptions often music students with such a background are lost when musical scores are removed; moreover, the idea of composition and "playing by ear" are sometimes quite alien to them. Teachers must protect the child with early verbal development from this suppression of his or her bimodal potential. It is ironic that the traditional superior student is many times *not* a creative thinker, *not* a problem formulator, not the one who sees multiple forms of reality.

NONVERBAL THOUGHT: THE POWER OF IMAGERY

Einstein's pathway to bimodality involved his powerful ability to think nonverbally. His problems that manifested themselves so clearly in school revolved around his verbal disabilities. We see him at age three playing silently, holding off the encroachments of verbal language into his spatial world. For as long as he could, he refused to accept the external discursive authority of verbalization, with its names and its rules that eventually force most creative children to surrender their curiosity and imaginative play and to enter the world of "civilization": the young marked by nonverbal imagic thought. By its very definition, this intuition-based world is very difficult to describe with its geometric and pictorial imagery and its resulting emphasis on patterns of symmetry and asymmetry. It is a world of nonverbal categorization that, when learned and practiced in the early childhood years, affects thinking styles throughout life.

And it did affect Einstein's entire life. In this early nonverbal orientation, the bimodal character of Einstein's thinking style found its origin. Gerald Holton argues that an extraordinary kind of visual imagery penetrated Einstein's very thought process. It was the creativity of this thought process that was responsible for liberating Einstein from the bonds of scientific orthodoxy that eclipsed most physicists' view of the possibilities that lay before them. Without this special bimodal perspective most physicists could not understand the limitations of Newtonian concepts of space, time, energy, mass, and light. According to Holton, most scholars could "simply not make the jump, although their own work prepared the labors of Einstein and others" (Patten, 1973, 17). This bimodal perspective, this combination of the logical and intuitive mode, lays the foundation for the leap from formal thinking to postformal thinking, the leap from logical procedural thinking that has been deified by modernism to intuitive, contextualized metacognition necessary to the formulation of the postmodern critique.

There is a propensity for great scientific and mathematical thinkers to employ bimodal thinking patterns that are visually based. Jacques Hadamard contended in *The Psychology of Invention in the Mathematical Field* that the world's noted mathematicians avoid thinking in words or mathematical signs. The more complicated a question, he argued, the more mathematicians distrust words. Vague visual images are better suited for decoding into mathematical formulas because such images can be more easily rearranged, altered, and manipulated. Indeed, the visual modality may be better suited than the verbal to the solution of certain types of math and physics problems. For example, a person intuitively knows that words have little to do with driving a car, flying an airplane, or estimating the trajectory of a baseball in order to catch it. In the initial recognition of patterns that ultimately lead to a scientific discovery, words may play an equally insignificant role (Patten, 1973).

Einstein's intuition-based visual thinking granted him the ability to scrape away the extraneous and proceed directly to the heart of a problem. Visual thinking like Einstein's bestows the capacity to see visual designs as images of the very patterns that compose the forces that direct the world and our existence in it. Such patterns are certainly to be found in physics, but they also underlie the functioning of our brains, our bodies, our societies, and our inventions. Einstein's application of visual thought in physics may inspire our physicists, but it should also provide insight into ways of viewing problems confronted by social scientists, artists, and even teachers.

Within the classroom context, imagery is associated with attempts to make sense of experience. As teachers construct their world and a view of science, they are guided by rich images that help them to reframe personal constructions of teaching. Language often consists of images that guide teachers' actions, even though they are less frequently revealed directly in speech. As teachers reflect on their practices, images give voice to individual ways of knowing. "Each of our images of what constitutes knowing, and hence knowledge, is part of what structures one's subjectivity: What is valued as truth or discarded as fiction, how one defines her relationship to the world and to others, what is believed about power and powerlessness, when one takes interpretive risks, feels the right to make interpretations and theorizes about experience, what is taken for granted in familiar and unfamiliar situations, and how one understands teaching and learning" (Britzman, 1991, 23–24). Here, Deborah Britzman is describing a form of postformal teacher thinking.

Our thinking about imagery is frequently limited to the idea of visual imagery. However, imagery exists in auditory and olfactory forms and in terms of how forces act upon us. Imagery can be thought of as consisting of conscious images that are context bound, specific, and rich in detail; i.e., the image formed when one is shown a detailed treasure map. Or imagery can be considered as consisting of the conventional images embedded in culture that are nonspecific, not context-bound; i.e., the nonparticular image of an elephant or people eating pizza (Lakoff, 1987, 445–47). In much the same way that imagery was a powerful visual and mental tool for Einstein as he constructed new ideas, it can be used throughout teaching as a vehicle for teachers giving meaning to their experiences through reflection.

When reading *Relativity, The Special and General Theory*, Einstein's popular book on relativity, one cannot help but be impressed by the awkward language and the rich visual imagery used to illustrate various concepts. The book on relativity was characterized by picturesque thought experiments that used watch readings, light signals, mirrors, positions of locomotives, and lightning. Whether or not one comprehends relativity is dependent upon his or her ability to visualize Einstein's thought experiments. It is an intuition-oriented process that is not contingent on the verbal linearity and sequential nature of the logical mode.

His book illustrated well his visually oriented bimodal thought. The origins of his thoughts and theories are grounded in the intuitive mode; the search for verbalization emerged in the second stage of his thought process when the visual image had been established and could be reconceptualized at will. Taking an example about the nature

Einstein's Unique Thinking Style 139

of gravity from his book, Einstein asked his readers to think of a large cage suspended in space. Standing in the cage is a man, and the cage is being pulled up at a uniformly accelerating rate by a large hook. If a man releases a ball in the cage it would appear to him *to fall* to the floor. The man in the cage assumes that the fall was the result of a gravitational field. But another observer, watching the situation from a different vantage point, would see the cage being pulled upward and perceive that the ball stood still in space, because of its inertia, and the floor of the cage moved up to meet it. By way of this visual thought experiment Einstein showed his readers that a gravitational field can be viewed in terms of inertia and uniform acceleration. Bernard Patten argues that the corollaries of Einstein's visual system of theoretical development presupposed an aesthetic respect for elegance, symmetry, and simplicity. This desire for simplicity, the distaste for extraneous complexity, is a key to understanding Einstein's bimodal process.

Einstein's thought and personality were shaped by his desire for simplified unity. Simplicity not only shaped his scientific work, but in his personal life his desire for simplicity was legendary. He preferred the simplest clothing and hated unnecessary and artificial restraints of all kinds. When asked why he used ordinary hand soap for shaving instead of a shaving cream, even though hand soap was less comfortable, he replied: "Two soaps? That is too complicated!" on another occasion he maintained that humans seek to form for themselves a lucid and simplified image of the world. This, he said, "is what the painter does, and the poet, the speculative philosopher, the natural scientist, each in his own way." Into this simple image, he continued, a person can place "the center of gravity of his emotional life, in order to attain the peace and serenity that he cannot find within the narrow confines of swirling, personal experience" (Holton, 1971–1972, 102–08).

Here the intuitive component of Einstein's bimodal thinking style sought holism in the most simple manner. His bimodal mind was searching for the most economical, simplistic, and formal principles upon which life rested, in other words, the barest bones of nature's frame, stripped of all that could be considered ad hominem, redundant, or unnecessary. The final goal of physics is the discovery of the unique solution, the most unified and comprehensive theory, which by necessity must be of the greatest simplicity (Rosenthal-Schneider, 1970). This desire for holistic simplicity was ever present as he called for physicists to content themselves with portraying the "simplest occurrences which can be made accessible to our experience" (Holton, 1971–1972, 108). In his own work he strived for simplicity, and in the context of theoretical physics he succeeded. Indeed, the simplicity of his thought experiments continues to amaze physicists. When all the questions that have remained unsolved since his early pronouncements on a variety of unexplained phenomena are considered, his success in formulating simple and empirically accurate scientific theories seems almost miraculous.

The innovative power of his holistic, bimodal simplicity freed Einstein from the isolated linearity that limited others. The bimodal thinking style was not just a tool used to ask new questions and solve problems, it shaped Einstein's life. His bimodal thought became the necessary mechanism for bringing out, in Gerald Holton's words, "one's strong side." In the light of the bimodal interpretation of Einstein's thinking style, "strong side" is an interesting phrase to use in this context.

As the bimodal thinking asserted itself, Einstein was liberated from what he called the "momentary and merely personal." These egocentric concerns were left behind as the holistic pattern of thought shaped Einstein's personality. Einstein the scientist could not be separated from Einstein the human being; they were one and the same. He was the humble man with the grandiose ambition to seek unity, expressing the concept in the sentence, "I am a little piece of nature" (Horton, 1971–1972, 102). Genius sees connections in many different areas; Einstein's bimodal thinking style allowed him to see a common thread that wove his lifestyle, his values, and the laws of nature together into a unique fabric.

Einstein's Search for Unity

The emergence of the ideas of relativity, quantum mechanics, and chaos in the twentieth century laid to rest the Newtonian clockwork universe defined by predictability, regularity, and order. Prevailing reductionistic beliefs had painted a complex world, assembled and disassembled in a multitude of ways and explained neatly through cause-and-effect schemes. A "fix-it" mentality was at the heart of this deterministic world and has continued to influence our approach to science and education today. This reductionist world, controlled by humans who attempt to fix it when it breaks is exemplified in Briggs and Peat's (1989) description of a science that attempts to fix the atmosphere by sending slingshots of frozen ozone into this atmosphere to repair the damage. In our schools, reductionist beliefs are recognizable in attempts to "fix" the system that are based on measuring students as quantities. When students do not fit the school with clockwork precision, gifted and title programs and diagnostic assessment and instructional practices are designed to fix the problem. Again we are confronted by the cognitive illness.

INHERENT ORDER WITHIN COMPLEXITY: THE SCIENCE OF CHAOS

Advances in mathematics and computer science have led scientists to see a world characterized by irregularity, unpredictability, and turbulence. Whereas Newtonian scientists explained the randomness, irregularity, and chaos in systems as a consequence of outside chance, new generations of scientists and theoreticians have searched for explanations that eliminated randomness and chance. These scientists drew attention to examples of irregularity and unpredictability everywhere: in biological, physical, political, economic, and education systems; in slime molds, evolving stars and growing cities (Briggs, 1990; Briggs & Peat, 1989; Davies & Gribbin, 1992; Ferris, 1988; Prigogine and Stengers, 1984; Stewart, 1989). Prigogine and Stengers described many instances of disequilibrium and self-organization in complex systems. In their description lies both paradox and promise.

The paradox. The ideas of chaos, in Prigoginian terms, are described by Toffler (1984) in the following way:

> All systems contain subsystems, which are continually "fluctuating." At times, a single fluctuation or a combination of them may become so powerful, as a result of positive feedback, that it shatters the preexisting organization. At this revolutionary moment . . . a singular moment or a bifurcation point—it is inherently impossible to determine in advance which direction change will take: whether the system will disintegrate into chaos or leap to a new, more differentiated, higher level of order or organization, which they call a dissipative structure.

It was nonlinear equations, which held little interest for Newtonian scientists, that provided Prigogine and others with insight into the nature of dissipative structures. The word "dissipative" brings forth images of scattering, dispersion, and chaos. But in the far-from-equilibrium states represented by nonlinear equations, scientists have discovered that matter has very different properties, ones which make self-organization possible.

The irony has not been lost on scientists discovering systems verging on chaos. "Chaos may have laws of its own." It may be, as Prigogine has suggested, that "the sudden appearance of order out of chaos is the rule rather than the exception" (Briggs and Peat, 1989, 84, 134). Attempts to understand chaotic systems through a reductionist lens are doomed to fail. Scientists are recognizing the futility of analyzing these systems by breaking them into parts that are isolated from the whole: such systems are constantly folding into each other by iterations and feedback loops. Thus, the discovery of chaos theory and the recognition that systems interact holistically has brought a revolution in perspective that holds much promise for the future, a promise that cognitively reveals itself in the ability to see facts as parts of larger processes.

The promise. At the intersection of chaos theory and the emerging science of wholeness, or holism, we see different schools and classrooms emerging. Physicists operating within a postmechanistic paradigm are creating multiple realities, developing alternative ways of looking at phenomena, and describing theories of parallel worlds (Davies and Gribbin, 1992, 219). In the same way, educators who are combining constructivist epistemology with holistic beliefs about teaching and learning are "seeing" new schools, cultures of learning in which teachers and students engage in a continual process of constructing personal meaning in response to their experiences. These educators recognize that the very nature of reality and of knowing is holistic. The rejection of a Newtonian-Cartesian view of the world has fundamentally altered our values and beliefs about the universe and our beliefs about the teaching and learning process.

STRETCHING THE METAPHOR: THE SPECIAL THEORY OF RELATIVITY

Newtonian clockwork or machine metaphors represented knowledge as a particular way of seeing the universe, or worldview. When these metaphors were stretched to their limit, they came up lacking in their ability to explain a world that is characterized by chaos. This raised fundamental questions about the construction of knowledge: What counts as real? How do we know? and Who decides in the first place?

It was Einstein's theory of relativity that provided an alternative metaphor and generated future metaphors and opened a whole new way of looking at the world. As the philosopher Max Black (1962) suggested, the process of stretching the Newtonian metaphors to their limit was accompanied by dramatic shifts in worldview. For Einstein, this worldview was characterized by his search for unity and "the belief that whatever laws are found should be applicable anywhere in the universe" (Briggs, 1990, 29).

A PERSONAL QUEST: EINSTEIN'S NEED FOR UNITY

What was the foundation of Einstein's genius? Was there any one factor that allowed him the ability to ask questions that had never been asked or to see what had never been seen? Such questions defy answers; but if there was one factor that runs through Einstein's work and sets him apart from his colleagues, it was his omnipresent search for unity. We can see his postformal desire to discover connections and seek unification in ostensibly dissimilar activities in almost every aspect of his work. Again, although we are not so naïve as to think that we can recreate or even explain genius, we can learn from Einstein's search for unity. Such a search and the awareness of the value of the search can be applied in almost every portion of human endeavor.

One of the most striking aspects of Einstein's character was his desperate need to find order in a chaotic world. The need was quasireligious in nature and seemed to manifest itself initially after he reached the conclusion that the stories of the Bible could not be literally true. Abandoning the certainty of religious answers, Einstein set out on the trail of the ultimate nature of things. "I want to know how God created this world," he exclaimed. "I want to know His thoughts" (Clark, 1971, 36–37). Such knowledge would possibly fill the vacuum left by the loss of religious certainty. The basis of his obsessive search for unity was emotional; he intimated that he would never rest until he finally arrived at logically connected concepts that provided insight into the cosmology.

And rest he never did; he spent the rest of his life searching for a unified world picture. The principles that shaped the work of Einstein the scientist were unity, generalization, and an egalitarian application of laws throughout the total realm of experience. Indeed, he was just quixotic enough to extend this desire for unity to the outlandish goals of attempting not only to discover the creator's blueprint but also a unified basis for all science.

It is ironic that such an ostensibly fatuous undertaking brought humanity closer in one leap to the secrets of the universe than any combination of leaps before it. Moved by this need to see the unity, Einstein began to discern patterns that had been previously overlooked. He recognized unity in a complex of phenomena that appeared to be entirely unrelated according to our sense perceptions. But our sense experiences can be viewed as a totality and they can be ordered, he maintained. Once one has recognized the unity, the totality of experience can be arranged through thought in a logical and orderly manner.

This glimpse of the unity that allows for the logical arrangement of the universe was a religious experience for Einstein. My religion, he confided, is expressed as a "humility and admiration for the superior intellect that reveals itself in world harmony" (Clark, 1971, 22, 24, 63). This superior intellect was the "God" of Benedict Spinoza, the seventeenth-century Jewish theologian who was excommunicated from the Amsterdam synagogue in 1656. Spinoza's excommunication was prompted by his belief in a God of nature and his rejection of the personal God of Jewish orthodoxy. In the seventeenth century few theologians had articulated a belief in harmony, beauty, and the ultimate comprehensibility of the universe any better than Spinoza (Woolf, 1980, 354).

Few twentieth-century thinkers articulated the Spinozan religious conception of universal harmony more creatively than did Einstein. "The religious feeling engendered by experiencing the logical comprehensibility of profound inter-relations is of a somewhat different sort from the feeling that one usually calls religious," Einstein maintained. "It is based on a feeling of awe one derives from sensing the unified scheme manifested in the material universe. This awe does not lead us to contriving a god-like entity formed in our own image who requires certain behaviors and who takes an interest in us as individuals. The awe leads us merely to further explorations of the unity of the divine plan" (Clark, 1971, 32). Indeed, the longing for a glimpse of what he considered the preestablished harmony of the universe was the source of Einstein's inexhaustible patience. And inexhaustible patience is certainly a prerequisite to genius.

A REVOLUTION IN PERSPECTIVE: UNITY IN EINSTEIN'S APPROACH TO SCIENCE

All of these perspectives contributed to Einstein's approach to science. He claimed that science was merely the attempt to make sense out of the chaotic diversity of our sense impressions by seeking a means of connecting the impressions with a logical system of thought. We must impose a structure of thought on the chaotic diversity of facts with which we are confronted, for such a process leads the observer to unity and order. In Einstein's system "single experiences must be correlated with the theoretic structure in such a way that the resulting coordination is unique and convincing."

Einstein made no apology for being dogmatic about his belief in the continuity of nature. His belief in it and his search for it were his driving forces. His intuitive sense of the continuity of nature had sustained him, it had to, for he admitted that he had no technical knowledge and that he often just "groped in the dark." What he did have, he was quick to point out, was the sense to look for and the ability to grasp the overview of physical connections. This orientation, he concluded, was far more valuable than the knowledge and routine of a specialist. His intuition in this situation seemed to separate him from more formalistic procedural (or routine) thinkers.

He applied these perspectives and this orientation directly to his study of physics, claiming that the final goal of physics is unity. When Einstein made this assertion, he meant that the role of the physicist is to establish some basic principles on which all known laws of physics can be grounded. He always hoped that such a set of unified principles would be established and worked diligently to accomplish this task. Throughout his life he had faith that even if he did not make it (which he didn't) that someday it would be done.

Once the laws of theoretical physics are established, Einstein argued, they will not only form the basis of explaining the physical world, but they will help establish the foundation for the understanding of all natural processes, and these would include the process of life itself. He understood the magnitude of his prediction and admitted that such a discovery would be a miracle. Still, however, he considered the task sufficiently realistic to continue the attempt. His search for unity pulled no punches; he wanted to discover a common basis not only for physical laws but for all sciences as well—physics, biology, psychology, and sociology, to name but a few.

The legacy Einstein left to physics was the universal hope as well as a method of achieving more comprehensive theories of unification. As physicists find connections between more and more physical phenomena, the search for unification is extended to larger and larger portions of the plane of experience. He maintained that we must push on until we uncover a system of the greatest conceivable unity, a system which by necessity will be marked by the greatest paucity of logical concepts. It is this desire for a unified system based on a minimal number of concepts that led him to reject quantum mechanics. It was too complex, random, and disunited for Einstein. An "inner voice" told him that it was "not the real thing." The theory of quantum mechanics says a lot, he admitted, but it "does not really bring us any closer to the secret of the Old one" (Clark, 1971, 18, 21, 23, 56).

These characteristics of Einstein's intellect were displayed early in his work and are apparent even in his first scholarly papers. In 1901 his first scientific paper was published in the *Annalen der Physik*. As he explored the phenomenon of capillarity, the surface tension that causes a portion of liquid coming in contact with a solid to be elevated or depressed, Einstein told a friend that it is a magnificent feeling to recognize the unity of a complex of phenomena which appear to be things quite apart from the direct visible truth" (Clark, 1971, 77). Here we see two foundations of his subsequent scientific work: the search for unity and the belief in a reality beyond the observable—a postformal concern with the identification of deep structures. These themes were instrumental in leading him to a variety of discoveries, including the theories of relativity.

His second paper took the search for unity to a new plateau. As he wrote about molecular forces, Einstein took a significant leap beyond his first paper. In his paper about capillarity he started with the phenomena, surveyed the literature on the subject, and in keeping with the protocol of the time, discussed the consequences of this previous work. In his second paper he hypothesized an extension of the second law of the mechanical theory of heat, which he understood to be outside the limits of observable phenomena. He then warned his readers that the extension would be assumed to be true throughout the paper. This was an important point in his intellectual development, for he then began to seek the discovery of postulates that were obviously beyond present experience. His attempt to find unity was asserting itself and was becoming the directive for his work. In his third and fourth papers he became more confident in his attempt to generalize, and embraced even broader phenomena to unify (Horton in Woolf, 1980, 51).

SETTING THE STAGE: THE SPECIAL THEORY OF RELATIVITY

It is this work that set the stage for the development of the special theory of relativity in 1905. Einstein was directed by postulates that could not be observed; he confided later that empirical facts had little to do with the formulation of the theory. The special theory emerged from his conviction that the universe was harmonious. The harmony of the universe was founded on the belief that ostensibly dissimilar phenomena rest upon the same physical laws. Relativity, as a reporter for the *London Times* put it, expresses what many

Einstein's Search for Unity

people are always doing—thinking in terms of something else (Clark, 1971, 6). Again, Einstein's postformality emerged, this time in his recognition of unique relationships.

This was exactly what Einstein was doing, thinking of mechanics in terms of electrodynamics. Indeed, the key word with relativity was unity, as Einstein united the momentum and energy principle and displayed the similar nature of mass and energy. In 1909, at a physics conference in Salzburg, he contended that relativity had indicated that energy and mass were equivalent magnitudes, as were heat and mechanical energy. The thought that there was no unity and constancy in the phenomenon of electromagnetism, he later wrote, was unbearable to him and "forced me to postulate the special relativity principle" (Holton in Woolf, 1980, 59).

The unifying principle that Einstein proposed was that the speed of light was a constant and was the ultimate speed limit in both the electromagnetic and mechanical worlds. Thus, light would travel at the same speed regardless of the bodies emitting or receiving it. Such a thesis would imply that while a ball thrown forward at x miles an hour from a train traveling at y miles an hour will apparently be traveling at $x + y$ miles an hour, something very different happens with light; whatever the speed of the train from which it is being emitted, light will travel at the same constant speed of some 186,000 miles a second. This seemed to be ridiculous and, as Bertrand Russell observed, "Everybody knows that if you are on an escalator you reach the top sooner if you walk up than if you stand still." But, he continued, "if the escalator was traveling at the speed of light you would get to the top at the same time whether you walked or stayed on the same step." Einstein took this assumption and linked it with his basic idea—that all natural laws appear the same to all observers moving uniformly relative to one another.

The problems created by the unification of Einstein's two assumptions—the similarity of all natural laws for all observers and the constant nature of the speed of light in both the electromagnetic and the mechanical worlds—become obvious when one examines Newton's traditional example of the sailor. Ronald Clark describes the following example:

> Consider him standing on the deck as his ship sails parallel to a long jetty. At each end of the jetty there stands a signal lamp and midway between the two lamps there stands an observer. As the sailor passes the observer, flashes of light are sent out by the two lamps. They are sent out, so far as the stationary observer on the jetty is concerned, at exactly the same time. The light rays coming from each end of the jetty have to travel the same distance to reach him, and they will reach him simultaneously. So far, so good. But what about the sailor on the ship, who will have been at an equal distance from both lamps as each sent out its light signal? He knows that both flashes travel with the same speed. Although this speed is very great, it is finite, and since he is moving away from one lamp and towards the other he will receive the light signals

at different times. As far as he is concerned, they will not have been switched on simultaneously.

The sailor provides the first outlandish result of the unification of Einstein's two assumptions. The idea of simultaneity is destroyed, as the events that appear to be simultaneous to the observer in the middle of the jetty are not simultaneous to the sailor. Thus, the concept of simultaneity is not absolute. Two events that are viewed as simultaneous from an original system of coordinates cannot be considered simultaneous when viewed from a system that is in motion relative to the original system. Thus, Special Relativity is grounded in the realization that one person's "now" is another person's "then." "Now" holds epistemological implications. It becomes a subjective perspective, meaningful only for an observer that is operating in one specific frame of reference (Clark, 1971, 119).

In the midst of this apparent chaos, Einstein found stability in the constancy of the speed of light. With its help all natural phenomena could be described in a way that was correct for all frames of reference in constant relative motion to each other. But the constancy of the speed of light destroyed the absolute nature of time. Consider the following statements. Velocity is found by dividing time by distance. Velocity of light is invariable. Then not only distance (or space) but also time is variable in Einstein's conception.

Thus, the absolute construction of the Newtonian universe was destroyed. Through his search for unity, Einstein had altered the very way scientists conceived of the universe. The power of Einstein's search for unity was not lost on the scientific community, but on the popular level it was lost and it remains an aspect of Einstein's genius not frequently noted.

BEYOND RELATIVITY: THE SEARCH FOR A UNIFIED FIELD THEORY

Einstein's zealous search for unity did not end with the special theory of relativity. After his early success he extended the search to ambitious new levels and sought to formulate a unified field theory. Gravity, electromagnetism, and even quantum mechanics must operate under the same laws, he postulated. The struggle to identify those laws became almost an obsession, and most of his subsequent work was devoted to this goal.

In 1913, Einstein published his general theory of relativity in which he treated the force of gravity as the result of a gravitational field. Matter produced a gravitational field, and this field in turn exerted an influence on other material bodies to cause certain forces to act. This was the basis of his suspicion that a unified field theory could be formulated.

Electrically charged particles, he argued, had an impact on all forces in the same manner as did gravitation. Electric charges formed an electromagnetic field, which exerted an impact on other charged particles. The gravitational field and the electromagnetic

Einstein's Search for Unity

field were analogous—a unified field theory could bring them together and thus could grant new insight into the nature of the universe. Einstein postulated that the same force that moves electrons around the nuclei of atoms is the same force that moves planets around the sun, and that it is the same force that brings light and heat to the earth that makes life possible. So Einstein began a lifelong search to explain the actions of planets and electrons in one mathematical set of equations (Michelmore, 1962, 128).

How did Einstein come to place such importance on unity? He explained his emphasis on unity with a wood-chopping analogy. "I know why so many people enjoy chopping wood," he said. "In that activity one immediately sees results." The search for unity, though a long-range process, was very similar to chopping wood, in that the results of the activity brought Einstein pleasure. Through the search for unity Einstein glimpsed the secrets of the universe and the joy of such an experience, he decided, was well worth the years of work it required.

To understand Einstein and the basis for his genius one must understand his dedication to the search for unity. A. F. Joffe, the Russian physicist, described a visit he made to Berlin to explain to Einstein his work on the mechanical and electrical properties of crystals. Joffe explained his work in about two hours and at that point he said that "Einstein began the process of turning the information to his own use." Joffe described this process as "the organic absorption of new information into an already existing uniform picture of nature" (Clark, 1971, 62, 505). In other words, Einstein approached new information on the lookout for how it contributed to his understanding of the unity. He had a matrix (a system of meaning) in which to fit the information—a matrix Joffe described as "an already existing uniform picture of nature." The fundamental concepts of this unified worldview had to be as narrow as possible: freely selected, but with attention to parsimony (Clark, 1971, 39). It was this quest for simplicity of concepts—the constant attempt to find basic generalizations—that grants us insight into the thought processes that characterized his search for unity.

THE SIGNIFICANCE OF UNITY: A PERSONAL CONSTRUCTION

By as early as 1905 Einstein had developed the method that he would use in his search for unity—the postulational method. The method rested on his need to see a uniform picture of nature, his desire for the simplicity of concepts, and the power of his imagination. To begin with, Einstein took an experimental rule, recast it in its most general form, and raised it to a postulate. If no experimental rule was available, as in the case of relativity, he made up his own experimental postulate—a classic example of accommodation. On this postulate he based his logical deductions. He then tested these deductions against experience. As a result, unique insights into the unity emerged, old mysteries were explained, and new questions presented themselves. With the proper postulates at the top, he argued, the correct consequences would naturally develop (Horton, 1979, 57).

By "correct consequences" he meant that through the postulational method and the right it grants to play freely with concepts, the researcher gains a unique thought structure. This mental matrix provides the seeker with a testable method of achieving a meaningful understanding of a wide variety of sense experiences that would normally appear to be separate and unconnected. Use of the postulational method is essential to the discovery of unity, he maintained, for it is through such a method that "we are able to orient ourselves in the labyrinth of sense impressions" (Clark, 1971, 60–61).

THE NATURE OF THE QUEST

Einstein's unity transcended the bounds of physics; he sought an interdisciplinary unity. Work performed in one field of inquiry influences others, and it was the job of the scientist to recognize and explore relationships between disciplines. It was Einstein's obsession with the search for unity through these interdisciplinary relationships that engendered a disdain of scientific trench work, e.g., the repetitive experiments of the laboratory.

Like his friend Bertrand Russell, Einstein became increasingly disinterested with the components of scientific study and more absorbed in the relationship between ostensibly unrelated fields. Commenting on the relationship between physics and biology, he said that when we "restrict ourselves to concepts and laws of physics, we are unable to get a reasonable view of the total events of life." In order to understand the totality, he argued, we must combine the perspectives of physics and biology—a slap in the face of the Newtonian-Cartesian tendency toward fragmentation. It was in this spirit that he consistently worked to apply the achievements of mechanics to areas that other scientists thought had little to do with mechanics (Clark, 1971, 16, 22, 35).

His interdisciplinary search for unity was not restricted to physics and the physical sciences. In 1912 Einstein signed a manifesto (also signed by Sigmund Freud) that contended that science must take on problems of a more general character. The theory of relativity, the manifesto maintained, touches the most searching question of epistemology—is knowledge absolute or relative? Is knowledge even conceivable? In psychological problems, the manifesto signers reasoned that physics and biology came together. And in the process, they argued, the anthropological sciences, especially history and sociology, find closer and closer connection with the biological concepts. Thus, in his association with the manifesto committee, Einstein's search for unity was extended beyond the frontiers of physics, mathematics, and biology, and was moved into the realm of the social sciences. From the social sciences, the search would eventually be extended into literature and art. Like his astronomer friend George Ellery Hale, Einstein accepted the unity between science, literature, and art, and recognized that creative imagination was the vital factor in all of them.

As he explored the connections between his physical theories and social realities, Einstein saw the unity between physical relativity and moral, philosophical, and cultural relativity. Different social, political, and ethical situations demanded different actions and attitudes—circumstances altered frames of reference even in nonscientific spheres of human endeavor. In the same way that time and space were devoid of absolutes, there was also nothing intractable about the means by which people should approach the complex and sometimes irrational actions of their brothers and sisters.

The tendency of relativity to connect the ostensibly unrelated was transferable—Einstein had helped to establish the lines between physical and social science. The unity of relativity's vision was not lost on contemporary observers, who sometimes had to remind Einstein of its comprehensiveness. At a meeting concerned with his work for the League of Nations in the early 1930s, Einstein was approached by Ernst Jackh, a director of the Hochschule fur Politik in Berlin. Jackh asked Einstein if the theory of relativity, Freudian psychoanalysis, and the League of Nations were all expressions of the same revolutionary way of looking at the world. Jackh reported that Einstein stared at him for a moment and said nothing. Surprisingly, his first response to the question was: "This synthetic vision is new to me. Let me think it over." Einstein held his response until after both men had sat through a formal dinner. At that point, Einstein walked over to him and said "You are quite right: I endorse your Holism" (Clark, 1971, 197, 208, 275, 443). One can only speculate about the meaning of Einstein's first response to Jackh: "This synthetic vision is new to me." Einstein had been in contact with Freud for years and Einstein's work with political affairs for the League of Nations was extensive. It is hard to believe that Einstein had not yet considered the mutual effects of his own relativity, Freud's psychoanalysis, and the League of Nations' work for peace. All three had contributed to the destruction of prevailing ways of viewing humanity and nature: relativity destroyed Newton's absolute laws of the universe; Freudianism discarded innocent explanations of the forces that motivate human behavior; and the League of Nations challenged popular conceptions of nationalistic loyalties.

By no means should Einstein's successors try to put words in his mouth or try to mold him into something he was not. But given his pronouncements on these subjects prior to his response to Jackh, it may be safe to assume that Einstein's response did not belie a naïveté in regard to the synthesis. It is quite possible that Einstein was searching for a more simplistic and common thread that united relativity, Freudianism, and the

League of Nations' search for peace. It was a common thread that subsequent historians and social analysts have discussed for decades and that has served to weave the unique fabric of the twentieth century.

THE SHARING OF A VISION

Just as Einstein helped weave the twentieth-century social fabric, he also produced the most important scientific discoveries of the century. The importance of Einstein's work emerged from his search for unity and has in turn contributed to the world's vision of unity. Because of Einstein's work human beings can now discuss the unity of the universe in a rational way. "After all," Dennis W. Sciama asks, "what could be more important than understanding everything else there is?" The general theory of relativity was the unifying tool that permitted rational discussion of the cosmology, for it was with the general theory that human beings for the first time had a means of laying out the spatial and temporal structure of the universe in a consistent manner.

Not only could physics students now discuss the unity of the universe, but laypeople too could think in terms of unification and could comprehend the value of seeking connections in ostensibly dissimilar events. In other words, through Einstein's search for unity, laypeople could share the synergistic energy that comes from synthetic thinking. The application of such thinking modes would not be lost on creative thinkers. While we don't have a comprehensive physical insight to replace Einstein, we do have a spate of attempts to identify and sophisticate the holistic thinking methodology that set him apart. It is still true that great syntheses are constructed in individual minds. Nigel Calder (1979) argues that "in detail Einstein is already being surpassed; all that is lacking is the new comprehensive insight, to match his."

TOWARD HOLISM IN EDUCATION: FRAMING AND ANSWERING QUESTIONS

Holistic beliefs and assumptions applied to the nature of science have transformed our ways of seeing the universe and approaches to scientific research. Not surprisingly, holism is now providing diverse ways of framing and answering questions that have profound consequences for the practice of education. David Bohm's theory of order as an enfolded process, the implicate order, logically follows Einstein's work. Like all chaotic systems, educational systems can no longer be analyzed in terms of behavioral objectives, task analysis, and other principles of reductionism that claim the superiority of objectivity. But how can our educational systems of the world restructure themselves so as to take advantage of holistic perspectives of teacher learning and curricula reform? Critical postmodernism is the nexus which ties holistic/constructivist perspectives on teaching and learning with curricular reform. This has critical implications for educational change,

Einstein's Search for Unity

that must be viewed as connecting the history and practice of schooling to larger structures of power and with race, class, and gender. It was ultimately this "unity" that enabled Einstein to see problems in the physical universe that no one else had ever seen. This postformal search for unity, for order, is a necessary condition for understanding and facilitating change that uncovers educational problems that were previously hidden.

What About Teaching?

Everyone has a stake in education reform. Yet differing viewpoints exist concerning the nature of reform efforts and how they can best be accomplished. These range from the traditional Victorian system to the neo-60s independent classrooms. This current state of affairs can be attributed, in part, to the conflicting perspectives of educators. The conduit metaphor has served teacher educators well for many years. They have been content to "train" teachers in the knowledge and content of pedagogy. In so doing, teacher educators have perpetuated a vision of teacher education in which the teacher's role is that of an empty vessel prepared to receive knowledge. Teachers are viewed, and come to believe, that they are incapable of constructing or changing their own knowledge in relation to teaching and learning. In much the same way, Belenky, Clinchy, Goldberger, and Tarule (1986) describe women as received knowers, with little or no voice in making sense of their experiences. It is only as constructed knowers that learning takes on significance, as women or teachers assume responsibility for working things out themselves and thus give voice to their ideas. Examples of science teaching are used often in this chapter to illustrate constructivist teaching, but the examples are valid for the teaching of any discipline.

CULTURAL MYTHS

Experience is embedded in culture. Thus learning should be considered in a cultural context. This includes both teacher knowledge and the curriculum. Tobin puts it best,

"Change can only occur if substantive changes occur in the culture in which the curriculum is embedded" (Tobin, 1991, 5).

Because of this cultural basis, experience can be interpreted in terms of the myths of a culture. Myths act as social referents for the actions of teachers and their underlying epistemologies. Unfortunately, too often the myths act as retardants rather than as catalysts. Britzman relates how myths can act as a framework for "repressing notions of pedagogy and identity" or as a vehicle for generating alternative images of teaching and learning (Britzman, 1991, 8). She provides examples of the myths that are rooted in teacher practice: teacher as expert, teacher as a product of experience, or teacher as sole bearer of power. Tobin suggests that an alternative to the myth of "school as workplace" might be "school as a learning place" (Tobin, 1991, 5). Numerous school and classroom practices reflect the way in which this myth has acted as a framework for school organization. A myth commonly associated with the development of middle school philosophy is the myth of "middle school as bridge to high school." Yet, if one considers the dynamic, changing nature of the middle school culture, one would have to question the folly of building a bridge on moving ground.

Another important myth that has pervaded teaching is that of objectivism. The acceptance of the myth of objectivism and its pursuit of "truth" hold important implications for teaching.

THE MYTH OF OBJECTIVISM

Many prevailing instructional practices continue to reflect traditional approaches to teaching, which are based on the assumption that teachers can generate learning only through information giving. In such a view of learning, knowledge is considered to be external to the minds and bodies of thinking beings. Classroom practices and curricular resources continue to reflect this myth of objectivism—the idea that knowledge is "out there" in the world and can easily be transferred to learners by their senses. When objectivism is the prevailing classroom practice, attention becomes focused on the milieu in which learning is assumed to be embedded at the expense of focusing on the learner.

As Ayn Rand's objectivist philosophy is based on the concept of the human as a completely definable rational machine, without emotion, social, or cultural responsibility—so too does objectivism in education put forth a concept of the world as a stable body of knowledge. It advocates two major suppositions: the notion of the unity of science and the notion of reductionism. These two basic assumptions of objectivism have been philosophically rejected for over twenty-five years; the rejection culminated in Thomas Kuhn's historical view of science activity. Kuhn's conception of the way science actually develops serves to illustrate the basic irrelevancy of an objectivist conception of the structure of scientific thought.

Despite the philosophical rejection of an objectivist concept of knowing, our approach to teaching is still shaped by objectivism as a referent; consequently, education in the postmodern era still reflects the search for truth, the preservation of the autonomy of individual sciences, and the perpetuation of the idea that scientific knowledge is omnipotent. Teachers who use objectivism as a referent may think about their own teaching practices in a way that parallels this epistemological conception.

An objectivist view of the world and of classroom culture requires the separation of thought and feeling. Such a separation is easily embraced, for it essentially releases the teacher from ethical responsibility. From this perspective, teachers are divested of any personal involvement in teaching. As a result, the many ethical dilemmas that teachers encounter daily are simply and clearly dichotomized as "ethical" or "nonethical." The ethical dimensions of teachers' practices are diminished, and teachers are deprived of the capacity for historical consciousness and self-criticism that is necessary to place oneself in the context of the larger culture.

A rethinking of school curriculum must reflect answers to basic questions about the nature of learning and the ways in which students make sense of their experiences in terms of what they already know. To do this, new insights are needed to dislodge the underlying structure of belief implicit in most of the current approaches to teaching. Such insights may ultimately lead to a revision of the educational system as we know it today; for example, disciplines may relinquish their subject matter boundaries and eventually be taught in an integrated manner. Students may become aware of their potential ability to modify culture, much in the same way that Einstein has modified the culture of our time.

THE MYTH OF CONSTRUCTIVISM

When teachers' actions are influenced by constructivism as a way of knowing and making sense of the world, learning is viewed as a process of making sense of new information in terms of what is already known. As a basic human characteristic, the process of making sense is an active process by which learners construct knowledge in a way that fits their personal experience. Because knowledge results from this active, constructive process, it cannot be conveyed to passive receivers. Since learners draw on their own background experiences in this process, their learning experiences are subjective and value laden. For example, when constructivism is used as a referent for science teaching, learners are provided with many opportunities to interact with scientific phenomena. In this way they can explore, construct, and reconstruct their own understandings of the way the world works. The consciousness of the knower, inseparable from the known, becomes essential when learning science is viewed as a way of coming to know the world.

From a constructivist perspective, ethical dimensions of teachers' practices are found in the sense-making process, and thus are deeply rooted in the professional lives of teachers. When ethical dilemmas are considered from this view, they reflect multiple perspectives and contradictions. Teaching thus involves a personal investment in the student-teacher relationships that are at the heart of many classroom dilemmas. Einstein alluded to the importance of the student-teacher relationship when he wrote about the significance of small colleges such as Black Mountain College:

> I am convinced that education without vivid personal relationship between all working together there, students as well as teachers, is far from the ideal, even if the teachers are of the highest standing (Einstein, 1954).

It is this relationship that van Manen alludes to when he describes his understanding of pedagogy. Differentiating from specific categories of pedagogy, i.e., critical pedagogy, emancipatory pedagogy, deconstructionist pedagogy, and so forth, van Manen says:

> ...the word pedagogy brings something into being. Pedagogy is found not in observational categories, but like love or friendship in the experience of its presence—that is, concrete, real life situations. It is here and here and here, where an adult does something right in the personal development of a child. Regardless of what we think parents or teachers do precisely, pedagogy is cemented deep in the nature of the relationship between adults and children. In this sense, pedagogy is defined not only as a certain relationship or a way of doing, but also pedagogy lets an encounter, a relationship, a situation, or an activity be pedagogical (van Manen, 1991, 31).

WHAT IS KNOWLEDGE?

There are two main questions that are important in the idea of constructivism: What is knowledge? What is learning? When knowledge is viewed from an epistemology rooted in the theory of constructivism, it is assumed to be the product of learning; that is, the process of making sense of experience in terms of extant knowledge. From this perspective, knowledge, which only resides in the minds of cognizant beings, can be represented as images, metaphors, propositions, beliefs, and actions. It is produced in philosophical, historical, cultural, and political contexts. Thus, there is a pressing need to examine the teacher's epistemological perspective and its relationship to knowledge. The examination of teachers' personal epistemologies in relation to knowledge should be part of a larger effort to construct new knowledge that takes into account the complex nature of teaching and learning and the process of change.

What About Teaching?   159

A perfect, albeit ad hominum, example is Ken Burns' film production about the United States Civil War. Burns, a northern white middle-aged male, influenced by both his artistry and the culture of America from 1950 to 1970 (the era of his growth) brought all of these cultural influences—geography, gender, race, background, artistic concepts—to his production. In turn, those who viewed the production allowed their own cultural influences to affect their perceptions. Thus, in the months that followed Burns was criticized for being pro-Southern, pro-Northern, antiblack, problack, promilitarist, antimilitarist, overly romantic, battle-happy, biased toward Lincoln, and biased toward the Confederate leadership. Similarly, the fifth grade student on Deer Isle, Maine, who sits within walking distance of his ancestors' graves (many of whom died to preserve the Union) is shown and thinks about a far different war than does the white student in Macon County, Georgia. Similarly the black student in Selma, Alabama, who even today must live with the cultural vestiges of his town and its people, will have a different view of the Civil War than a twelve-year-old black student in south Los Angeles, who daily exists in an ongoing urban civil war.

TEACHER AS FACILITATOR OF KNOWLEDGE

Teachers who adopt a constructivist approach will move away from teacher-dominated classrooms in which their primary roles consist of disseminating knowledge and delivering services of an administrative and custodial nature. They will become advocates for empowering students to learn. Fosnot considers learning to be "something a learner does, not something that is done to a learner" (Fosnot, 1990, 5). From this perspective, teachers assume the role of facilitators of learning. Their job will be to identify what sense, in terms of extant knowledge, students are making of the learning experiences.

Science teachers can become facilitators of knowledge by recognizing the importance of familiarizing students with theoretical ideals of science and presenting them with many experiences that are designed to challenge existing conceptions. But in order to become facilitators, all teachers should be equipped with an understanding of how knowledge develops in children. They should develop a repertoire of cooperative learning and problem-solving strategies that advance the learner's construction of meaningful experiences and open the classroom to authentic conversations.

TEACHER AS ASSESSOR OF KNOWLEDGE

Alternative assessment means many things. Historically, the goal of most assessment practices was equity, but such an approach was reductionistic. Evidence from past practices reveals the ways in which assessment has generally skewed the curriculum in the direction of easily measurable basic skills and isolated facts. More recently, alternative assessments, defined as "authentic" or "performance" have been attempts to capture equity in the contexts of the discipline and of the school and the learner. This has spurred the development of alternative forms of assessment such as writing tests, open-ended experiences in math, hands-on minds-on experiences in science, portfolio collections, and culminating exhibitions.

We propose another interpretation of alternative assessment—one that is epistemologically alternative and is grounded in critical constructivism. In a constructivist approach to assessment the point of reference becomes what the learner understands. What the student knows is used to facilitate further learning. Accordingly, assessment involves the representation of knowledge and a judgment about the viability of knowledge. It should be dependent on context, should reflect the domain-specific nature of the subject matter, and should address the unique cultural aspects of the class, the school and the community of learners.

Constructivism provides a different conceptual apparatus from which to view assessment. From a constructivist perspective, the knower personally participates in all acts of understanding. Consequently, as teachers construct new knowledge and attempt to change their practices in relation to assessment they negotiate with each other. They address important questions such as: How can specific knowledge be represented? To what extent should students be given control over the what, how, and when of an assessment? How can the viability of student solutions to problems be judged? In this way teachers can test new knowledge and meaning about their changed practices in relation to assessment.

A teacher's role as an assessor of student progress is critical to structuring appropriate experiences and to asking questions that encourage and probe. From a constructivist perspective, assessment reveals to the teacher the method by which students organize conceptual knowledge. Assessment allows the teacher to understand individual motivation and individual progress.

Assessment practice should reflect the nature of classroom instruction. Traditional assessment tools, driven in part by the move toward accountability, have emphasized the measurement of factual knowledge. Meng and Doran have stressed the need for assessment to match the inclusion of organizing concepts, process skills, and problem-solving strategies into the science curriculum. But assessment is a complex and controversial issue that is intertwined with local, state, and national policy. From a constructivist perspective, the teacher as assessor is one who challenges the traditional power of assessment to shape the nature of curriculum and instruction. This is essential to the determination of what type of science students will be doing in the next decade and beyond (Meng and Doran, 1990).

REJECTING THE MYTH OF OBJECTIVISM IN FAVOR OF THE MYTH OF CONSTRUCTIVISM

The rejection of the myth of objectivity and the recognition of the value in all we do and come to know has important implications for our understanding of teachers' practices. Millar has suggested that the "potential to achieve something very special with students" is lost when science is taught in a way that represents absolute truth.

In rejecting the myth of objectivism in favor of the myth of constructivism, science educators have expressed concern for how cognizant beings construct knowledge that is personally meaningful; a type of personal constructivism. However, constructivism as a way of knowing should not be confused with the notion of discovery learning, which has been a popular science education theme in recent years. As Millar explains:

> ...constructivism is not the same as discovery learning. There is no ideological requirement here that the teacher wait until pupils "discover" the scientific idea for themselves. She can legitimately introduce the accepted scientific view, but needs to be aware that it may be reconstructed by individual students as they make personal sense of it (Miller, 1989, 56).

It might be nice if we could have our students learn in the discovery manner of Thoreau, but sadly this oftentimes develops into a novel contemplation, and we should remember that a great many of those who clung to this philosophy in the 1960s and 1970s have become Wall Street bond sellers today—Walden Pond meets Gordan Gecko. This initial concern led to student conception research, the focus of which was understanding how students' knowledge of photosynthesis, for example, might compare with the epistemological "truth" of science. This led to the development of a conceptual change model and a dearth of research to investigate student misconceptions or alternate conceptions. Cobern emphasizes, "conceptual research was important to constructivists because they considered learning to be the process of deconstructing misconceptions and reconstructing valid scientific conceptions in their place" (Cobern, 1991, 4).

Some science educators, dissatisfied with what they considered to be an inadequate model of conceptual change, began to look more closely at the epistemological, social, and cultural contexts of science teaching and learning (Cobern, 1991; Millar, 1989; Solomon, 1987). The move away from a single focus on personal constructivism toward a contextual constructivism (a precursor to critical constructivism) invited those concerned with science teaching and learning to consider student knowledge construction within the cultural context that gives meaning to personal constructions. The following vignette illustrates how culture is related to the individual meaning that students construct from their experiences and interactions with their environment. In a study conducted by Kagan and Tippins (1991), a student teacher described her perceptions of student learning:

> There's Candace staring out into space again. I think she's got a problem with that, because she is constantly like that. Even with an activity, she still has to be kept constantly busy. Yesterday she was sitting there just talking to the floor. She doesn't seem to pay attention but when you ask her a question, she's smart. She always makes A's and everything. Maybe she's just so intelligent that things bore her.

This particular student teacher valued active involvement during science class as an indication that learning was occurring. Without a broader awareness of culture and learning styles she was unable to realize that Candace may have placed a value on abstraction and imagination. The child may actually be penalized in relation to a learning style that the teacher preferred. There is a need for increased sensitivity to aspects of culture and diverse learning styles that may be present in the classroom. We suggest that contextual constructivism falls short when it fails to critically examine the broader social and political forces that encompass the cultural context—a type of *critical* constructivism. Our understanding of the sense-making process can only occur when teachers and researchers gain insight into the ways that the struggle for power shapes our ways of knowing, and ultimately the image of epistemology that prevails.

TEACHER LEARNING

The type of theoretical base that teachers need to develop is neither purely scientific nor purely interpretive, but rather, critical, in the sense that individuals are able to develop a clear understanding of those aspects of their culture, beliefs, and actions that inhibit the attainment of educational goals. Carr and Kemmis state:

> Educational theory must always be oriented towards transforming the ways in which teachers see themselves and their situation, so that the factors frustrating their educational goals and purposes can be recognized and eliminated (Carr and Kemmis, 1986, 130)

Teacher learning, when viewed from a constructivist perspective, requires opportunities for the teacher learner to directly experience and critically reflect on the problems associated with teaching and learning. Teacher learning occurs when teachers form "self-critical communities of inquirers" to examine the culture of teaching, teacher beliefs, and practices. As teachers interact in social settings from which they develop meaning they are able to develop a critical understanding of the teaching profession and the culture in which it is embedded. When teacher-researchers begin to develop an understanding of the way in which competing forces shape curriculum and instruction, they use the process of action research, an intimate and powerful process of "coming to the mirror." When they understand their own culture, beliefs, and practices, teachers can make conscious choices about what should and should not be done to facilitate student learning.

THE ROLE OF LANGUAGE AND DISCOURSE IN TEACHER LEARNING

The conviction that teaching is an inherently moral endeavor has been fundamental to the recent rhetoric of teacher professionalism. Attempts to "professionalize teaching" (Soder, 1991, 295) have been grounded in the value of subject-matter knowledge and pedagogical knowledge, and have ignored the critical ethical dimensions of teaching. Einstein expressed the same concern for the moral dimensions of teaching nearly forty years ago:

> It is not enough to teach a man a specialty. Through it he might become a useful machine but not a harmoniously developed personality. It is essential that the student acquires an understanding of and a lively feeling for values. He must acquire a vivid sense of the beautiful and morally good. Otherwise he, with his specialized knowledge, more closely resembles a well trained dog than a harmoniously developed person. (Einstein, 1959)

Central to the concern for ethical dimensions of teaching and teachers' growth has been the notion of control. In the classroom, where teachers traditionally hold more power over students, there is an inherent tension that occurs within the dynamic interplay of power on the part of the teacher and acts of resistance on the part of students. It is a tension that parallels the role of power in society:

> Society is typically constituted by structures and relations of power, exercised or resisted; it is characterized by conflict as well as cohesion, so that the structures of meaning at all levels, from dominant ideological forms to local acts of meaning will show traces of contradiction (Hodge and Kress, 1988, 8).

The realization that power relationships inhibit and mold our language and conversation means that we must investigate language to understand meaning in the classroom and to encourage reflection by teachers. The use of semiotics, metaphors, images, referents, and metonymy, in particular, can contribute greatly to our knowledge of how students daily learn (or are inhibited from doing so) and construct meaning.

The inherent tension associated with relationships of power reflects a more fundamental question concerning the purposes of education. Should education serve as "a source of social reproduction, serving to reproduce social relations as they are?" (O'Loughlin, 1991, 31). Or, as Ginsburg suggests, should education enable people "to act individually and collectively to expose, challenge, and transform unequal and contradictory class, gender and race relations" (Ginsburg, 1988, 17). Ethical dilemmas arise when the power relationships of schooling are considered:

> Can a teacher be truly democratic in the classroom? If not, is the presence of egalitarianism more debilitating for the powerless than naked assertion of power? If teaching is not value-free, how do we avoid being impositional on our students when our values and theirs conflict? How are we to reconcile the conflicting impulses between schooling as reproduction versus school as transformation? (O'Loughlin, 1991, 31)

Semiotics, as a way of understanding how meaning is constructed in classrooms, has the potential to significantly change classroom practice. As a qualitative research tool, semiotics involves the decoding of systems of symbols and signs in which culture is embodied. This decoding process enables humans to derive meaning from their surroundings. When culture is understood as a system of signs used in communication, the tacit beliefs and ideas of the culture are revealed.

As learners are engaged in the personal construction of meaning they are continually shaped by existing networks of meaning in the context of their social environment. Semiotics can provide insights into many of the hidden structures of communication that support and give meaning to educational practices. It can provide clues to understanding power structures and social and psychological processes. When teacher-researchers use semiotics as a tool for research, they are also concerned with exploring semiosis, the process of generating signs, and the hidden messages that are communicated to students in the process. What are the communication structures one might encounter upon entering a science classroom? The arrangement of lab tables and desks? The location of special objects such as a clock? The activities performed in the classroom and the way they are structured? The choreography of time and space, and the patterns of verbal interchange (Groisman, Shapiro, and Willinsky, 1990)?

Language can be used to frame the personal meaning individuals give to events. Referents in the form of metaphors, images, metonymies, and beliefs are important aspects of language and knowing. They provide another means of representing and constructing a teacher's practical knowledge in relation to teaching and the culture in which it is embedded. They promote investigation into the sense-making process by enabling such questions to be asked as: What referents are used to make sense of actions. How do they apply to particular situations in classrooms (Lakoff, 1987)?

The essence of metaphor, for example, is the implicit, hidden comparison that provokes an element of surprise, and allows the familiar to become strange. Because the basis of comparison revealed in a metaphor is created by the addressee of the metaphor, different individuals will make sense of the same metaphor in unique ways. As teachers use metaphors and images to talk about what they do in the classroom, the different beliefs associated with the metaphors emerge. When Eric and Kathryn, two secondary science teachers, discussed their use of the "teacher as police officer" metaphor, they used the same metaphor to conceptualize teaching in different ways. Teaching behaviors that Eric associated with this metaphor reflected beliefs about the teacher as a disciplinarian and authority figure. Kathryn, however, saw the "teacher as police officer" as the protector of individual rights within the classroom.

Language has the potential to facilitate teacher change by providing alternative metaphors and images with which to conceptualize teacher roles and clarify beliefs, in both preservice and in-service teacher education contexts. The recognition that teachers' personal images and metaphors may at times be inappropriate has important implications: for professional growth to occur, teachers need opportunities for the self-reflection that is essential if they are to modify and reconstruct images, metaphors, and beliefs about teaching. We can see just how this might occur by focusing on a middle school science teacher on the path to becoming a constructivist.

TRANSLATING THEORY INTO PRACTICE:
BECOMING A CONSTRUCTIVIST SCIENCE TEACHER

"Greg" was introduced to constructivism while teaching middle school science. Because he found constructivist-oriented beliefs to be most consistent with his vision for teaching and learning, he gradually rejected the myth of objectivism in favor of the myth of constructivism. Although Greg used constructivism as a referent for his actions, he encountered many constraints to his efforts to implement his "ideal curriculum." Greg described his ultimate curriculum in the following way:

> Curriculum is that meshing of everything—how it all interacts. How you play out all those things. But if you ask what my ultimate curriculum would be, basically it would be students deciding what they want to learn and having a big input into what they want to learn—a lot of negotiation about what's learned. Students being excited about learning. They walk in the classroom and they don't want to leave. Students choosing what they want to learn and they're basically learning through each other by helping each other. I think there's a lot of people including the state—whoever writes all those objectives and stuff—that just say you have to memorize these things, know these facts; and they're isolated little bits. They don't tie biology with chemistry. There's no meshing or blending, neither with other science disciplines, nor with English, writing, math. That learning does not occur. So in my ultimate curriculum I would see it as students picking up on a unit or idea—whether it be muscles, hormones, nervous response—and presenting their findings to the rest of the class. And the rest of the class could either choose to continue or choose another experiment or project. Students would become seekers of problems and solvers of problems.

Einstein also encouraged a vision of schooling in which students would be excited about learning for learning's sake. Writing in the freshman publication at Princeton he said:

> Never regard your study as a duty, but as the enviable opportunity to learn the liberating influence of beauty in the realm of the spirit of your own personal joy and the profit of the community to which your later work belongs (Einstein, 1979, 15–20).

Greg translated his image of curriculum into practice by developing a project-centered curriculum in which students were free to select scientific areas of interest to study, i.e., water quality parameters or alternative energy sources. Greg provided students with opportunities for firsthand experiences that would lead to the development of important constructs. He helped students to move from a dualistic to a multiple understanding of scientific phenomena. In the process of becoming a constructivist, however, Greg's actions in the classroom were not always consistent with his beliefs—tension existed between what was happening and what Greg thought should be happening.

A team of three researchers that included Greg and two science educators actively participated in the data collection and interpretation necessary to construct new knowledge and bring about change. Greg worked together with the other team members and within their multiple frames of reference to develop a vision of what science education ought to be, and to design and implement strategies to support that vision. Constructivism served as a referent for the planning and actions of the team. In order to develop a vision it was first necessary for Greg to understand his classroom practice and the context in which his actions were grounded. In a collaborative effort, the team looked at metaphors, images, referents, beliefs, and constraints that drive practice. In the process they uncovered ways in which social values, personal epistemologies, and worldviews unconsciously influenced Greg's beliefs about science teaching.

The team identified classroom situations for which inconsistent mindsets were evident; e.g., the need to shape instruction for individual students while gaining control over the group. Social interactions involving cooperative learning, classroom assessment practices, questions of what to teach and how best to present the material to students, issues of safety, and interactions involving subject matter knowledge were areas in which inconsistencies were identified.

REFERENTS FOR MAKING SENSE

One way in which Greg made sense of science teaching was in terms of referents that guided his actions. These referents acted as organizers of his knowledge and provided insight into the beliefs and metaphors that influenced his actions. Although construc-

What About Teaching?

tivism served as a referent, Greg's preference for higher-level referents was context-dependent in relation to the sense he made of particular classroom circumstances. In some cases, Greg's actions were constrained by the referents he used to frame events. In other situations, referents helped to clarify and define the conditions at hand. In order to bring to light the implicit aspects of teacher knowledge, we use vignettes to illustrate some of the situations and the referents Greg associated with them, many of which resulted in conflicting actions and led Greg to act in ways different from what made sense.

Greg encountered many situations in his daily practice in which he had to make decisions about methods of assessment. He expressed beliefs about assessment that were consistent with a constructivist approach to science teaching:

> I don't think you should have to grade students in the classroom. The students should want to learn for learning's sake. I see grades as a reward or punishment. It would be nice if we didn't have to use grades—no rewards or punishments. The ideal class would internalize rewards. Rewards would be the satisfaction of doing well, facing adversity and beating it, increasing one's understanding of self and the world. In the past I believed that the teacher was the final authority—the expert not only in the content area, but also in the areas of teaching students and assessing their knowledge. Tests were based strictly on the prestated objectives and were of the fill-in-the-blank variety. If the students had a disagreement with an answer, they would really have to convince me to see their point of view. My response would be that I told you the answer and that's what is in the book, and the book is always right. I was very stubborn and unbending.

As Greg became a constructivist his beliefs about assessment and his practices changed. His rejection of the myth of objectivity, a philosophy that often grounds assessment strategies in a practice of behavior modification and reinforcement in the form of rewards and punishments, led him to seek alternatives to the traditional forms of assessment. He began to use a variety of alternative assessment tools, including concept maps, oral interviews, scrapbooks, dialogue journals, and portfolios. His actions no longer revealed the belief that assessment should reflect mastery of certain objectives or prestated goals. He tried to get a handle on the problem of having to assign a letter or number to achievement by involving students in the negotiation process:

> Whole class negotiation is used to determine "weight" of each grade. This process allows the students to have input about which projects they learned from and valued the most. By teacher-student and student-student interactions the strengths and weaknesses of each student are discussed and a letter that both parties can agree on is determined.

While Greg made changes in his actions with regard to assessment, he continued to express frustration with his inability to implement his ideal vision of assessment:

> Still, because there are new beliefs conflicting with well-entrenched beliefs, I sometimes revert to old methods of assessment when feeling unsure of myself. Social factors such as parents and other teachers cause a conflict between my beliefs and undesirable alternatives.

Greg's ability to implement the curriculum in a preferred way was made less effective when referents such as social expectations, control, time, and personal epistemology acted as constraints on the way he thought and acted in relation to assessment. Because constraints can deter an individual from acting in a manner that makes sense, they have a strong influence on the curriculum. In many classroom situations, conflicting actions stem from the use of different referents. Certain referents are used to justify one set of actions over another.

SOCIAL EXPECTATIONS AS A REFERENT. Greg's classroom practice was influenced by perceived constraints in the form of implicit and explicit expectations of parents, colleagues, administrators, and students. These constraints, in effect, "drove" Greg to assign grades to student learning. The influence of these social expectations was felt throughout the curriculum: while Greg did not value lecture as a form of instruction, he chose to lecture at times, because he believed others valued a lecture form of instruction. Greg was particularly influenced by the perceived expectations of other colleagues. Although Greg believed that the purpose of schooling was more than raising test scores, he expressed conflict resulting from his belief that other teachers valued testing and grades:

> Are alternative methods of assessment fair to the student? I would say yes—students should be able to demonstrate what meaning they have constructed in their own manner. Alternative assessments are the fairest way to determine student constructions of science. But what of the future? Standardized tests are used to determine if students graduate from high school, what college they get into, what scholarship they receive. Do alternative assessments which provide opportunity for students to show what they know prepare them for taking tests that are looking for specific answers to author-determined questions? Do they prepare them for future classes where other teachers will have expectations about grades and testing?

Social expectations also acted as a referent when Greg made a decision to present basic chemistry information via lecture during the last few weeks of school. Concerned that his eighth grade students might not fulfill the expectations of the ninth grade teacher, Greg chose to "cover" the periodic table by lecturing. Reflecting on this decision Greg said:

> I believe that it is best to learn a few things very well instead of covering many things. But what value do parents, administrators, and other teachers place on this? A lot of these things I'm going to be doing these next three weeks are things that I might not necessarily believe in. But I'm doing them because I believe Mark (the ninth grade teacher) values them.

What About Teaching?

CONTROL AS A REFERENT. In the process of teaching science, Greg appeared to legitimate his actions with regard to assessment, presentation of subject matter, and other areas by relating them to the referent of control. When control served as a higher-level referent, Greg experienced inherent tension between his desire to control and his desire to see students have the power to make choices about learning and assessment. Greg understood the ways in which power and control influenced the production of knowledge. He expressed his personal evolution toward understanding the role of power in the production and legitimization of knowledge, and the ways in which power relations ultimately shaped the negotiated and experienced curriculum:

> Earlier in my teaching I believed that content should be determined by a central authority because the authority knew best. Well, I first rested on the State Department of Education to determine what students should learn. But my mind was changed with the realization that the people at the state level did not have any idea about the nature of science, the nature of science education, or the nature of students. So following the notion of "curriculum should be determined by the community" I became dependent on the county-level curriculum. But that community was still too large. A more intimate community was needed to make curriculum choices—at the school level. Unfortunately, I thought at the time [that] schools do not determine curriculum. For what reasons, I cannot say. I then became the ultimate authority for the curriculum content. But I began to doubt my right to determine what should be taught. Who am I to determine what is relevant to individual students? At this point I turned toward students having the autonomy to select the content of the curriculum. This process was supported by my readings on emancipatory interests and constructivism. How does this fit into assessment? How can a single teacher assess all of the different curriculum contents being studied in the classroom, much less in five classes? Each student would require individual assessment. Constructivism supports individual assessment because even when students are studying the same content, they will have different understandings. This also fits with other things I have learned, especially the "doubling time of science." With so much new information generated each year, what does a teacher teach? Let the students focus on what they want to learn and consider important.

Greg's use of control as a referent repressed many of the changes he desired to make. Greg explored the use of many alternative assessment strategies and instructional alternatives to the lecture. He focused on coming to know his students so that he could bring the life experiences and personal interests of students into the learning process. Yet he continued to experience tension when his need to gain control over assessment or presentation of subject matter conflicted with his desire to show care and respect for personal autonomy. As he reflected on this dilemma, he actively reconstructed his experience in terms of an image:

> My need to have control stems from either my image of a teacher standing at the front of the room managing students' behavior or the protestant work ethic that I was raised with. My parents always said "idle hands are the devil's tools." Although I believe for myself that students need mental breaks, my fear is that students will take advantage of my easygoing nature and never get on task. Is that their choice? Should students be allowed to opt out for a day, week, [a] unit, or the year?

As a teacher, Greg participated in constructing his own story in order to make sense of the ways in which power shaped both his personal self-representations and the experienced curriculum. For Greg, imagery was a valuable tool for uncovering hidden meanings in the sense-making process. In much the same way, Einstein's ability to unveil hidden meanings was nurtured through his ability to make mental images. To his friend Max Wertheimer, Einstein affirmed this nonverbal formulation of images in the thought process when he said: "I very rarely think in words at all. A thought comes, and I may try to express it in words afterward" (Wertheimer, 1959, 213–28).

Einstein relied on an intuitive mode of thought, with its imagery and spatial skills, throughout most of his scientific life. It influenced his choice of axioms, the direction of his investigations, and his choice of leisure pursuits. As we increase our knowledge of processes that involves the intuitive mode, we may better be able to encourage the use of imagery as a tool in the sense-making process of science teacher education programs.

TIME AS A REFERENT. Greg expressed beliefs consistent with an approach to science teaching that stresses depth as opposed to breadth. In such an approach there is a decreased emphasis on facts and definitions and an increased emphasis on encouraging learners to construct individual meaning. Time, however, is a referent that constrained Greg's ability to implement the curriculum in this way. For Greg (and for the school), time was viewed as a scarce commodity; consequently, Greg was a victim, caught up in a power struggle for a scarce resource. It is a struggle that devalues the need for reflection and analysis in the teaching and learning process. Greg described the nature of this struggle:

> Time controls everything that we do. I mean, I don't want it to be that way. But it seems like every time we start doing something I look at my watch and they're expected to be in another class. And if they are not there when the time strikes, other teachers get real irritated and come down and say something. The way the structure of our school is designed, I'm supposed to be able to dash up there and let other teachers know that I'm running over . . . but it's not happening that way.

Time, seen as an organizer of efficiency, a scarce commodity, emerged as an important constraint that shaped the curriculum and influenced the way that students made sense of science in their lives. Time is revealed in the many decisions teachers make on

What About Teaching? 171

a routine basis; decisions about field trips for students, decisions about implementing and following safety procedures, decisions about what should be taught and how it should be taught. From a critical constructivist perspective, time is a reflection of social order, a major referent for an industrial society. Greg metaphorically described the way in which time acted as a referent to influence the way he thought about presenting material:

> ...it's like a book, and the teacher is that book. And you're determined, but it's not like you want to get through *BSCS Green*. It's the content you determine for the year. And you get into time going along and you realize that you're going to have to tear out these pages here. And you get down to a real thin book by the end of the year. And you're not going to get to all those pages you want to—that's my idea of time, not getting to all those pages.

In the process of disassembling Newtonian physics, Einstein demolished the notion of time as an absolute, a river flowing from the past toward the future: in his relativistic world, time was dependent on the relative motion of the observers. He distinguished the physical time that is experienced from mathematical time. The humorous way in which Einstein made this distinction is often described:

> When a pretty girl is sitting in your lap, an hour seems like a minute. But a minute sitting on a hot stove seems like an hour (Parker, 1986, 24).

The familiar representation of time—the clock—is prominently displayed on the walls of almost any classroom one enters today. It is a stark reminder of the reductionism that dominates education, a measure of a learning process that is fragmented into intervals of time. As a semiotic message, the clock occupied a prominent position in Greg's room. However, upon close inspection it was observed that someone had neglected to plug this electronic clock into the outlet. Greg admitted that the clock was displayed solely in adherence to school policies and was actually running only when an administrative visit for evaluation purposes was expected.

EPISTEMOLOGY AS A REFERENT. Greg had an implicit stance toward knowledge that suggested an obvious paradox in his explanation of knowledge and truth. His explanation was very similar to the way in which a critical constructivist might address the issue: while there may be a reality that exists, we cannot experience that reality in any way that approximates truth. Accordingly, we make sense of our experience in terms of what we already know and have previously experienced, taking into account the influence of historical, political, and social forces on the development of consciousness. Greg clarified his epistemological beliefs in the following conversation:

Greg: I do believe that there is a truth out there. The problem is [that] with our technology we can never really be sure if we have the truth and what is truth. We can all raise the idea of truth, but will we ever really notice the truth? Some say when we die we'll know all the truths. But as we live now, will we ever know if we have the truth? So when it comes to science you really can't teach truth at all. You can talk about best accepted theories, but there's really no guarantee that this is the way it's going to be or the way it is universally.

Team Member: Let me press you on this just a little. Initially you implied that it was a question of technology. Through the technology we have available now, will we know the truth? Is it a question of technology or is it the nature of human beings? If we had better technology, would we be able to know the truth?

Greg: People will always interpret the truth differently. Unless you have something that everyone can agree upon, like when you use technology to make a measurement or reading. Even then, people aren't always going to agree on what the measurement is telling us.

Team Member: Then let me say something that may surprise you. Your beliefs that you spoke about today are very consistent with radical constructivism. People might say, Greg is becoming a constructivist.

Greg: That's what I'm afraid of... It's not always carried out though, because it's ingrained for twenty-something years—you've always been told this is the truth, this is the way it's going to be. You still have that side pulling you that way. It's real uncomfortable not having the truth—not having something you can count on.

Science and epistemology are uniquely interwoven. This idea is essential for understanding science teaching and learning. Sensitive to this relationship, Einstein wrote:

> The reciprocal relationship of epistemology and science is of noteworthy kind. They are dependent on each other. Epistemology without contact with science becomes an empty scheme. Science without epistemology is—in so far as it is thinkable at all—primitive and muddled (French, 1979, 154).

Perhaps that is why scientists and educators alike often turn to philosophical analysis as a device for unlocking the mysteries of their field. If it is nothing else, postformal thinking is a form of cognition that is always epistemologically aware, regardless of the object of contemplation.

RECONSTRUCTING KNOWLEDGE: IMPLICATIONS FOR CHANGE

The path to becoming a critical constructivist is not an easy one. Significant changes must occur. Along the way there are many obstacles in the form of constraints—social constraints, control, time, the myths of the traditional culture and many others. Many of these constraints are socially negotiated and frequently are reinforced throughout the culture of teaching.

Teacher education programs should seek ways to enable teachers to overcome constraints and create change in practice. They should empower teachers to formulate new ways of knowing. They should facilitate an understanding of the ways in which dominant worldviews affect the construction of consciousness in students and in relation to knowledge of the discipline. But just how this should be accomplished remains unclear. Should the focus be on the development of an image of "self-as-teacher" in order to encourage reflection and stimulate postformal thinking? Or should we look to the personal lives and stories of teachers to construct a vision for teaching and learning?

The process of becoming a teacher is rooted deeply in our personality and experience as a learner. It is not a neutral process, considering the complex relationships between power and knowledge. Inferences can be drawn about the appropriateness of a constructivist model of teaching and learning for education. Critical constructivism offers an approach to identifying and solving problems and can act as a referent with which to gauge beliefs about teaching and learning, but cannot serve as the single ideology that will bring about educational reform. Ultimately a postmodern vision of teacher education must include a critical dimension in which our approach to reconstructing knowledge about the world of teaching is deeply rooted in the social structures of the past, the present, and the future.

And Beyond Modern Education...

When the kids were little, we went to a parents' meeting at their school and I asked the teacher why all her students were geniuses in the second grade? Look at the first grade. Blotches of green and black. Look at the third grade. Camouflage. But the second grade—your grade. Matisses everyone. You've made my child a Matisse. Let me study with you. Let me into second grade! What is your secret? And this is what she said: "Secret? I don't have any secret. I just know when to take their drawings away from them."

Six Degrees of Separation, J. Guare

How many "geniuses" were created when their drawings were taken away? How many teachers have defined and classified their students by weighing accomplishments against their own expectations? Can educators recognize genius? Can they encourage it? Can we go beyond modern education to an understanding that genius carries a stigma that is introduced by the evaluations of society and standardized testing? Is it important to define a genius? Is it possible to encourage genius in even the nongenius? Who is a nongenius? Where do we go from here? How do we allow a child to develop his or her genius unencumbered by outside classifications?

The second grade teacher who knew when to take away the drawings was engaged in creativity control. Modern education cries for such an essentialist point of view—the reduction of creativity and genius into controllable parcels which fit into the expected mold. This essentialism is symptomatic of the cognitive illness which pervades modern education, as it forces us to engage in a constant quest for certainty. Creativity is _____. Intelligence is _____. Students should _____. We are forced to come up with normalized definitions into which we must fit the student. To move beyond this, we have to forsake the need for certainty. We must celebrate ambiguity as we allow children to find their own categories, guided only in a general sense. As postformal educators and students we must lead the revolt against this cognitive illness to emancipate our educational systems.

ON THE OTHER HAND...

Contrasting modern education with postmodern education allows us to weigh the characteristics of both. We deconstruct what is said about modern education and postmodern education and create a space in which to define what is and is not needed in education. Viewing education as tactile, we pull against the tightness of modern education and "go with" the elasticity of the postmodern. The Newtonian-Cartesian restrictions of modernism define what should and should not be taught, and what the expected outcome should be; postmodern educators allow a give and take, never defining what "must be," instead searching with students in a democratic quest which will benefit all. Postmodern education cannot accommodate restrictions; there are no sequenced and linear "ways" to define education. One cannot "pull paradise and put up a parking lot" with knowledge. We do not search for limits and painted lines, rather we search for more questions and multiple meanings as lines become fluid, disconnected, and ever changing.

Modern education uses reason as an absolute for success. Empirically proven formulae, models, and categories darken the lines that define the boundaries of learning. The postmodern teacher encourages the use of intuition, imagery, and metaphor and contextually grounds what is being learned. Reason is not negated in postmodern ways of knowing. Rather, it is redefined and used as a vehicle to examine and enlighten—to disprove or improve upon. The neutral language of reason is replaced with a socially meaningful language, which recognizes power and its effects. Definition is replaced with metaphor and students receive knowledge that is integrally involved with self-production, with their own world.

Instead of a search for answers, postmodern education is engaged in a search for questions. Questions which are divergent rather than convergent; they do not require a certain percentage of right or wrong answers. There are not four categories from which to chose, nothing is keyed to an answer sheet, and everything is negotiable. Knowledge is intimately tied with asking, not answering, and learning becomes insight into what to ask and what asking means. Einstein's theories were not developed by answers; they became reality as they developed from questions about questions.

Modern education is obsessed with the product. Courses are taught around a curriculum that is designed to lead to a final exam. Art is evaluated by a final picture, drama

And Beyond Modern Education...

is concerned with the Christmas play or the all-school musical; songs are learned in music class to be sung at the spring concert; essays are written and rewritten in order to select the best piece for the bulletin board; multiplication tables are timed so that students can do them within a two-minute limit... and so the list goes on. Postmodern education is surrounded by the process. The goal is not to evaluate. In fact there isn't a goal in the traditional sense. Teaching must be concerned with the actual process of learning. Knowledge is active rather than passive, and one does not expect a final product in order to empirically determine whether or not success was achieved. Assessment of the process guides teachers and students to determine what is "next." Assessment in place of evaluation opens up a *whole* view, a look into the "great wide open." By going beyond the goals, definitions, and products of modern education we are empowered by our own understanding of what relating the knower to the known means.

Product orientation is a development from authoritative ways of seeing the world. Schools that are controlled from top-down authority are trapped naturally in a force field of reason, empirical evaluation, and authority. This authority pervades the administration of a school as well as knowledge by demanding the Newtonian-Cartesian authority of science and reason. In postmodern education we develop a critical, emancipatory form of authority, one that allows principals, teachers, parents, and school boards to use a metaperspective to apply social context in order to understand the multiple purposes of schooling. Ideas of "liberal" school reform do not go beyond the force field. However, they still confine themselves to the "outer limits" of knowledge. Critical postmodern reform transcends these limits and becomes limitless and without linear design—cognition is never limited or scientized. Postmodern reform demands a cognitive revolution, by which there is nothing to lose but the shackles now placed upon the imagination. Instead of the modern school, which is the last place one would go for excitement and the romance of learning, a postmodern school is the obvious place to discover and develop multiple intelligences and talents.

WHAT DO CRITICAL POSTMODERN SCHOOLS LOOK LIKE?

We have seen what modern education is, and more importantly, what it is not. Let us sculpt a soft piece of clay that resembles postmodern school reform. What might it look like? In order to present a visual image of our criteria for reform, listed below are thirteen points that would fit well into postmodern visions of schooling. Following this list (which could easily be expanded) is a discussion of each criterion. (Numbering our ideas merely serves to make words more readable; there is no priority in mind.) Our hope is that teachers and students will add and delete from these thirteen points as they explore their own notions of postformal education.

Criteria for Reform

1. School leaders and teachers need to understand what schools are for and why reform is needed.
2. Knowledge is produced in the classroom through the interaction of student experience with information derived from the disciplines.
3. Knowledges and understandings of the world that have previously been devalued and excluded are made useful.
4. Postformal thinking is encouraged.
5. Facts are contextualized.
6. The community and the school must cooperate in all educational endeavors.
7. Learning networks must be built between schools and communities, making use of recent developments and innovations in communications technology.
8. Teachers and students are researchers.
9. Schools become places that support teachers as learners.
10. The inability of orthodox methods of studying education to explain the world of schooling in the late twentieth century is recognized.
11. Genius and intelligence are redefined.
12. Appropriate modes of assessment are developed.
13. The ways that power shapes the everyday life of schools are recognized.

Discussion of Criteria for Reform

1. School leaders and teachers need to understand what schools are for and why reform is needed.

Larry Cuban writes in *How Teachers Taught* (1984) that regardless of *what* reforms have been prevalent in American education, teachers have taught their classes, and administrators have managed their schools in traditional ways. Even after extensive in-service training in new methods and techniques, schools have remained fact-oriented institutions based in linguistic and mathematical logic that are isolated from the outside world and the lives of students. A key term here is "trained." Because they have not been given the professional respect they deserve, teachers have often been *trained* for their roles, not *educated*. In other words, teacher educators have assumed that teachers need only learn how to execute their tasks, much as an assembly-line worker need only learn his or her job. Focusing on training teachers to follow directions, to implement strategies devised by experts of one type or another, teacher educators have neglected to teach teachers the larger social, psychological, and pedagogical understandings that provide a justification for particular ways of teaching.

And Beyond Modern Education...

When teachers revert back to familiar and comfortable ways of teaching, such teacher educators should not be surprised. Of course, many teachers pick up on their own larger understandings, but typically they gain their knowledge with little help from in-service teacher education. Principals, supervisors, and superintendents, like teachers, have not been exposed to the larger understanding that justifies particular educational strategies. Too much of the professional education of school leaders is of a technical variety, focusing on management and effective supervision. What is neglected is the analysis of the role that schools *have* played in the society and the cultivation of a vision of the role schools *could* play in the society. This understanding of the purposes of education should be a central dimension of preservice and in-service teacher and administrator education. Without such grounding, any reform effort will continue to spin its wheels in the sand of the status quo.

2. Knowledge is produced in the classroom through the interaction of student experience with information derived from the disciplines.

Most of our teaching and present efforts for educational reform operate on the assumption that knowledge is an external body of information independent of human beings. Thus, the role of the teacher is to take this knowledge and insert it into the minds of students. The knowledge becomes a body of isolated facts to be committed to memory by generally uninterested students. Evaluation procedures that emphasize retention of isolated bits and pieces of data strengthen this view of knowledge. Conceptual thinking is discouraged; schooling trivializes learning. Students are evaluated on the lowest level of human thinking—the ability to memorize. Thinking skills that involve the ability to ask unique questions, to see connections between concepts, or to apply conceptual understandings are seen as unimportant. The point at which the information of the disciplines intersects with the understandings and experience students carry with them to school is the "zone" in which knowledge is created. The skillful teacher encourages this interaction, helping students to reinterpret their own lives and uncover new talents as the result of their encounter with school knowledge. Unless students are moved to incorporate school information into their own lives, schooling will remain merely unengaging rite of passage into adulthood. Indeed, the social activities will continue to outweigh the classroom activities.

3. Knowledges and understandings of the world that have previously been devalued and excluded are made useful.

Schools unconsciously identify what it means to be educated with the particular social groups. The belief systems, definitions of citizenship, views of success, and histories of these groups are seen and understood as privileged while the perspectives and histories of other groups are devalued. One of the basic criteria of our reform effort is to incorporate the cultural knowledge that all students bring to school into the curriculum. Everyone profits from such understandings: students from the dominant culture gain insights into the struggles of those who are different from themselves—invaluable knowledge in a society that values harmony based on understanding; and students from the dominant cultures gain an appreciation of their heritage—an appreciation that becomes a source of self-respect and the basis on which family and community solidarity can be constructed. As we come to value excluded understandings, we include voices in the school that grant us new perspectives on the world. For example, the foot soldier's perspective on war, a grandmother's perspective on women's history, the union member's perspective on labor management relations, or the freedom marcher's view on race relations provide a perspective from the bottom up instead of the top down. In this way, new questions are raised and new ways of relating to information are created (Kincheloe and Steinberg, 1997).

4. Postformal thinking is encouraged.
Our reform effort seeks to produce self-conscious students who are cognizant of how they have come to think as they do and are aware of the theories of thinking in general. Such students learn about what constitutes postformal thinking as a beginning stage in their attempt to achieve such knowledge. Students who think about thinking in this manner examine the ways that their own assumptions have come to be formed. They seek not only to solve problems but to discover how problems originate. In this way they move beyond the limitations of common sense, as they begin to see beyond the expected. This is what Albert Einstein was able to do, to understand how his thinking about physics was shaped and then to look beyond the official perspectives. In doing so, he recognized relationships between ostensibly unrelated entities such as electromagnetism and gravity. As he exposed these undiscovered relationships, he found keys to unlock mysteries of the physical universe. This is what we want from our students—an awareness of how thinking is shaped—that allows them to move beyond. In order to reach such goals, *teachers must first learn to think about their own thinking*. Only then can such awareness be transferred to students.

5. Facts are contextualized.
A central concept of our notion of school reform involves the idea that educational success does not mean filling students' heads with pieces of information which can be measured on a standardized test. Facts are irrelevant if they are not seen as a part of some

larger context. Einstein in his search for unity displayed this appreciation for the contextualization of facts. He undertook no scientific investigation, no exploration of the physical universe in isolation from the larger attempt to understand the relationship between the components of the universe. While gravity, for example, was originally conceived by Newton as a fascinating, but isolated force, Einstein's conception of gravity revolutionized the way we conceive space. The famous "space as a stretched rubber sheet indented by the stars and planets" has captivated many a young mind with its novel portrayal of the connections between matter, empty space, and gravity. In the spirit of Einstein, teachers must come to understand that no body of facts should ever be taught in isolation. Our reform movement envisions teachers who refuse to teach decontextualized information, who always ask from where data came, and how this information can be used to help students confront the world and understand themselves. We must make every effort to provide teachers with experiences that help them act on such pedagogical understandings.

6. The community and the school must cooperate in all educational endeavors.
The school must take seriously its role as a part of the community. It must draw on *all* constituencies within the community—not just the dominant few. As a school takes seriously its role as a part of the community, it coordinates educational activities within it. In this context teachers and school leaders must become students of their communities who are aware of the multiplicity of educational resources that every community offers. Teachers and students must come to view the community as a mini laboratory for democratic participants. All communities have their successes and their failures, and students and teachers must be encouraged to explore and learn from them. The community's history is extremely important to our reformed schools as students and teachers explore it for its own sake and for its connections to the history of the state, the nation, and the world. It becomes the microcosm through which world events and their effects can be analyzed. Understanding the place we come from and the ways it has shaped our consciousness is an important function of the vibrant schools we envision. Einstein was a student of the communities in which he was reared. Intensely aware of everything from the community's perception of the physical universe to its view of the role of the military to its expectations for schools, Einstein constantly reexamined the impact of such ideas on his own belief systems. It was through this deep understanding of the community that he was empowered to speak about its reform.

7. Learning networks must be built between schools and communities, making use of recent developments and innovations in communications technology.

Teachers are traditionally protective of their own lesson and unit plans. Probably an early trauma occurred the first time that as a student teacher, perhaps daily journals, logs, lesson plan books, and entire unit plans were dissected by the cooperating teacher and methods professor under a frightening microscope called a "conference." When a student finally becomes a teacher there is an instinctive need to keep one's plans private and to share only the tidbits required of faculty lounge conversations. Many teachers love to get "goodies" at conferences and accumulate wonderful plans that may never see the light of day because an hour-long workshop or in-service does not serve to allow authentic conversation about integrating new ideas into the classroom. An ethic of cooperation that includes peer conferences, unit sharing, and proclaiming open season on digging through colleagues' files are ways of networking in a nonthreatening way in order to enhance each other's resources.

Computer networking opens up a new dimension that can link school districts, libraries, and individual schools. Instead of allowing computer banks to languish in the bowels of the resource room, we are empowered by the expansion of sharing information, brainstorming, and asking questions of other educators. Instead of letting dictates from "the top" design our curricula, we must enter into an ongoing conversation with other educators. Teachers need to talk about teaching. Talk about students, "work," and parents is not critical discourse—talk about teaching is. It is important for educators to see themselves as professionals engaged in ongoing conversations about teaching. Engaging the internet with classroom pedagogy can also facilitate these conversations. Students are part of the network because they are able to access technology to communicate with educators and other students. Knowledge becomes kinetic, moving in all directions, unencumbered.

8. Teachers and students are researchers.
If schools are to teach students to think beyond a concrete, rote-based level, we must encourage one of the most important activities that teaches thinking—research. The creation of knowledge to which we referred in criterion one is contingent on our ability to engage teachers and students in research. Not only will teachers as researchers be better able to control their own professional lives, they will also better understand their students' past and present life histories, their concerns, their strengths and weaknesses. Such understandings will enhance their ability to motivate, appreciate, and evaluate their students. As researchers, teachers will gain the skill to question their own practices, question their own assumptions, and to understand contextually their own situations. We are referring here to a higher level of teacher cognition: postformal thinking. Anyone who is able to engage in such activities has moved into a realm of higher-order conceptual

analysis. Based on their research-driven analysis, teachers will be able to develop curricula for their schools, they will be able to research problems and share their findings with other teachers during in-service meetings and team planning sessions, and they will be able to devise methods to bring dignity and intelligence to their self-evaluation procedures.

Students as researchers will become similarly empowered as they learn fieldwork skills: observing, interviewing, photography, video taping, taking notes, and collecting life histories. In the process students will learn and sophisticate the traditional skills we value in curriculum: reading, writing, arithmetic, listening, interpreting, and thinking. Students will learn to uncover the forces that shape their everyday lives—their place in the social hierarchy of their peer group, their romantic relationships, their vocational aspirations, their relationships with teachers. Teacher and student researchers will work together to explore one another's life histories. In this process they will exchange stories of everyday life, their hopes, their fears, their joys, and sadnesses. They will explore one another's dreams and the factors that have worked to interfere with those dreams. Together student and teacher researchers will construct interpretations of various events and their relationship to the community and its larger social and cultural influences. In addition to basic academic skills, students as researchers will learn to derive meaning from themselves and the world around them (Steinberg and Kincheloe, 1998).

9. Schools become places that support teachers as learners.
School leaders and the community must endeavor to make teaching good work—a profession in which teachers are supported in their efforts to carry their knowledge of students, subject matter, the community, and pedagogy to new levels. Understandings of psychological theory, socioeconomic context, and the political outcomes of learning must be viewed as information worth knowing. At all costs the teacher-deskilling that results from standardized-test-driven curriculum, top-down authoritarian management strategies, and prepackaged (teacher-proof) curriculum materials must be avoided. In many present classrooms, teachers have little time for anything more than daily survival—time for further learning, reflection, and analysis seems remote and silly given the low esteem in which they are held, the crisis management atmosphere, and the immediate attention that survival necessitates. In such a climate those who would suggest that more time and resources be delegated to reflective and growth-inducing pursuits are viewed as impractical visionaries devoid of commonsense. Thus, the status quo is perpetuated and the cycle of deskilling rolls on with its culture of low morale. If schools are to be reformed, this cycle must be broken. Teachers must be treated with the respect they are due; they must be supported in their attempts at professional improvement.

10. The inability of orthodox methods of studying education to explain the world of schooling in the late twentieth century is recognized.

After Einstein and the discovery of quantum physics, the use of Newtonian physics was irrelevant in subatomic new contexts. In Newtonian terms, the quantum dimension was unexplainable, an irrational land of mystery where objects instantly transformed themselves from particles to waves, and where matter walked through two doors at once. The "Newtonian" world of education no longer exists. We live in a media-propelled landscape that is markedly different from the world of one-room schoolhouses and quilting bees. Late-twentieth-century education and the society that shapes it are unlike the culture that gave birth to teacher education and the methods for studying education that are still employed. Students are confronted with a world of computers, sound bytes, and sophisticated manipulative strategies directed at consumers and political participants. Much of the research conducted on education fails to take into account the ways that information access and media technologies affect our students and our teachers. In order to capture these effects we need to use new methods of research that have been developed to study media effects. Educational researchers and teachers must move beyond surface appearances to uncover the hidden effects of the technologies of the contemporary era. Using techniques borrowed from anthropology, film studies, literary criticism, and history, we can uncover the subliminal codes, and the unintended effects of computers, television, video games, advertising, earphone stereo systems, and other contemporary influences. Given such realities, we must be open to new ways of doing what educators have traditionally done. Our vision of educational reform refuses to change our strategies for change's sake. Instead, we propose that educational changes undertaken to confront contemporary social and cultural realities be firmly grounded in recent advances in research.

11. Genius and intelligence are redefined.

When Albert Einstein came to the United States after winning the Nobel Prize in Physics, he was already regarded as the most intelligent person in the world, a genius. As he left his ship and walked to the pier in New York, he was confronted by a swarm of reporters. A journalist shouted this question:

> "Dr. Einstein, what is the speed of sound?"
> "I don't know," Einstein replied.
> The baffled journalist responded, "But you're the smartest man in the world. Why don't you know?"
> "I don't need to know," Einstein told the reporter. "I can look it up if I need the information."

The reporter's question reflected the naïveté of the twentieth-century view of intelligence. We still seem to associate it with the mind's capacity to store information. There are forms of intelligence that go beyond this concrete ability to commit information to memory. Indeed, there are forms of intelligence that move beyond what Jean Piaget described as formal thinking.

Schools at the start of the new millennium must redefine intelligence in light of what we have learned about cognition in the last few decades. Howard Gardner's work alerts us to multiple forms of intelligence. In addition to the linguistic and logico-mathematical intelligences that traditional schooling has emphasized, Gardner contends that humans possess musical, spatial, bodily-kinesthetic, intrapersonal, interpersonal, and maybe many more forms of intelligence (Gardner, 1983). The intelligences interact with and build upon one another throughout one's life. Gardner's theory has powerful implications for the reform of schools. If these different forms of intelligences do interact and build upon one another, then it becomes essential that teachers develop the capacity to research their students in order to discover talents. These talents can then be drawn upon to improve a student's skills that are underdeveloped for social or psychological reasons. For example, Einstein's powerful spatial intelligence could have been drawn upon to help his linguistic difficulties, thus releasing him from his miserable experience in school. While many reasons exist for us to move beyond the standardized-test-driven curriculum that has emerged from the reforms of the last decade, few are more compelling than the arguments offered by those who point out the tests' neglect of a range of human intelligences (Kincheloe, Steinberg, and Villaverde, 1999).

12. Appropriate modes of assessment are developed.
Many critics of school reform may fear that a "cognitive revolution" will not include methods of assessing how "well" a student is doing. There are complaints that reform will lead to "touchy-feely" schooling that does not prepare or qualify students for adulthood—that students will "get out" of having to take standardized tests that really show how they are doing. Proponents of modern methods of evaluation demand definitions, categories, and a delimiting use of knowledge. For them, students must be shaped to meet the characteristics of the evaluation—squished, stuffed, and pushed into a bordered category that displays ranks and percentages.

The use of an elastic approach to schooling—divergent thinking, asking questions, intuitive teaching, socially constructed languages of metaphor and imagery—does not negate an ability to assess students and their progress. Students in critical, emancipatory classrooms have a voice in their own assessment. Their progress is assessed by their own abilities and aptitudes, not ranked against national norms and standardized tests.

Assessment in a postformal classroom allows students to show what they can do, they are assessed on *what they know*, not *what they don't know*. Postformal assessment is a situational form of evaluation in that it takes into account the context in which the learner has operated to produce knowledge.

13. The ways that power shapes the everyday life of schools are recognized.
Power operates in school by muzzling the very people it sets out to empower through education. In modern schools we don't learn how curricular knowledge is produced. In modern teacher education we don't ask which social voices are represented in the curriculum and which voices are excluded. Reform proposals view teaching as a narrow practice, a technique that has little, if anything, to do with knowledge production or the analysis of questions of ethics or justice. How does schooling contribute to the production of our identities, our self-concepts, our ability to function in the world? Does it matter that we come from rich or poor homes, white or nonwhite homes? These questions are not recognized as questions about power—indeed, they are often not recognized at all. The idea that school is a social practice that operates within a society characterized by unequal power relations is simply not a part of the public discourse about schooling.

In a school reform that goes beyond modern education, that is grounded in a critical postmodern social vision, these questions of power are central. As schools confront the subtle forms of racism, sexism, and class bias that keep the disempowered powerless, educators will begin to understand the emancipatory force of postformal thinking—the sociocognitive orientation that attunes us to questions of power and the insidious ways that power is unequally distributed in schools. Einstein, like "different" students of all stripes and in all eras, was crushed by the grand power narratives of intelligence and success that existed in the Germany of his boyhood. The pain of his disempowerment festered in him throughout his life, expressing itself in a passion for democracy. Critical postmodern educators have inherited this democratic passion. In the postmodern world, with its hyperreality of multiple representations and exploding images, passion is necessary but insufficient in the quest for social justice in education. Beginning with our passion we learn to decode the power codes, the repressive ways in which ideological interests invade not only the schools but the popular culture as well. Our postformal concern with reading the world as text reemerges at this point, impressing us with its ability to expose the invisible workings of postmodern power. Teachers who are concerned with democracy must possess these deconstructive abilities in the twenty-first century if we are to help children understand where they are in the web of sociopolitical reality. If schooling is to empower its students rather than muzzle them, our work as lovers of democracy is set out for us. The journey beyond modern education, on which Einstein was a pioneer, has begun.

BUT HOW DO WE ANSWER THE CHALLENGES?

In our work of school reform, it is simply not enough to articulate an educational vision. We must anticipate the arguments of those that oppose a postformal school reform. We find that the following arguments are often presented to oppose critical school reform:

1. School leaders and teachers need to understand what schools are for and why reform is needed.

The Challenge

Few would make overtly the argument that school leaders and teachers don't need to understand what schools are for and why reform is needed. The way in which the challenge to this proposal often manifests itself is not with an explicit confrontation but in institution of reform procedures that consist of top-down sets of guidelines that must be followed. This all takes place in a context where lip service is given to the need for the participation of teachers and administrators. The language of inclusion and democracy is frequently invoked. A classroom teacher recently remarked that his school's reform effort consisted of allowing teachers to take part in decision making. His first decision was between blue and mauve—what color to paint the teachers' lounge.

The Postformal Response

The only way to counter such a challenge is to demand constantly that authorities show how teachers and administrators are included, that they understand how the reforms that are planned match the practitioners' perceptions of the purposes of schools and the reasons the reform is needed. We have found that because teachers have traditionally been removed from discussions of school purpose they need help to understand the contextual factors that have brought about the need for change. Thus, an important portion of a reform package may involve the provision of institutes for practitioners to encourage them to think through the purposes of their institutions.

2. Knowledge is produced in the classroom through the interaction of student experience with information derived from the disciplines.

The Challenge

The common argument issued against the idea that knowledge is created in the classroom involves the epistemological assumption that knowledge is "out there" and simply needs to be inserted into the passive minds of students. This is the way that we have always done it and we see no reason to change now. The great ideas have been established, and tradition dictates that these great ideas be passed along to the next generation. Adler's *Great Books* and Hirsch's *Cultural Literacy* give us the guidelines to perpetuate our culture, our canon.

The Postformal Response
The implications of the argument that knowledge is simply "out there" must be explored. If we accept this notion, then instruction is trivialized and the teacher becomes little more than a conduit through which ideas may pass on their way to students. No purpose is served by educating thoughtful, knowledgeable teachers if they simply insert existing knowledge into the minds of students. Questions of social context and power are irrelevant. The "genius" of great thinkers has not involved their ability to retain the information they encountered, but has revolved around their ability to produce new knowledge. When school operates at a postformal level, knowledge is produced by the collision of student experience with the information of the disciplines. This does not mean that traditional knowledge is thrown into the garbage heap of history. We may indeed reexamine what constitutes traditional knowledge, the traditional canon, but we also recognize value in that which others have produced. The salient point here is that we interrogate this knowledge and think about it in light of new contexts and new questions. Such analysis is an important step in the creation of new knowledge, as it precludes the simple concrete-level "mastery" of secondhand data.

3. Knowledges and understandings of the world that have previously been devalued and excluded are made useful.

The Challenge
Why would we want to know such "inferior" and "un-American" ways of seeing, opponents ask. The arguments invoked in response to this reform criterion can become quite ugly in their Anglocentrism, racism, and sexism. Opponents typically argue that this is a European, Christian nation that requires a common culture to unite us.

The Postformal Response
The greatness of this country involves the wide diversity of peoples who have settled here across the centuries. We are indeed a Christian country—but we are also a Jewish country, a Muslim country, an agnostic country, and an atheist country. Indeed, the diversity of beliefs among Christians is so great that any precise meaning of what "a Christian coun-

try" means is impossible. We do not envision a nation of religious and ethnic enclaves, each separate and hostile to one another. Such was the case in the past and one need only see the ugliness of such a system—from the Salem witch trials to the burning of crosses by the Ku Klux Klan. Instead, we see a nation united by the concept of difference; a predisposition to seek solidarity through our desire to learn from one another. Solidarity is not achieved through consensus only. With our cultural diversity as a great American attribute, why not play to our strength? We must draw inspiration from and build our curricula and our ways of seeing around our differences. Modernity seeks to melt difference, to make us "all the same." Postmodernity celebrates difference and enhances our realities by these differences, making them equally valid.

4. Postformal thinking is encouraged.

The Challenge
Such proposals are simple attempts to politicize cognition and thus undermine the neutral role of the school. The school has no business asking how facts become certified—we are not there to judge the facts, we are there to teach and learn them.

The Postformal Response
We must learn to think about the nature of the political. All forms of cognition have political implications. For that matter, all educational decisions are in some way political. This is not wrong, it is simply the nature of the beast. Just as Whom do we teach? What do we teach? and How do we teach it? are political questions in that they involve dimensions of power, the question of How do we think? is a political question as well. For example, take what Piaget calls concrete and formal thinking. Concrete thinking involves the ability to commit information to our memory and formal thinking involves the ability to utilize formal particular procedures as we attempt to solve the problems that confront us. If the school does not transcend these forms of thinking, particular political solutions will be privileged over others. We will not learn to deconstruct the unspoken dimensions of particular political processes such as racism or sexism, which often operate most effectively in unspoken and encoded ways. Thus, if we fail to think at a postformal level, particular forms of power will tend to remain unquestioned and unchallenged. The ways which power shapes our consciousness and molds our belief structures will elude our awareness. All forms of thinking hold political implications. The question is not about how to keep politics out of education, but about *which* political disposition is most consistent with principles of democracy, egalitarianism, and justice.

5. Facts are contextualized.

The Challenge
How can we possibly worry about the contextualization of facts when students are not learning the facts they are now presented? These criteria of reform are unrealistic pronouncements of ivory tower dreamers. They sound good but they will never work.

The Postformal Response
The reason that students are often unmotivated now (and have been in the past) is the direct result of this decontextualization. When facts are presented as isolated fragments of data to be inserted in an orderly manner into the mind, the raison d'être for learning is undermined. Only when learning makes sense, when it is understood in the context of their own lived experiences, will students become motivated to learn. When information is decontextualized, no way exists to create knowledge in the classroom. This creation of knowledge is a key to alleviating the crisis of motivation that plagues our schools. The critics are operating with an inverted logic. Rendered cynical as a result of contact with unmotivated students, they reject the very points of reform that aim to restore meaning and thus enhance motivation. Theirs is the unrealistic argument that students will be motivated to learn a body of abstract, unconnected facts; it is a pipe dream.

6. The community and the school must cooperate in the educational endeavor.

The Challenge
Many would see this statement as an insult to an already "pleasant" school-community relationship. Arguments that the school has an active PTA and that parents are busy with fund-raising and carnivals will fall upon critical reformers' ears. Many schools maintain a good public relations image within their community; they may even cite awards as "model schools" and show volumes of newspaper clippings about the performances and rewards of their students and teachers. Many schools hold open houses and invite the community to come and view the classrooms and bulletin boards (put up especially for the open house). Parents are often invited to attend classes "any time you would like," yet very few ever take a teacher up on the offer. Why do parents feel uncomfortable in the classroom? What were their own school experiences?

The Postformal Response
Public relations and strong parent group involvement do not equal an authentic involvement. Rewards by state officials who come in to a school with a predetermined checklist

do not stand up to critical light. As postformal schools become empowered with critical viewpoints about schooling, so also should parents and community officials. Authentic involvement may consist of parent-student writing nights, in which parents come into classrooms, write along with their children, and then engage in a discussion about their writing. Community participation in the form of open forums about race or gender relations is essential to a well-informed group of parents. Parents and community members should feel that they are not only welcome in the schools, but that they play an important part in the process of schooling. Mentor programs are an excellent way to encourage authentic community involvement. Utilizing parents as speakers within the classroom is also an important way to integrate the community and school. Parents are more valuable as partners in the learning experience than as committee members for selling peanuts in the fall fund-raiser. New bulletin boards and open houses are not enough in postmodern educational reform.

7. Learning networks must be built between schools and communities, making use of recent developments and innovations in communications technology.

The Challenge
If the purpose of schooling is to teach the basics, then what does the community have to do with teaching the curriculum? Communities should support schools through fund-raising and activities, but there is no purpose for any other involvement. Computers are to be used for calculations and in learning centers. Of course, every student should learn to use computers and to "surf" the internet.

The Postformal Response
If one defines school as a place to learn the basics and to prepare a student for a "job," then there is no need for intrinsic relationships between communities and school. However, when one examines school as an extension of the community, the reflection of a multiplicity of different attitudes and cultures, then there is a critical need to join the school and community to create an understanding of all of the forces that shape our students. Instead of being a financial support (through donations and fund-raising drives), and a ready audience for performances, the community and school can join in a critical partnership of mutual conversation about what is needed in postmodern education. Community School Programs, where a school becomes a literal extension of the community, promote authentic partnerships. Adopt-a-school or a-classroom programs, community centers within the school, and city-school newspapers are other ways of utilizing and sharing.

Computers are not just vehicles for getting a better-paying job. It is not enough to use the net and send e-mail. A critical understanding of media and computers leads to students learning how to critically apply the production of technology with knowledge. I am reminded of a discussion with a woman who was buying a computer for her son. She remarked that she knew nothing about computers, that they were a mystery to her. After further discussion, she mentioned that she worked all day inputting data at the telephone company. She laughed at the realization that even though her permanent vocation was with a computer, she knew absolutely nothing about it. Students who are truly "literate" with technology enter into a world without boundaries around the potential of what they can do to manipulate and add to the technology. Computers are to be used and extended, not to be viewed as a way to learn another skill—another "basic." Critical media literacy teaches us to understand not only how to use a computer, but the implications of this technology on our lives (Semali and Pailliotet, 1998).

8. Teachers and students are researchers.

The Challenge
Teachers simply are incapable of engaging in such a sophisticated activity. With all the other responsibilities that teachers have to face in their professional lives, we are simply setting them up for failure when we ask them to become researchers. It will never work.

The Postformal Response
Given the prevailing structure of the schools, the critics make good points. One aspect of the power of the teachers-as-researchers proposal is that it necessitates the restructuring of the school workplace. One of the unfortunate dimensions of modern schooling is that teachers are deskilled. We expect teachers to think at such a low level. The idea of teachers engaging in sophisticated classroom research does not fit with the picture of teachers painted in technicist teacher education programs and in the in-service education fostered by school districts. This is the degraded picture of teachers found in the minds of politicians who approve the top-down reform legislation that has dominated the schools of the late twentieth century. Critical postmodern reform demands that we reconceptualize our picture of deskilled teachers. It demands that we restructure the workplace to accommodate professionals who have sophisticated skills such as research. Teachers must be given the freedom and the time to reflect on their practice—we will have to convince the public to pay for that right.

9. Schools become places that support teachers as learners.

The Challenge

Schools are for students. Teachers have already had their education. We already have four in-services a year, and try to give our teachers preparation time—a half an hour each day. Most schools cannot afford these reform efforts—once a teacher finishes college, they should be ready to teach. One can't be taking courses forever. Teacher education programs should reflect the reality of teaching. Student teachers should enter the school ready to work one hundred percent of the time; they need to know *what it is really like* to be a teacher.

The Postformal Response

Teaching is often viewed as a "eight to three" job, including a three-month vacation. Teachers are not considered professionals. The factory metaphor dominates the modern view of teaching. One "punches" in and spends the day in the classroom. Teachers are often seen as workers who "have it easy." "You have all summer off, and Christmas and Easter as well. Teachers don't know what it is like to *really* work."

For most teachers, preparation periods serve as a time to catch up on grading, recording marks, and duplicating exams and work sheets. There are not many teachers who have time during a normal day to upgrade their own work, or to study the newest research on education. Teachers must become reflective practitioners; people who are respected as professionals and who constantly seek to learn more about teaching and knowledge. A nonreflective orientation undermines all aspects of the educational enterprise. In the student teaching phase of teacher education, for example, the experience is often viewed as a trial to see if the student can "really handle it." Such practicum experiences should provide the opportunity for student teachers to mature as reflective practitioners. In-service meetings of a day or two do not traditionally have a lasting effect. Teachers are usually so glad to get out of the classroom that workshops serve as a release. Many teachers leave workshops with exuberant ideas and commitments to changing their methods and curriculum, only to find that the heavy dose of an "Amway" approach to teaching leaves a let-down when the chants and vows wear off.

Teaching must become a profession. Schools cannot afford not to find authentic and lasting ways to allow teachers as professionals to upgrade and continue their education. Teachers need to talk about teaching. Attempts to upgrade education should not be based on a higher pay scale, but the knowledge that continuing research and critical reflection leads to the emancipation that a postformal teacher must have.

10. The inability of orthodox methods of studying education to explain the world of schooling in the late twentieth century is recognized.

The Challenge
The objection to the use of new research methods to study the postmodern socioeducational reality is very simple: we need precise, scientific tools of measurement to answer the important questions about education. The tools proposed by the critical postmodernists are unscientific devices that produce unverified knowledge. Modern statistics and psychometric research have devised ways of precisely measuring most anything in the world of education. If we are to do our jobs as educators effectively, we need their precision.

The Postformal Response
Statistics and psychometric research have failed in their attempts to produce knowledge that is germane to the lives of educational practitioners. Because not all educational questions lend themselves to quantification, such methods are limited to particular types of questions—often questions involving the most trivial aspects of schooling. Questions of consciousness, of power, of self-production almost always will be ignored by empirical research. If we have any hope of understanding the impact of schools on our students or the role that schools play in the constructions of their consciousness or the relationship between school and society, we will have to expand our research vocabulary to include both qualitative and quantitative methods.

11. Genius and intelligence are redefined.

The Challenge
Cultural traditions, the dominance of empirical research methods, and the power of discursive practices will form the basis of the challenge to the critical postmodern attempt to redefine intelligence. Modern Western societies have been privileged with logico-mathematical and linguistic forms of intelligence for several centuries. When this cultural tendency is coupled with the dominance of research methods that are capable of measuring only logico-mathematical and linguistic intelligence, the possibility for a redefinition of what constitutes genius is rendered remote. Add to these factors the realization that such limited perspectives are embedded in our language; we have developed very little language that would aid our attempt to reconceptualize intelligence. While forms of overt opposition would be expressed, the most damaging opposition would involve these tacit structural forces.

The Postformal Response
Once again the value of nonempirical, qualitative forms of inquiry is demonstrated. To reveal the structural forces that shape our views of education, we must employ ethnographic, historiographic, phenomenological, and semiotic forms of research. Postformal

educators must be able to show those who are interested that it is not a logical argument that undermines our efforts to transcend modern cognitive barriers. Through our innovative research strategies critical postmodernists will reveal the ways in which power and tradition operate to squash emancipatory cognitive innovation. Through these same research methods, we will have to prove that individuals who come from outside the white, male, middle-class mainstream are punished by the limited ways that intelligence is presently defined. Postformal educators will have to convincingly articulate the idea that ways of thinking exist that go beyond Piagetian formality. To be convincing, we will have to demonstrate specific ways of thinking that can be used to improve the human condition.

12. Appropriate modes of assessment are developed.

The Challenge
Standardized tests are the only fair way to evaluate students. Charges of test bias are absurd. The Educational Testing Service and The College Board have performed extensive analyses of the tests and have eliminated questions that were biased.

We need to specify precisely what students need to know and then check to see if they know it. We need to specify precisely what teachers need to do and then check to see if they are doing it. We already know what it is that students need to learn. The new forms of evaluation, like portfolios and student teacher-created assessments, muddle the issue and shift our focus from that which is important.

The Postformal Response
Evaluation procedures utilized in contemporary schools simply fail to take into account social, cultural, and economic factors which position students in the web of reality. It is not simply a manifestation of intelligence that a student from a two-parent, white, upper-middle-class home, who has traveled extensively, has been read to nightly, and has a home full of books and learning games scores highly on a elementary-level standardized test. Such a performance also reflects the experience this child has had with language, his or her understanding of the importance of test-taking procedures, and the value of schooling generally. To compare this student's "intelligence" with a child of poverty's simply on the results of the test is the height of naïveté. The tendency toward social decontextualization is a manifestation of the cognitive illness. Because of his early-childhood language disability, Einstein would never have scored highly on standardized tests. The characteristics that the world used to label him as a genius would have never been tapped into by such evaluation procedures.

The centralization of the testing industry in the twentieth century represents society's blindness to the diversity of expression of intelligence, its regional flavors, its multi-dimensionality. The unfortunate aspect of this narrow view involves its condemnation of the economically, culturally, and (in Einstein's case) the psychologically different. The very characteristics that have fueled genius historically are ignored by these tests.

When students and teachers together design methods of assessment, students enter into a democratic partnership that gives them personal ownership of their educational expectations. Assessment is not an isolated device which serves to alienate the student from knowledge, but an extension of the process of learning. The only way to measure qualities and talents traditionally attributed to genius is to allow students to express what they know, not what they don't know.

13. The ways that power shapes the everyday life of schools are recognized.

The Challenge
Many will argue that reality is what we can see and that power operates in an overt, linear, cause-and-effect manner. The progeny of the Enlightenment remain uncomfortable with the critical position that we must penetrate surface appearances if we are ever going to understand reality. As a result, traditionalists will scoff at the postmodern portrayal of the covert operation of power in the educational process.

The Postformal Response
In the response to so many of these traditionalist challenges, it becomes extremely important for postformal educators to confront the way that reality is typically portrayed. As critical postmodernists go beneath the surface to illustrate the hidden ways that the forces of race, class, and gender shape an individual's educational experiences or how discursive practices bind us to particular constructions of our lives and the world, they must formulate accessible and convincing ways to communicate this information to those concerned with educational reform. Until postformal teachers are able to convince the public that to "know" is to understand power configurations such as, How is knowledge validated? Who has the opportunity to know it and who doesn't? and Why is some knowledge dismissed as unworthy? all of our talk about tacit manifestations of power will remain mysterious and irrelevant.

RESUSCITATING OUR SCHOOLS

In 1938, Einstein wrote that "knowledge exists in two forms—lifeless, stored in books, and alive in the consciousness of men" (Einstein, 1938). Einstein intuitively understood one of the cardinal tenets of our attempt to escape modern education: the schools effectively destroy the will to learn by treating knowledge as a prepackaged commodity, to be memorized and recited just as items are bought and sold in the market. The Einsteinian flame of curiosity and rebellion against deadening convention has burned at one time in all of us. In the cognitive revolution we promote, this flame can ignite our schools into a reassessment of their policies. In the process, we must find out how educational leaders allow the flame in their lives to be doused by the unholy water of the modern schools. Why are they so vulnerable to the cognitive illness?

When we listen to the TV talk shows about educational reform, we are told we need to try harder, to commit more community time to education, to allow business leaders to serve as educators, and to promote educational quality and educational excellence. Amid the flurry of these discussions with experts, few concrete proposals for school reform are heard. Americans are befuddled by the school crisis that faces them. Blinded by Newtonian-Cartesian frameworks of reality, political leaders don't know where to begin the process of reform. Albert Einstein's sacred intuition provides the light in the darkness.

References

Adelman, K., & Adelman, H. (1987). Rodin, Patton, Edison, Wilson, Einstein: Were they really learning disabled? *Journal of Learning Disabilities, 20* (5), 270–79.

Albert, R. S. (1974, February). Toward behavioral definition of genius. *American Psychologist*, 140–151.

Arnheim, R. (1969). *Visual thinking*. Berkeley, CA: University of California Press.

Aronowitz, S. (1973). *False Promises*. New York: McGraw-Hill.

———. (1989). The new conservative discourse. In H. Holtz et.al. (Eds.), *Education and the American dream*. Granty, MA: Bergin and Garvey.

Aronowitz, S. And H. Giroux (1991). *Postmodern Education: Politics, culture, and social criticism*. Minneapolis: University of Minnesota Press.

Becker, G. (1978). *The mad genius controversy: A study in the sociology of deviance*. Thousand Oaks: Sage Publications, Inc.

———. (1979, August). Two developments in the rise of the modern intellectual. *School Review*. The University of Chicago, 398–411.

Belenky, M., Clinchy, B., Goldberger, N., & Tarule, J. (1986). *Women's ways of knowing: The development of self, voice, and mind*. New York: Basic Books.

Besag, F. (1986). Striving after the wind. *American Behavioral Scientist, 30* (1), 15–22.

Best, D. (1979). *Expression in movement and the arts; A philosophical inquiry*. London: Lepus.

Bigelow, W. (1990). Inside the classroom: Social visions and critical pedagogy. In S. Tozer, T. Anderson and B. Armbruster (Eds.), *Foundational studies in teacher education: A re-examination.* New York: Teachers College Press.

Black, M. (1962). *Models and metaphors: Studies in language and philosophy.* Ithaca: Cornell University Press.

Bloom, A. (1987). *The closing of the American mind.* New York: Simon and Schuster.

Bohm, D., & Peat, F. (1987). *Science, order, and creativity.* New York: Bantam Books.

Briggs, J., & Peat, F. (1984). *Looking glass universe: The emerging science of wholeness.* New York: Touchstone.

———. (1989). *Turbulent mirror.* New York: Harper and Row Publishers.

Briggs, J. (1990). *Fire in the crucible.* Los Angeles: Jeremy Tarcher, Inc.

Britzman, D. (1991). *Practice makes practice: A critical study of learning to teach.* Albany, NY: State University of New York Press.

Buck-Morss, S. (1975). Socio-economic bias in Piaget's theory and its implications for crosscculture studies. *Human Development,* 18, 35–49.

Burich, K. (1987). The moral and philosophical origins and implications of relativity. In D. Ryan (Ed.), *Einstein and the humanities.* New York: Greenwood Press.

Calder, N. (1988). *Einstein's universe.* New York: Viking Press.

Calinescu, M. (1987). *Five faces of modernity: Modernism, avante-garde, decadence, kitsch, post-modernism.* Durham, NC: Duke University Press.

Callahan, R. (1962). *Education and the cult of efficiency.* Chicago: University of Chicago Press.

Carr, W., & Kemmis, S. (1986). *Becoming critical: Education knowledge and action research.* Philadelphia: Falmer Press.

Central Elementary School Letter, September 17, 1990.

Clark, B. (1983). *Growing up gifted.* Columbus, OH: Charles E. Merrill Publishing, Co.

Clark, R. (1971). *Einstein: The life and times.* New York: Avon Books.

Cobern, W. (1991). *Contextual constructivism: The impact of culture on the learning and teaching of science.* Paper presented to the National Association for Research in Science Teaching, Lake Geneva, NY.

Cochran-Smith, M. (1991). Learning to teach against the grain. *Harvard Educational Review,* 61 (3), 279–309.

Combs, A., & Holland, M. (1990). *Synchronicity: Science, myth, and the trickster.* New York: Paragon House.

Courtney, R. (1988). *No one way of being: A study of the practical knowledge of elementary arts teachers.* Toronto: MGS Publications.

Cuban, L. (1984). *How teachers taught.* White Plains, NY: Longman Inc.

Culler, J. (1982). *On deconstruction: Theory and criticism after structuralism*. Ithaca, NY: Cornell University Press.

———. (1981). *The pursuit of signs: Semiotics, literature, deconstruction*. Ithaca, NY: Cornell University Press.

Danesi, M., & Mollica, A. (1988). From right to left: A "bimodal" perspective on language teaching. *Canadian Modern Language Review*, 45 (1), 76–90.

Davies, P., & Gribbin, J. (1992). *The matter myth: Dramatic discoveries that challenge our understanding of physical reality*. New York: Simon and Schuster.

Doyle, D. (1989). Education, excellence, and the free market. In H. Holtz, et.al., (Eds.), *Education and the American dream*. Granley, MA: Bergin and Garvey.

Driver, R. (1989). The construction of scientific knowledge in school classrooms. In R. Millar (Ed.), *Doing science: Images of science in science education*. London: Falmer Press.

Einstein, A. (1934, July 3). To National Council of supervisors of Elementary Science. *Einstein Papers*. Princeton University.

———. (1938). Remarks about class year book, The Elm Tree. *Einstein Papers*. Princeton University.

———. (1948, January 3). To Wallace Spears. *Einstein Archives*. Princeton University.

———. (1950). To Peter Van Dore. *Einstein Papers*. Princeton University.

———. (1951a, June 19). To O. John Rogge. *Einstein Papers*. Princeton University.

———. (1951b, November 9). To Lt. J. G. Guy, H. Raner, Jr. *Einstein Papers*. Princeton University.

———. (1952a, October 5). Transcript of Interview by Benjamin Fine. *Einstein Papers*. Princeton University.

———. (1952b, March). Message to the Ben Schemen Dinner. *Einstein Papers*. Princeton University.

———. (1952c, January 28). To Archibald Watson, *Einstein Papers*, Princeton University.

———. (1954, March 3). *Einstein Papers*. Princeton University.

———. (1954a, January 16). Notes on Black Mountain College. *Einstein Papers*. Princeton University.

———. (1954b, May 14). To Simon W. Heimlich. *Einstein Papers*. Princeton University.

———. (1959). *Ideas and opinions*. New York.

———. (1970). Autobiographical notes. In P. Schilpp (Ed.), *Albert Einstein: Philosopher-Scientist*. LaSalle, Illinois.

Eisner, E. (1983). Anastasia might still be alive, but the monarchy is dead. *Educational Researcher*, 12, 13–14, 23–24.

Fee, E. (1982). Is feminism a threat to scientific objectivity? *International Journal of Women's Studies, 4,* 378–92.

Ferguson, M. (1980). The aquarian conspiracy: Personal and social transformation in our time. Los Angeles: J. P. Tarcher, Inc.

Ferris, T. (1988). *Coming of age in the Milky Way.* New York: William Morrow and Company, Inc.

Fiske, D. (1986). Specificity of method and knowledge in social science. In D. Fiske, and R. Shweder, *Metatheory in social science: Pluralisms and subjectivities.* Chicago: University of Chicago Press.

Fleming, R. (1987). Einstein and the limits of reason. In D. Ryan, *Einstein and the humanities.* New York: Greenwood Press.

Fosnot, C. (1988). *The dance of education.* Paper presented to the Annual Conference of the Association for Educational Communication and Technology, New Orleans.

———. (1990). *Enquiring teachers, enquiring learners.* New York: Teachers College Press.

Foucault, M. (1977). *Language, Counter-memory, practice,* edited by F. Bouchard. Ithaca, NY: Cornell University Press.

Fox, R. (1989). What is a meta for? *Clinical Social Work Journal, 17* (3), 233–44.

Frankel, B. (1986). Two extremes on the commitment continuum. In D. Fiske and R. Shweder, *Metatheory in social science: Pluralisms and subjectivities.* Chicago: University of Chicago Press.

Freire, P. (1990). *Pedagogy of the oppressed.* New York: The Continuum Publishing Company.

———. (1970). *Pedagogy of the oppressed.* New York: Continuum

French, A. (1979). *Einstein: A centenary volume.* London: Heinemann.

Frye, C. (1987). Einstein and African religion and philosophy: The hermetic parallel. In D. Ryan, *Einstein and the humanities.* New York: Greenwood Press.

Gallagher, J. J. (1975). *Teaching the gifted child.* Boston, MA: Allyn and Bacon, Inc.

Ganyadean, A. (1987). Ontological relativity: A metaphysical critique of Einstein's thought. In D. Ryan, *Einstein and the humanities.* New York: Greenwood Press.

Gardner, H. (1983). *Frames of mind: The theory of multiple intelligences.* New York: Basic Books, Inc.

Garman, N. & Hazi, H. (1988). Teachers ask: Is there life after Madeline Hunter? *Phi Delta Kappan, 6,* 670–72.

Gerard, A. (1966). *An Essay on Genius.* B. Fabian, Ed., Reprint, Wilhelm Fink Verlag, Munich.

References

Ginsburg, M. (1988). *Contradictions in teacher education and society*. Philadelphia: The Falmer Press.

Giroux, H. (1989). Educational reform and teacher empowerment. In H. Holtz, et al., (Ed.), *Education and the American Dream*. Granby, MA: Bergin and Garvey.

———. (1989). Rethinking education reform in the age of George Bush. *Phi Delta Kappan*, 728–30.

———. (1991). Introduction: Modernism, postmodernism, and feminism: Rethinking, the boundaries of educational discourse. In H. Giroux, *Postmodernism, Feminism, and Cultural Politics: Redrawing Educational Boundaries*. Albany: New York State University of New York Press.

———. (1988). *Schooling and the struggle for public life*. Minneapolis: University of Minnesota Press.

———. (1988). *Teachers as intellectuals: Toward a critical pedagogy of learning*. Granby, MA: Bergin and Garvey.

Giroux, H., & McLaren, P. (1989). Introduction: Schooling, cultural politics, and the struggle for democracy. In H. Giroux and P. McLaren, *Critical pedagogy, the state, and cultural struggle*. Albany, NY: State University of New York Press.

Goertzel, V., & Goertzel, N. (1962). *Cradles of eminence*. Boston: Little, Brown.

Gordon, E., Miller, F., & Rollock, D. (1990). Coping with communicentric bias in knowledge production in the social sciences. *Educational Researcher*, *19* (3), 14–19.

Gramsci, A. (1988). *An Antonio Gramsci reader*. In Forgacs, D. (Ed.), New York: Schocken Books.

Groisman, A., Shapiro, B., & Willinsky, J. (1990). *The potential of semiotics to inform understanding of events in science education*.

Grumet, M. (1988). *Bitter milk: Women and teaching*. Amherst, MA: University of Massachusetts Press.

———. (1995). The curriculum: What are the basics and are we teaching them? In J. Kincheloe & S. Steinberg, *Thirteen questions: Reframing education's conversation*. 2nd ed. New York: Peter Lang.

Guare, J. (1990). *Six degrees of separation*. New York: Vintage Books.

Guilford, J. P. (1986). *Creative talents: Their nature, uses, and development*. Buffalo, NY: Bearly Limited.

Hardison, O. (1989). *Disappearing through the skylight: Culture and technology in the twentieth century*. New York: Penguin Books.

Haring, N. G., & McCormick, L. (Eds.). (1986). *Exceptional children and youth*. Columbus, OH: Charles E. Merrill Publishing Co.

Hauptman, R., & Hauptman, I. (1987). The circuitous path: Albert Einstein and the epistemology of fiction. In D. Ryan, *Einstein and the humanities*. New York: Greenwood Press.

Hawking, S. (1989). *Foundation for science and the handicapped newsletter, 13,* 5–6.

Hebridge, D. (1989). *Hiding in the light.* New York: Routledge.

Held, D. (1980). *Introduction to critical theory: Horkheimer to Habermas.* Berkeley, CA: University of California Press.

Heshusius, L. (1982). At the heart of the advocacy dilemma: A mechanistic worldview. *Exceptional Children, 49* (1), 6–11.

———. (1989). *Holism, or: There is no substitute for real life purposes and processes.* Paper presented at the Preconvention Training Program, CFC's 6th Annual Convention, San Francisco.

Hodge, R., & Kress, G. (1988). *Social semiotics.* Ithaca, NY: Cornell University Press.

Hoffman, B., & Dukas, H. (1972). *Albert Einstein: Creator and rebel.* New York: The Viking Press.

Holton, G. (1979). What Precisely is "Thinking"? Einstein's Answer. *The Physics Teacher, 17,* 157–60.

———. (1972). On trying to understand scientific genius. *The American Scholar, 16,* 91–108.

Howe, K. (1985). Two dogmas of educational research. *Educational Researcher, 14,* 10–18.

Hutcheon, L. (1988). *A poetics of postmodernism.* New York: Routledge.

Inge, K. (1990). *The experience of a supervising teacher: A biographical ethnography of a high school science teacher.* Unpublished master's thesis, Tallahassee, Florida State University.

Jaki, S. (1987). The absolute beneath the relative: Reflections on Einstein's theories. In D. Ryan, *Einstein and the Humanities.* New York: Greenwood Press.

James, M., & Ebbutt, D. (1981). Problems and potential. In J. Nixon, (Ed.), *A teachers' guide to action research.* London: Grant McIntyre.

Janson, H. W., & Janson, D. J. (1966). *The story of painting.* New York: Harry N. Abrams, Inc., Publishers.

Johnson, J. A., Collins, H. W., Victor, L. D., & Johnansen, J. H. (1988). *Introduction to the foundations of American education.* Needham Heights, MA: Allyn and Bacon, Inc.

Jones, R. (1951, July 7). Editorial. *Tulsa Tribune.*

Kagan, D., & Tippins, D. (1991). Helping student teachers attend to student cues. *The Elementary School Journal, 91* (4), 343–56.

Kegan, R. (1982). *The evolving self: Problem and process in human development*. Cambridge, MA: Harvard University Press.

Kincheloe, J. (1991). *Teachers as researchers: Qualitative inquiry as a path to empowerment*. Bristol, PA: Falmer Press.

———. (1992). Introduction: The questions we ask, the stories we tell. In J. Kincheloe and S. Steinberg (Eds.), *Thirteen questions: Reframing education's conversation*. New York: Peter Lang.

———. (1993). *Toward a critical politics of teacher thinking: Mapping the postmodern*. Westport, CT: Bergin and Garvey.

———. (1995). *Toil and Trouble: Good work, smart workers, and the integration of academic and vocational education*. New York: Peter Lang.

———. (1996). "The New Childhood: Home Alone as a way of life." *Cultural Studies*, 1, pp. 221–40. Greenwich, CT: JAI Press, Inc.

———. (1998). "Critical research in science education." In B. Fraser and K. Tobin (Eds.), *International Handbook of Science Education*, Part 2. Boston: Kluwer Academic Publishers.

———. (1999). *How do we tell the workers? The socioeconomic foundations of work and vocational education*. Boulder, CO: Westview.

Kincheloe, J. and S. Steinberg (1993). "A tentative description of post-formal thinking: The critical confrontation with cognitive theory." *Harvard Educational Review*, 63, pp. 296–320.

———. (1997). *Changing Multiculturalism: New times, new curriculum*. London: Open University Press.

Kincheloe, J. and S. Steinberg (Eds.) (1998). *Unauthorized methods: Strategies for critical teaching*. New York: Routledge.

Kincheloe, J., S. Steinberg, and A. Gresson (Eds.) (1996). *Measured Lies: The Bell Curve examined*. New York: St. Martin's Press.

Kincheloe, J., S. Steinberg, and P. Hinchey (Eds.) (1999). *The post-formal reader: Cognition and education*. New York: Falmer Press.

Kincheloe, J., S. Steinberg, N. Rodriguez, and R. Chennault (Eds.) (1998). *White Reign: Deploying whiteness in America*. New York: St. Martin's Press.

Kincheloe, J., S. Steinberg, and L. Villaverde (Eds.), (1999). *Rethinking Intelligence: Confronting psychological assumptions about teaching and learning*. New York: Routledge.

Kincheloe, J., & Pinar, W. (1991). Introduction. In J. Kincheloe & W. Pinar (Eds.), *Curriculum as social psychoanalysis: Essays on the significance of place*. Albany, NY: State University of New York Press.

Knight-Ridder News Service, September 17, 1990.
Koestler, A. (1970). *The act of creation.* London, PAN.
Lakoff, G. (1987). *Women, fire, and dangerous things: What categories to reveal about the mind.* Chicago: The University of Chicago Press.
Lavine, T. (1984). *From Socrates to Sartre: The philosophic quest.* New York: Bantam Books.
Leshan, L., & Margenau, H. (1982). *Einstein's space and Van Gogh's sky: Physical reality and beyond.* New York: Macmillan Publishing Company.
Lieberman, A. (1982). Practice makes policy: The tensions of school improvement. In A. Lieberman and M. W. McLaughlin (Eds), *Policymaking in education* (81st yearbook of the National Society for the Study of Education). Chicago: University of Chicago Press.
Liem, T. (1989). *Invitation to science inquiry.* El Cajon, CA:: Science Inquiry Enterprises.
Lincoln, Y., & Guba, E. (1985). *Naturalistic Inquiry.* Beverly Hills, CA: Sage Publications.
Longstreet, W. (1982). Action research: A paradigm. *The Educational Forum, 46* (2), 136–149.
Lowe, D. (1982). *History of bourgeois perception.* Chicago: University of Chicago Press.
Lyotard, J. (1984). *The postmodern condition.* Minneapolis: University of Minnesota Press.
Madaus, G. F., Kellaghan, T., & Schwab, R. L. (1989). *Teach them well: An introduction to education.* New York, NY: Harper & Row, Publishers, Inc.
Mahoney, M., & Lyddon, W. (1988). Recent developments in cognitive approaches to counseling and psychotherapy. *The Counseling Psychologist, 16* (2), 190–234.
Mandell, S. (1987). A search for form: Einstein and the poetry of Louis Zukofsky and William Carlos Williams. In D. Ryan, *Einstein and the humanities.* New York: Greenwood Press.
McCutcheon, G. (1981). The impact of the insider. In S. Nixon (Ed.), *A teachers' guide to action research.* London: Grant McIntyre.
McLaren, P. (1989). *Life in schools.* New York: Longman.
Meeker, R. (1981). *SOI systems* (brochure). Vida, OR: SOI Systems.
Meng, E., & Doran, R. (1990). What research says . . . Appropriate methods of assessment. *Science and Children, 28* (1), 42–45.
Michelmore, P. (1963). *Einstein: Profile of the man.* London.
Mies, M. (1982). Toward a methodology for feminist research. In G. Bowles and R. Klein, *Theories of women's studies.* Boston: Routledge and Kegan Paul.

Millar, R. (Ed.). (1989). *Doing science: Images of science in science education.* Philadelphia: Falmer Press.

Moore, M. (1989). *Problem finding and teacher experience.* Paper presented to the annual meeting of the Eastern Educational Research Association Meeting, Savannah, Georgia.

Morrison, R. (1987). Einstein on Kant, religion, science, and methodological unity. In D. Ryan, *Einstein and the Humanities.* New York: Greenwood Press.

Myers, L. (1987). The deep structure of culture: Relevance of traditional African culture in contemporary life. *Journal of Black Studies, 18* (1), 72–85.

Nyang, S., & Vandi, A. (1980). Pan-Africanism in world history. In M. Asante and A. Vandi, *Contemporary Black thought: Alternative analyses in social and behavioral science.* Beverly Hills, CA: Sage Publications.

Oldroyd, D. (1985). Indigenous action research for individual and system development. *Educational management and administration, 13,* 112–18.

Oliver, D., & Gershman, K. (1989). *Education, modernity, and fractured meaning: Toward a process theory of teaching and learning.* Albany, NY: State University of New York Press.

O'Loughlin, M. (1991). *Beyond constructivism: Toward a dialectical model of the problematics of teacher socialization.* Paper presented at the symposium on Emerging Role of Constructivism in Changes in Teachers' Beliefs, American Educational Research Association, Chicago, IL.

Ornstein, A. C., & Levine, D. U. (1989). *Foundations of education.* Boston, MA: Houghton Mifflin Company.

Ornstein, R. (1977). *The psychology of consciousness.* New York.

The Oxford Dictionary of Quotations (3rd Ed.) (1980). Oxford University Press.

Pagano, J. (1990). *Exiles and communities.* New York: SUNY Press.

Parade Magazine. September 15, 1990.

Parker, B. (1986). *Einstein's dream: The search for a unified theory of the universe.* New York: Plenum Press.

Patten, B. (1973). Visually mediated thinking: A report of the case of Albert Einstein. *Journal of Learning Disabilities, 6,* 15–20.

Peat, F. (1990). *Einstein's moon: Bell's theorem and the curious quest for quantum reality.* Chicago: Contemporary Books.

Penrose, R. (1991, March 28). The biggest enigma. *New York Review of Books,* 37–38.

Pinar, W. (1975). The Analysis of Educational Experience. In W. Pinar, *Curriculum theorizing: The reconceptualists.* Berkeley, CA: McCutchun Publishing Company.

Plotkin, A. (1955, April 24). Einstein hated snobs, haircuts. *Boston Globe.*

Poplin, M. (1988). Holistic/constructivist principles of the teaching/learning process: Implications for the field of learning disabilities. *Journal of Learning Disabilities, 21* (7), 401–16.

Poster, M. (1989). *Critical theory and post-structualism: In search of a context.* Ithaca, NY: Cornell University Press.

Powell, P. M. Genius. *Roeper Review, 10* (2), 96–98.

Prigogine, I., & Stengers, I. (1984). *Order out of chaos.* New York: Bantam Books.

Reinharz, S. (1979). *On becoming a social scientist.* San Francisco: Jossey-Bass.

Renzulli, J. S. (1977). *The enrichment triad model: A guide for developing defensible programs for the gifted and talented.* Mansfield Center, CT: Creative Learning Press, Inc.

Resnick, R. (1980). Misconceptions about Einstein. *Journal of Chemical Education, 57,* 12, 857–62.

Reynolds, R. (1987). Einstein and psychology: The genetic epistemology of relativistic physics. In D. Ryan, *Einstein and the humanities.* New York: Greenwood Press.

Rifkin, J. (1989). *Entropy: Into the greenhouse world.* New York: Bantam Books.

———. (1987). *Time wars: The primary conflict in human history.* New York: Simon and Schuster.

Rosenholz, S. (1989). *Teacher's workplace. The social organization of schools.* New York: Longman.

Rosenthal-Schneider, I. (1970). Presuppositions and anticipations in Einstein's physics. In P. Schlipp (Ed.), *Albert Einstein: Philosopher-scientist.* La Salle: Illinois.

Russell, M. (1983). Black-eyed blues connections: From the inside out. In C. Bunch & S. Pollock, *Learning our way: Essays in feminist education.* New York: The Crossing Press.

Sagan, C. (1978). The other world that beckons. *The New Republic,* 129, 11.

Samples, B. (1979). Mind cycles and learning. In F. Schultz (Ed.), *Education: Annual editions.* Sluice Dock, CT: Dushkin Press.

Sampson, E. (1981). Cognitive psychology as ideology. *American Psychologist, 36,* 730–43.

Schlipp, P. (Ed.). (1944). *The philosophy of Betrand Russell.* LaSalle: Illinois.

Scholes, R. (1982). *Semiotics and interpretation.* New Haven: Yale University Press.

Schon D. (1987). *Educating the reflective practitioner.* San Francisco: Jossey-Bass Publishers.

———. (1983). *The reflective practitioner: How professionals think in action.* New York: Basic Books.

———. (1973). *Beyond the stable state.* New York: Norton.

Sciama (1979). In Aichelburg, P. and R. Sexl (Eds.), *Albert Einstein, his influence on physics, philosophy, and politics*. Germany: Vieweg and Sohn.

Semali, L. and Ann Watts Pailliotet (Eds.) (1998). *Intermediality: The teachers' handbook of critical media literacy*. New York: Peter Lang.

Semali, L. and J. Kincheloe, (Eds.) (1999). *What is indigenous knowledge? Voices from the academy*. New York: Falmer Press.

Shweder, R., & Fiske, D. (1986). Introduction: Uneasy social science. In D. Fiske & R. Shweder, *Metatheory in social science: Pluralisms and subjectivities*. Chicago: University of Chicago Press.

Slaughter, R. (1989). Cultural reconstruction in the post-modern world. *Journal of Curriculum Studies, 3*, 255–70.

Soder, R. (1991). The ethics of the rhetoric of teacher professionalism. *Teaching and Teacher Education, 7* (3), 295–302.

Solomon, J. (1987). Social influences on the construction of pupil's understanding of science. *Studies in Science Education, 14*, 63–82.

Stacks, D., & Sellers, D. (1986). Toward a holistic approach to communication: The secret of "pure" hemispheric reception on message acceptance. *Communication Quarterly, 34* (3), 266–85.

Steinberg, S. and J. Kincheloe (Eds.) (1997). *Kinderculture: The corporate construction of childhood*. Boulder, CO: Westview.

Steinberg, S. and J. Kincheloe, (Eds.) (1998). *Students as researchers: Creating classrooms that matter*. Bristol, PA: Falmer Press.

Stewart, I. (1989). *Does God play dice? The mathematics of chaos*. Cambridge, MA: Penguin Books Ltd.

Talbot, M. (1986). *Beyond the quantum*. New York: Bantam Books.

Tannenbaum, A. J. (1983). Problems in assessing creativity. *Gifted children: Psychological and educational perspectives* (pp. 273–77). New York: Macmillan Publishing Co., Inc.

Terman, L. W. (1916). *The mismeasurement of intelligence*. Boston, MA: Houghton Mifflin Co.

———. (1951). The Stanford studies of the gifted. In P. Witty (Ed.), *The gifted child*. Boston: Heath.

———. (1954). The discovery and encouragement of exceptional talent. *American Psychologist, 9*, 221–30.

Thompson, E. (1967). Time, work-discipline, and industrial capitalism. *Past and Present, 38*, 79–92.

Thompson, L. (1971). Language disabilities in men of eminence. *Journal of Learning Disabilities, 4,* 39–40.

Tobin, K. (1991). *Referents for making sense.* Paper presented to the annual meeting of the American Educational Research Association, Chicago, Illinois.

Toffler, A. (1984). Science and Change. In I. Prigogine & J. Stengers, *Order out of chaos.* New York: Bantam Books.

Van Dore, P. (1950, November 9). To Albert Einstein. *Einstein Papers.* Princeton University.

Van Hesteran, F. (1986). Counselling research in a different key: The promise of human science perspective. *Canadian Journal of Counseling, 20* (4), 200–34.

Van Manen, M. (1991). *The tack of teaching: The meaning of pedagogical thoughtfulness.* Albany: SUNY Press.

Vann, C., & Walkerdine, V. (1977). The acquisition and production of knowledge. *Ideology and consciousness, 3,* 67–94.

Voorhees, B., & Royce, J. (1987). Einstein and epistemology. In D. Ryan, *Einstein and the humanities.* New York: Greenwood Press.

Walker, B. G. (1983). *The woman's encyclopedia of myths and secrets.* New York: Harper & Row, Publishers.

Walker, J. H., Kozma, E. J., & Green, R. P. (1989). *American education: Foundations and policy.* St. Paul, MN: West Publishing Company.

Welch, S. (1985). *Communities of resistance and solidarity.* Maryknoll, NY: Orbis Books.

Wertheimer, M. (1959). *Productive thinking.* New York: Harper.

Wheatley, G. (1991). Constructivist perspectives on science and mathematics learning. *Science Education, 75* (1), 9–21.

Whitson, J. (1986). Interpreting the freedom of speech: Some first amendment education cases. In J. Delly (Ed.), *Semiotics: 1985.* New York: University Press of America.

Wirth, A. (1983). *Productive work in industry and school.* Lanham, MD: University Press of America.

Wood, P. (1988). Action research: A field perspective. *Journal of Education for Teaching, 14* (2), 135–50.

Woolf, H.(Ed.). (1980). *Some strangeness in the proportion: A centennial symposium to celebrate the achievements of Albert Einstein.* Reading, MA: Addison-Wesley Publishing Co.

Young, M. (1971). *Knowledge and control: New directions for the sociology of education.* London: Macmillan.

Index

abstract rationality 102
accommodation 70, 149
Adler, M. 188
Afrocentric ways of knowing 82
Albert, R. 111
Alexander, L. 11
algebra 1
alienation 79
alternative assessment 160, 168
androcentrism 81
Annalen der Physik 35, 146
Apple, M. 6
Aquinas-Aristotle synthesis 14
Aristotle 78
Aronowitz, S. 89
Asian students 24
assessment 168, 195, 196
atoms 67
authority 81

Bacon, F. 15, 19, 52
Baudrillard, J. 90
Becquerel, H. 122
behavior modification 53

behavioral problems 134
belief in absolute space, time and motion 22
Bennett, W. 11
bimodal thought 123, 133, 135, 139, 140
Binet scale 105
Binet, A. 103
Black, M. 143
Black Mountain College 158
Bloom, A. 6, 7
Bloom's Taxonomy (Benjamin Bloom) 109
Bohm, D. 64, 67, 73, 87, 91, 92, 152
Bohm's theory of order 152
Bohr, N. 86, 92
Born, M. 10,
Bouguereau, A. 111
Brigham, C. 74
Britzman, D. 138
bubonic plague 14
Burns, K. 159

calculus 45
Calder, N. 152
Calinescu, M. 3
Calvin, J. 80

captitalism 33, 34
capitalist social system 33
capitalistic class 32
capitalistic competition 34
Cartesian dualism 14, 19
Cartesian logic 99
cause and effect 25, 100
Cézanne, 111
chaos 141, 142, 143, 145, 148, 152
citizenship 180
Christianity 14
Clark, R. 147
class division of society 32
Classical Age 96
cognition 65, 117, 188
cognitive disease 20
cognitive dissonance 123
cognitive growth 130
cognitive illness 11, 197
cognitive revolution 11, 12, 20, 22, 26, 50, 75, 177, 185
College Board, The 195
common sense 2, 26, 65
community school programs 192
computer networking 182
computers 184
conceptual thinking 179
consciousness and reality 21
consciousness 10, 14, 18, 20, 25, 54, 67, 71, 165, 167, 190
constructivism 10, 91, 58, 59, 60, 117, 118, 157, 158, 160
constructivist epistemology 118, 142
constructivist teachers 70, 159
constructivist view of learning 135
contextualization 13, 69
contextualization of facts 190
Copernicus, N. 19
creativity 12, 175
critical
    constructivism 44, 58, 60, 61, 62, 63, 69, 71, 161, 162, 171
    epistemology 84

media literacy 192
perspectives 90
postmodern educators 72, 83
postmodern epistemology 83
postmodernism 47, 68, 152, 177
school reform 186
spaces 58
system of meaning 3, 50, 61
theory 68, 60, 81, 90
Cuban, L. 178
Cubism 21
cultural myths 155
cultural signs 61
culture(s) 4, 53, 74
culture and class 23
current of linearity 22
currere 64
curriculum 42, 50, 51, 64, 83, 157, 160, 165, 166, 169, 183, 191
curriculum theory of place 69, 71
Cushing, H. 134

da Vinci, L. 23, 73, 130
daemon 96
Darwin, C. 19, 98
David 111
Decartes, R. 14, 15, 19, 52
Decline and Fall of the Roman Empire 39
deconstruction 25, 26, 71, 95, 97, 99, 101, 110,
decontextualization 102
Degas, E. 111
democracy 50, 187
democratic citizenship 63
democratic communities 3
Derrida, J. 25, 90
deskilling of teachers 56, 57, 183, 184, 193
determinism 85
developmental stages 59
developmental theory 117
Dickens, C. 9, 25
dissonance 122
divergent thinking 186

Index

djinni 96
dominant culture 65
dominant views of the world 51
double consciousness 5, 52
DuBois, B. 66
Duchamps, M. 22

economic profit 24
Edison, T. 134
education system 69
educational
    change 153
    discourse 53
    psychology 18
    reductionism 62
    reform 155, 179
    science 22
Educational Testing Service 195
egocentricity 52
Einsteinian physics 22
Einsteinian relativity 25
electrodynamics 13, 147
electromagnetism 147, 148
emancipation 5, 7, 11, 13, 61
emancipatory education 13
emancipatory source of authority 61
Emerson, R. 97
emotion 132
empathy 68
empirical methods of inquiry 64
Enlightenment 97, 129
epistemological defeatism 86
epistemological pluralism 85
epistemology 83, 85, 158, 171
ergo cogito 52
essentialism 175
etymological construction 96
etymology 68
Euclidean geometry 45
explicate order 64, 65

factoid syndrome 16
facts 2, 55, 181

Faulkner, W. 73
feminist constructivism 66
feminist educators 81
feminist epistemologists 82
feminist notions of knowing 82
feminist pedagogy 131, 132, 133
feminist perspectives 56, 90
feminist theory 55, 81, 82, 114, 131
formal operations 11
formal thinking 11, 100, 101, 188, 189
forms of intelligence 23
Foucault, M. 7, 53, 57, 90
fragmentation 55, 90, 155
fragmentation of meaning 54
Frankfurt School 60, 81
freedom of inquiry 35
Freire, P. 110, 131
Freud, S. 26, 98, 111, 150
Freudian psychoanalysis 151

Gallagher, J. 101
Galton, F. 98, 111
Garbut, J. 23
Gardner, H. 185
genealogy 7
generalization 70
genie 96
genius 2, 4, 7, 9, 95, 96, 97, 98, 102, 107,
    110, 119, 130, 134, 140, 143, 144, 175,
    184
Gestalt psychology 119
Gibbons, E. 39
Gilbert, F. 39
Godfather II 73
Gramsci, A. 54
grand narratives of legitimation 4
gravitation 148
Great Search 12
Great Tradition 84
Greek science 14
Grossman, M. 46
Grumet, M. 55, 62, 66
Guilford, J. P. 106, 107

Habermas, J. 80, 90, 137
Hale, G. E. 151
Hardison Jr., O.B. 87
Hegelian dialectic 122
Heidegger, M. 22, 92
Heisenberg, W. 26, 59, 78, 86
hemispherical research 127
Hereditary Genius 98
Heshusius 42
Hesse, H. 10
higher-order intelligence 7, 13
Hirsch, E. D. 6, 188
history 10
history of science 122
holism 73, 74, 88, 140, 142, 152
holistic teaching 40
holographic quantum perception 21
Holton, G. 120, 122, 123, 137, 140
human cognitive activity 11, 102
human experience 12, 14
humanness 54
Hume, D. 121
Hussein, S. 72
hyper-rationality 102

ideology 17, 44, 51
illiteracy 57
imagery 137, 138
implicate order 64, 65, 67, 68, 73, 88
Impressionism 111
indigenous people's subjugated knowledge 83
Ingresn J.A.D. 111
inner experience 14
intelligence 7, 24, 104, 184, 185,
intelligence of ethnic groups 74
Internet 182
intuition 54, 136, 138
IQ 1, 103, 104, 106

Jackh, E. 151
Jameson, F. 89
Japanese families 24
Joffe, A. E. 149

Jung, K. 26, 67
juno 96, 114

Kafka, F. 19
Kant, I., 77, 97, 130
Keller, H. 52
Kepler 19
Kincheloe, J. 60, 69, 71, 99
Klee, P. 65
Knapp, R. 23
knower and the known 14, 58, 81, 91
knowing 131
knowledge 6, 58, 59, 78, 81, 117, 158, 159, 177, 196
  makers 28, 29
  of connection 132
  users 28, 29
Kohlberg, L. 102
Kuhn, T. 156

language 67, 92, 127, 132, 134, 163, 164, 165
Laplace, P. 15, 16
learners 20
learning 158
learning disabled 134
Lebenswelt 73
left brain 127, 130
liberation theologians 69
linguistic codes 61
logocentrism 3,
Lowell, J. R. 95
Luther, M. 80
Lyotard, J.F. 4, 89, 90, 93

Mach, E. 121
madness 97, 110
Magritte, R. 23
Manet, E. 111
Mann, H. 100
mathematical knowledge 77
mathematics 137
McCarthy Era 5

Index

McLaren, P. 50, 58, 64, 74
mechanics 13
media 93
melancholy 97
meta-awareness 52, 55
metaphor and imagery 186
metaphors 15, 22, 28, 30, 31, 32, 143, 155, 158, 163, 164, 165, 177, 186
metaphysical frameworks 17
Middle Ages 96
mind and matter 14
modern
    anthropology 33
    knowers 82
    linearity 73
    objectivity 82
modernism 3, 13, 17, 18, 19, 20, 24, 58, 68, 93
modernist concepts of genius 98
modernist education 176, 186, 197
modernist schools 16
modernity 15, 16
molecules 67
Monet, C. 111
Mozart, W. A. 26, 73
multiple ways of knowing 118
Munich Gymnasium 35
myths 156, 161

nationalism 15
Native American epistemologies/ways of knowing 82
natural laws 147
natural phenomena 14
nature 145
New Right 68
Newton, I. 15, 19, 84
Newtonian
    concept 21
        physics 2, 86, 171, 184
    scientist 12
    ways of seeing 22

Newtonian concepts of space, time, energy, mass and light 137
Newtonian-Cartesian
    absolutism 84
    authority of science and reason 177
    boundaries 22
    cause and effect linearity 17
    compass 15
    definitions 82
    epistemology 79, 83, 84, 88
    frameworks of reality 197
    linearity 127
    love 88
    models of genius 97
    modernism 90, 176
    modernity 16, 23, 54, 55, 56, 69, 70, 102, 176
    paradigm 110, 124
    perspectives 69, 89
    physics 86, 93
    problem solving formalism 66
    scientists 93, 141
    thinkers 126
    universe 73
    view of knowlege 79
    way of organizing the world 14, 143
    way of seeing 22, 60, 74, 85
    world 11, 54, 82, 92, 99
    world of science 70
neural biomodality 128
Nietzsche, F 20
nonverbal thought 137

O'Keefe, G. 23
O'Neill, E. 4
objectivism 156, 157, 160
Orton, S. 135

Pagano, J. 132
Paine, T. 8,
particularity 70
passion and emotion 56

patriarchial expansion 15
patriarchal methodology 132
patriotism 34
Patten, B. 133
patterns 138
Patton, G. 134
pazzia 96
pedagogical nihilism 51
pedagogy 18, 182
pedagogy of democratic schools 50
Pedagogy of the Oppressed 110, 131
personal knowledge 56
personal constructivism 161
personal, social, and cultural construction of meaning 41
Pestalozzi, J. 46
physicists 21
physics 36, 37, 38, 39, 58, 59, 70, 73, 80, 87, 88, 91, 93, 100, 117, 118, 123, 140, 145, 147, 150, 188
Piaget, J. 59, 100
Piagetian formalism 11, 63, 195
Picasso, P. 26
Pinar, W. 64, 69, 71
Plank, M. 85
Plato 77, 96
Poe, E.A. 95
poetry 132
Polanyi, M. 78, 79, 80, 82
political neutrality in education 27
portfolios 195
positive reinforcement 53
positivism 102
post for teacher thinking 138
post-Einsteinian science 21
post-formal
    cognition 26
    genius 102
    observers 65
    search for unity 152, 153
    teachers 71
    thinking 11, 13, 22, 32, 63, 64, 65, 67, 69, 71, 74, 136, 180

postformalism 12, 146, 147, 153
postmodern
    analysis 99
    cognitive revolution 12
    concept of knower participation in knowing 79
    condition 12, 54, 93
    critique 7, 11, 12, 18, 20, 63, 93, 137
    education 176, 177
    educators 11, 52, 57
    epistemology 58, 93
    insurrection 75
    perspective 81
    reform 177
    school reform 177
    schooling 26
    science 21
    simultaneity 127
    students 4
    teacher 21, 51, 52
    thinkers 56
    Western 20
    world 26, 75, 93
postmodernism 3, 4, 18, 20, 58, 74, 83, 85, 88, 91, 176
poststructural perspectives 90
Powell, P. 130
power 57, 60, 61, 81, 163, 186, 188, 190
power elites 110
pre-Einsteinian universe 10
premodernism 79
Prigogine, I. 142
primitive cultures 33
product orientation 177
production of knowledge 50
progress 3
psychology 58
purposes of schooling 63
Pythagoras 77, 119

qualitative research 164
quantitative universe 15
quantum epistemology 86

Index

quantum mechanics 141, 148
quantum physics 21, 59, 78, 85, 86, 87, 89, 90, 126, 184
quantum reality 91
quantum theory 3, 21, 88, 90, 92
quantum world 93

radiation 122
Rand, A. 156
randomness 141
Raphael 111
rational mode dysfunction 136
rationalism 10
rationality 15
rationality of the universe 85
Reagan Era 9
Reagan, R. 11, 50
Reagan-Bush reforms 16
Realism 111
reality 10, 59, 84
Red Dawn 72
reductionism 99, 100, 156
reflection 138
reform 197
reformers 28, 30
relativity 59, 141, 147
Relativity: The Special and General Theory 139
Renaissance 96
Renoir, A. 111
Renzulli, J. 109
researchers 28, 29, 30
Rifkin, J. 13,
right brain 130
right-wing libertarian ideologue 50
right-wing reform 16
Rodin, A. 134
role of education 32
Romantic Era 97, 111
Russel, B. 40, 78, 147, 150
Russell, M. 51

scientific thought 126

Schon, D. 65
school
   failure 23
   performance 24
   reform 185, 186
Schopenhauer, 22
Sciama, D. 152
science 171
   and education 13, 15
   educators 161
   and technology 3, 15
scientific method 132
scientific objectivity 87
self-criticism 71
semiosis, 164
semiotics 163, 164
sensation 14
Skinner, B.F. 79
social
   class 4
   conditioning 53
   context 50, 67, 188
   expectations 168
   justice 3, 125, 186
   responsibility 125
   theory 90
socialism 32, 33
socialist economy 34
Socrates 78, 96
space and time 121
Special Relativity 148
special theory of relativity 17
speech 127
speed of light 147, 148
Spinoza, B. 144
Stanford-Binet Intelligence Scale 104, 109
Structure of Intellect (SOI) 106
Stuart, G. 26
student consciousness 51
student progress 160
students 51
subatomic particles 85
success 58

Sullivan, A. 52
synergistic cycle 55
system of meaning 61
system of values 32

Tannenbaum, A. 107
Taylor, F. W. 24, 25
Taylor model of efficiency 24
teachers and students as researchers 164, 182, 183, 192
teachers as learners 22, 142, 162, 183
teachers facilitating learning 159
technology 182, 192
Terman, L. 103, 104, 11
testmakers 101
tests (intelligence) 80
text 25, 71, 104, 109, 183, 187, 196
theme of abstraction 55
theory
    generators 28 , 29
    translators 28, 29
    of indeterminancy 78
    of knowledge 83
    of personal knowlege 78
    of relativity 2, 13, 67, 68, 72, 78, 85, 121, 143, 145, 146, 148, 150
    of special relativity 85
thinking 99
Thompson, L. 134
thought experiments 121
Tianiman Square 54
time and space 85
time 73, 170, 171
Tobin, K. 155
Toffler, A. 142
Torrance Test for Creativity 109
transformative intellectuals 28, 30, 57
truth 156

unanticipated realities 22
unity 143, 149, 150

Van Gogh, V. 23, 26
van Manen, M. 158
Veblen, T. 33
verbal problems 134
visual thinking 138

Wallace, G. 65
Watson, J. 79
Wertheimer, M. 119
Wesley, J. 80
Western canon 84
Western commonsense 2, 22
Western culture 82
Western logic 25
Western philosophy 90
Wheeler, J. 86
Whitehead, A. 51
Whitman, W. 18
wholeness 89
Williams, W. C. 22
Wilson, W. 134
Wittgenstein, L. 78, 92
Wolfer, A. 35
women's ways of knowing 4
Women's Ways of Knowing: The Development of Self, Voice, and Mind 132

Young, M. 61

Zeitgeists 68
Zurich Federal Institute of Technology 35

Studies in Criticality

General Editor
Shirley R. Steinberg

Counterpoints publishes the most compelling and imaginative books being written in education today. Grounded on the theoretical advances in criticalism, feminism, and postmodernism in the last two decades of the twentieth century, Counterpoints engages the meaning of these innovations in various forms of educational expression. Committed to the proposition that theoretical literature should be accessible to a variety of audiences, the series insists that its authors avoid esoteric and jargonistic languages that transform educational scholarship into an elite discourse for the initiated. Scholarly work matters only to the degree it affects consciousness and practice at multiple sites. Counterpoints' editorial policy is based on these principles and the ability of scholars to break new ground, to open new conversations, to go where educators have never gone before.

For additional information about this series or for the submission of manuscripts, please contact:

> Shirley R. Steinberg
> c/o Peter Lang Publishing, Inc.
> 29 Broadway, 18th floor
> New York, New York 10006

To order other books in this series, please contact our Customer Service Department:
> (800) 770-LANG (within the U.S.)
> (212) 647-7706 (outside the U.S.)
> (212) 647-7707 FAX

Or browse online by series:
> www.peterlang.com